Barth and Schleiermacher: Beyond the Impasse?

DEDICATED TO HANS W. FREI
1922–1988
Distinguished scholar and esteemed colleague

Barth and Schleiermacher: Beyond the Impasse?

Edited by
JAMES O. DUKE and ROBERT F. STREETMAN

Fortress Press   Philadelphia

Excerpts from *The Theology of Schleiermacher* by Karl Barth, copyright © 1982 by
Wm. B. Eerdmans Publishing Co., are used by permission of Wm. B. Eerdmans
Publishing Co.

Biblical quotations, unless otherwise noted, are from the Revised Standard Version
of the Bible, copyright 1946, 1952, © 1971, 1973 by the Division of Christian
Education of the National Council of the Churches of Christ in the U.S.A., and are
used by permission.

Library of Congress Cataloging-in-Publication Data

Barth and Schleiermacher: Beyond the Impasse?
  Includes index.
  "This work had its origins in a joint session of the
Barth Society of North America and the Schleiermacher
Consultation of the American Academy of Religion, held
at the 1983 annual meeting of the American Academy
of Religion and the Society of Biblical Literature."
  1. Barth, Karl, 1886–1968—Congresses. 2. Schleier-
macher, Friedrich, 1768–1834—Congresses. I. Duke,
James O. II. Streetman, Robert F. III. American
Academy of Religion. IV. Society of Biblical Literature.
BX4827.B3B36 1988   230'092'2   88–45236
ISBN 0–8006–0888–7

3508E88   Printed in the United States of America   1–888

Contents

CONTENTS

PART 3
THE PROSPECTS FOR FURTHER DIALOGUE: ASSESSMENTS

Preface

Twenty-first-century theology is already with us. It is a seedling hidden beneath the surface of things or among familiar "contemporary trends." Where it is and what it will become are for the moment open questions. This much is certain: with its taproot sunk in twentieth-century soil, its well-being depends on a healthy theological environment. There is much ecological damage to repair before the century ends. The cleanup effort might well begin by removing misconceptions about what was, and is, at stake in Karl Barth's effort to come to grips with the thought of Friedrich Schleiermacher. Without clarity on this point, twenty-first-century theology will be left unnourished by a genuine dialogue between the heirs of neo-orthodoxy and neo-Protestantism.

Genuine dialogue is always difficult, and the difficulties faced by theologians who cannot forget the concerns of Schleiermacher and those who cannot shake the concerns of Barth are formidable. Are we not dealing here with two paradigms, two rival visions, of the theological enterprise as a whole? On what basis can dialogue even begin when differences are so deep, so broad, and so intractable? Conventional wisdom suggests that discussion is at an impasse: theologians must choose either to stand their ground without flinching or to seek open paths elsewhere.

The suggestion has been warmly received in the last half of the twentieth century. Theology does go on and on. Yet even as Schleiermacher and Barth pass into history, issues that they, more than anyone else, forced theology to address—for example, concerning theological method, the meaning of church doctrine, God, and the Christian life—pass over into the future. To go about our theological business as though we no longer need to take stock of the claims and counterclaims that led to this impasse is nothing less than a disservice to twenty-first-century theology. Commitments to the future, not the past, prompt a fresh examination of the relationship between Barth and Schleiermacher.

This volume reports on just such an examination conducted by an international team of scholars who realize that talk about a theological impasse is not wisdom merely because it is conventional. Their findings cast new light on the contest between Barth and Schleiermacher and in so doing raise serious questions about familiar, indeed all-too-stylized, accounts of their relationship. Ongoing research, which has granted the English-speaking audience a wider view of the writings of Barth and Schleiermacher, has also brought about revisionist readings of those writings. Thus, for example, Schleiermacher appears more a "church theologian" and Barth more a "narrative theologian" than once thought, and Barth appears no less concerned for the "public character" of church dogmatics than Schleiermacher for the "Word of God" in the church's *Glaubenslehre*.

News that Barth and Schleiermacher are now found to have been in fundamental agreement would likely be the occasion for alarm rather than celebration. Twenty-first-century theology would still be left unnourished by a genuine dialogue between the heirs of neo-orthodoxy and neo-Protestantism. Readers of these reports may rest assured that upon fresh examination it is found that the two theologians remain divided by deep and broad differences. Yet by no means does all remain as it was. Taken together, these studies redraw the dividing lines, probe new areas of connection, and detect openings for movement toward dialogue.

This work had its origins in a joint session of the Barth Society of North America and the Schleiermacher Consultation of the American Academy of Religion, held at the 1983 annual meeting of the American Academy of Religion and the Society of Biblical Literature. The essays and responses are arranged into three parts. The first invites readers to look again, this time with a more trained eye, at the terms of Barth's debate with Schleiermacher. The second explores, from a variety of perspectives, the prospects for an improved understanding of the similarities and differences between Schleiermacher's and Barth's theological concerns. The final section offers assessments of the effort at advancing beyond an impasse to a dialogue about the legacy of these two theologians.

JAMES O. DUKE
Pacific School of Religion

Contributors

JAMES J. BUCKLEY is Associate Professor of Theological Studies at Loyola College, in Maryland. His publications include articles in *Theological Studies*, the *Thomist*, the *Heythrop Journal*, and in *Modern Christian Theologians*, edited by David Ford (forthcoming).

DANIEL B. CLENDENIN, who has served as a Guest Professor at the Faculté de theologie evangélique de Bangui, in the Central African Republic, is Assistant Professor of Theology at William Tyndale College, in Michigan. He is author of *Theological Method in Jacques Ellul* (1987).

RICHARD CROUTER, Chair of the Department and Professor of Religious Studies at Carleton College, in Minnesota, has published articles on nineteenth- and twentieth-century theology in the *Journal of Religion*, the *Journal of the American Academy of Religion*, and the *Journal of Religious Ethics*. His new edition and translation of Schleiermacher's *On Religion: Speeches to Its Cultured Despisers* is forthcoming in the Texts in German Philosophy series of Cambridge University Press.

JAMES O. DUKE, Professor of Church History at the Pacific School of Religion, is also a member of the Doctoral Faculty in Historical Studies of the Graduate Theological Union, Berkeley, California. His latest work in Schleiermacher studies, with Howard Stone, is *Christian Caring: Selections from Schleiermacher's* Practical Theology (1988).

HANS W. FREI, A. Hoober Professor of Religious Studies at Yale University, is an internationally known authority on modern theology. Among his major publications are *The Eclipse of Biblical Narrative* (1974) and *The Identity of Jesus Christ* (1975).

DANIEL W. HARDY is Van Mildert Professor of Divinity at the University of Durham, and Residentiary Canon of Durham Cathedral, in Durham, England. His publications include *Jubilate: Theology in Praise* (with David F. Ford; published in the United States under the title *Praising and Knowing God* [1985]) and many articles.

RICHARD R. NIEBUHR, Hollis Professor of Divinity at Harvard Divinity School, is the author of *Schleiermacher on Christ and Religion: A New Introduction* (1964) as well as numerous essays and articles on various aspects of Schleiermacher's thought.

ROBERT F. STREETMAN, Professor of Religious Studies at Montclair State College, in New Jersey, is cofounder of the Schleiermacher Consultation of the American Academy of Religion and the *New Athenaeum: A Scholarly Journal Specializing in Schleiermacher Research and Nineteenth-Century Studies*. Among his publications are articles in the *Journal of the American Academy of Religion* and in *The Interpretation of Belief: Coleridge, Schleiermacher, and Romanticism*, ed. David Jasper (1986).

STEPHEN W. SYKES is Regius Professor of Divinity, University of Cambridge, Hon. Canon, Ely, and Fellow of St. John's College, Cambridge. He is widely published, and his major contributions to nineteenth- and twentieth-century studies include *Friedrich Schleiermacher* (1971), an edited work, *Karl Barth: Studies of His Theological Method* (1980), and *The Identity of Christianity* (1984).

JOHN E. THIEL is author of *God and World in Schleiermacher's* Dialektik *and* Glaubenslehre (1981) and of articles appearing in the *Heythrop Journal* and *Theological Studies*. He is the Chair of the Department and Professor of Religious Studies at Fairfield University, in Connecticut.

RONALD F. THIEMANN is Dean and John Lord O'Brian Professor of Divinity at Harvard Divinity School. He is author of *Revelation and Theology: The Gospel as Narrated Promise* (1985).

TERRENCE N. TICE is Professor of Philosophy in the School of Education and Research Science in the all-university doctoral program in Urban, Technological, and Environment Planning at the University of Michigan. He is a noted translator and interpreter of Schleiermacher's work, and his most recent publication is *Schleiermacher on Academia* (1988).

Barth and Schleiermacher: Beyond the Impasse?

Introduction

ROBERT F. STREETMAN

The only certain consolation which remains for me is to rejoice that in the kingdom of heaven I will be able to discuss all these questions with Schleiermacher extensively . . . for, let us say, a couple of centuries. "Then I will see clearly *that*—along with so many other things, also that—which on earth I saw through a glass darkly." I can imagine that that will be a very serious matter for both sides, but also that we will both laugh very heartily at ourselves.

—Karl Barth[1]

At the same time as he sought to be a Christian theologian Schleiermacher also felt responsible—I should like to understand and weigh this as earnestly as possible—for the intellectual and moral foundations of the cultural world into which a man was born at the end of the eighteenth century. He wanted in all circumstances to be a modern man as well as a Christian theologian—we must not seek to decide whether he was striving for the former aim with the same or perhaps with even greater earnestness than that with which he sought to be a Christian theologian, at any rate he did so with similar earnestness.

—Karl Barth[2]

In both partners of the theological dialogue to come, there is an unflinching commitment to church dogmatics, to the best ecumenical impulses of the day, to the highest standards of theological scholarship, to the practical demands and needs of the pastorate, as well as to pressing sociopolitical issues. It is this extraordinarily rare combination of theological and pastoral talents that sets Karl Barth and Friedrich Schleiermacher far apart from their colleagues, who by comparison are like performers on only a single string. Learned theologians are not

1

impossible to find, nor does one have to mount a safari to locate caring and dynamic pastors. But to find both strengths in the same person is cause for celebration!

Both of the subjects of this study began their theological revolutions as working pastors, and both were to retain their interest in the everyday problems of pastoral work throughout their careers. Indeed, as we shall soon see, one of them continued in a university pastorate throughout his lifetime while becoming the most celebrated German theologian of his day. The other was catapulted from a modest pastoral appointment into an academic career to which he had never aspired and for which he felt unprepared.

Early in his teaching career, Schleiermacher wrote that every person, clerical or lay, holding a position of church leadership is obligated to have an acquaintance with theology that is commensurate with the amount of leadership responsibility he or she holds. To ensure that his message would not be lost in translation, Schleiermacher added that the very reason for doing theology is church leadership (*Kirchenleitung*) and that anyone whose study of theology is not grounded in personal conviction does not really deserve to be called a theologian. Rather, such a person is a humanist, a historian of religion, or perhaps a social scientist, who is doing no more than pursuing a serious academic *interest* in theology.[3] For Schleiermacher, then, the only valid systematic theology must be *church dogmatics,* and in our time he wins the agreement of Karl Barth on this point, although disagreement of these two persons over the proper method of translating systematics into church dogmatics is as wide as could be imagined. The concurrence is reflected in the titles of their respective systematic works—*The Christian Faith Presented Systematically according to the Fundamental Propositions of the Evangelical Church* (Schleiermacher) and *Church Dogmatics* (Barth)— and the disagreement was never more evident than in their methodological introductions to these works, as will be seen in some of the essays of this volume.

Following the example of his grandfather and father, Schleiermacher entered the ministry as a Reformed chaplain to the Charity Hospital in Berlin. Although he prepared for an academic career, he combined the teaching of theology with a series of pastoral appointments, the last of which was at the Trinity Cathedral in Berlin—a prestigious pulpit, where he was eventually to instruct the young Otto von Bismarck in the faith and prepare him for communion. Although Schleiermacher was acknowledged in Germany as one of the most gifted preachers of his day, his prowess in the pulpit and his contributions in other areas of practical pastoral work have rarely been recognized outside Germany until our own time. Recently Brian A. Gerrish published an excellent volume that is a crystallization of several lectures on Schleiermacher before pastoral conferences and university audiences.[4] His focus on the high value of Schleiermacher's pastoral work is representative of a great deal of contemporary thinking.

Karl Barth also followed his grandfather and father into the pulpit, beginning as a vicar in Geneva, but after twelve years in various pastoral appointments he was called, mainly on the basis of his epoch-making studies of the *Epistle to the Romans* (1918–19), as Honorary Professor of Reformed Theology to the University of Göttingen (1921), which then had a "predominantly Lutheran faculty."[5] Despite the trauma of being thrust into the limelight and of inheriting a mantle for which he did not feel fully prepared academically, Barth entered the lecture hall. Nevertheless, pastoral concerns were never far from his mind, and the critique he was to make of Schleiermacher was predicated on the thesis that it was in Schleiermacher's sermons that the fundamentals of his theology were to be discovered.

AN OVERVIEW OF BARTH'S REACTIONS TO SCHLEIERMACHER

If we survey our own century for confirmation of Schleiermacher's belief that the systematic task of theology, as church dogmatics, is discharged responsibly only when it is undertaken anew in each generation, we discover that in this respect Schleiermacher has had at least one thoroughly consistent disciple—Karl Barth.[6] There is, however, a curious irony in the identification of Barth as Schleiermacher's disciple in the reconstruction of theology *ab ovo*. The irony is that in the travail of Barth with the legacy of many of his theological predecessors, the root ran directly back to Schleiermacher, whom Barth felt bound to refute in order to make a new beginning of his own.

So fundamental was Barth's break with the neo-Protestant heritage stemming from Schleiermacher that he was forced to work his way through a number of changes in approach before he was finally free to go his own way to the production of an affirmative church dogmatics. The account of these various changes is one of the most fascinating studies in Western Christian history, yet most of the details of this development are not immediately relevant to the present topic.[7] Hans Urs von Balthasar speaks for many interpreters of Barth when he asserts that, these changes notwithstanding, Barth ought to be understood as "holding on to the same basic insight throughout his career, trying to find the proper way to express it, and discarding one form of expression after another."[8]

Although, from Barth's developing standpoint, the negative influences of his neo-Protestant predecessors could only be overcome by attacking the original source—in Schleiermacher's *On Religion* and *The Christian Faith*—his campaign does not take the form of a massive monographic onslaught. On the contrary, he speaks against Schleiermacher mainly in class lectures, in individual essays, and in books on other topics. Nevertheless, until 1931 the polemic is always there, even when only by implication.[9] It is almost as if Barth fears that an extensive refutation may achieve the opposite effect of spreading Schleiermacher's influence even further.

The Contrast of Methods

It is necessary at this point to gain a clear understanding of the basic contrast of theological methods between Schleiermacher and Barth. This contrast can be clarified through minor modifications of some words of Paul Tillich:

> One can distinguish two ways of approaching God: the way of overcoming estrangement and the way of meeting a stranger. In the first way man discovers *himself* when he discovers God; he discovers something that is identified with himself although it transcends him infinitely, something from which he is estranged, but from which he can never be separated. In the second way man meets a *stranger* when he meets God. The meeting is accidental. Essentially they do not belong to each other. They may become friends on a tentative and conjectural basis. But there is no certainty about the stranger man has met. He may disappear, and only *probable* statements can be made about his nature.[10]

The first approach, which is akin to Schleiermacher's, Tillich calls the "ontological type," and the second, akin to Barth's intended correction of the first, the "cosmological type." Although these labels may offer some help, it is preferable to examine Tillich's contrast by means of the attributions respectively of "continuity" (immanence) and of "discontinuity" (transcendence), since they seem to do more justice to the spirit of Barth's reaction to Schleiermacher.

The term "continuity" indicates the belief that there is some sort of relational bond (ontological, epistemological, and/or ethical) between God and man. According to T. F. Torrance, the term "continuity" denotes here "every attempt to erect a synthesis between man and God from the side of man." In his words,

> Neo-Protestant theology was impregnated with an instinctive abhorrence of all discontinuity so that it was consciously and unconsciously determined to break down barriers, to pare away the edges of difference, and to bring everything within one continuous dimension of reality. Hence the great differences between God and man, eternity and time, Christianity and humanism, were eaten away until the precipice that separated them was transformed into a slope leading gradually from one to the other.[11]

In the first of Tillich's two ways of approaching God, the "way of overcoming estrangement," a previously established relationship (of continuity or spiritual kinship) has been disturbed because the parties to the relationship have been alienated from each other. In this case, the relationship is the way of redemption or reconciliation, which would remove the disturbance and put the relationship back on a positive basis. In the system of Schleiermacher—for whom religious self-consciousness is the prerequisite for mature personhood—the "relation to God" is another name for the "feeling of absolute dependence."[12] Thus, God, although unknowable in essence, is the correlate of the religious self-consciousness by virtue of being the cause of one's being in such a state.

Tillich's alternative way, that of "meeting a stranger," emphasizes discontinuity—a recognition of the absence of a preestablished relationship as well as a recognition of an "essential" difference between the two parties. Thus, strictly speaking, it is not an "approach" by a seeker at all. It is in fact an "accidental" meeting, because in this case all initiative is attributed to the "stranger," who elects to be known by one previously unacquainted.

A striking example of the self-manifesting stranger illustrates Barth's emphasis upon discontinuity. It is the encounter of Job with the strange God who speaks to him from the whirlwind (Job 38—42:6). Up to the moment of encounter, Job has stubbornly—and rather impatiently—maintained his innocence of any wrongdoing that would justify his suffering. He has even insisted on pleading his case directly before God:

> He condemned God to human finiteness in an attempt to justify himself. He conceived divine justice, not in relation to a God-revolving macrocosm but as a function of his self-centered microcosm. He denied the theocentricity of the universe by living anthropocentrically.[13]

Yet when confronted with the voice of God out of the whirlwind, Job hung his head in repentance. He did so because he saw for the first time that the God before whom he was innocent was not real at all but only a figment of a religious and cultural value system. Indeed, there was an "antithesis between the traditional belief by hearsay, inherited through the intellect from a past now dead, and the actual experience, as piercing as burning coals, as real as death, as warm as life."[14]

The God of the whirlwind was a stranger—a God so different from the one Job had previously worshiped that he had no case left to plead. Job confessed, "I had heard of thee by the hearing of the ear, but now my eye sees thee; therefore I despise myself, and repent in dust and ashes" (Job 42:5–6). Originally Job is like the neo-Protestant whom Barth is criticizing, one who trusts in religious and moral observance to deliver him or her blameless before God. This is the believer in continuity. Conversely, the God of divine initiative, in Barth's way of discontinuity, is analogous to the self-manifesting stranger—the God who transcends all that Job had seen and heard—and the encounter with the true God reduces the person to repentance. Once Job has lost all pretense of worth before God, he is justified before God even in the face of his detractors (Job 42:7–8). Emphasis on this divine yes, which comes only on the other side of the initial no, to the way of religion, is characteristic of Barth, especially during his earlier period.[15] Until Barth could shake free of Schleiermacher's influence, he conceived of his task as exposing the tenuous thread of the relational bond of continuity, which allegedly breaks under the stress on human initiative by neo-Protestants. On the contrary, Barth insists upon discontinuity— the view that God transcends any knowledge or reconciliation arising from human initiative.

The Barthian case against Schleiermacher is likely well known. The translation of Barth's early Göttingen lectures, published under the title *The Theology of Schleiermacher*, is perhaps only the most recent reminder of it. To recall Barth's quarrel with Schleiermacher, however, is to think of an even more massive and fateful turn in twentieth-century theology generally—the neo-orthodox critique of its liberal heritage. Thus the confrontation between Barth and Schleiermacher represents the trial by ordeal between the champions of neo-orthodoxy and those of neo-Protestantism, and its outcome holds contemporary no less than historical interest. Theology that seeks its bearings in an age of pluralism, an age that is in crucial respects both postliberal and post-neo-orthodox, can only be served by reassessing the debate that has brought it to its present position.

In this regard the present volume is a breakthrough. It challenges customary, and often facile, readings of Barth and Schleiermacher, and reconsiders the nature and extent of the two theologians' differences. Some of the essays, building upon ongoing revisionism in Schleiermacher studies, suggest that—to paraphrase the words of Dietrich Ritschl in another context—Barth's interpretation of Schleiermacher teaches us more about Barth than about Schleiermacher.[16] Others, penetrating to foundational issues upon which Barth and Schleiermacher disagree, cast fresh light on the theological stakes involved in the attempt to wrestle with perennial concerns of Christian theology. Overall, the essays reorient thinking about the supposedly irreconcilable claims of neo-orthodoxy and neo-Protestantism and thereby contribute to a more adequate understanding of the theological task itself.

NOTES

1. Karl Barth, "Concluding Unscientific Postscript on Schleiermacher," trans. George Hunsinger, in Barth's *The Theology of Schleiermacher: Lectures at Göttingen, Winter Semester of 1923/24,* ed. Dietrich Ritschl, trans. Geoffrey W. Bromiley (Grand Rapids: Wm. B. Eerdmans, 1982), 277.

2. Karl Barth, *Protestant Thought: From Rousseau to Ritschl,* trans. Brian Cozens, rev. H. H. Hartwell et al. (New York: Harper & Bros., 1959), 314.

3. F. D. E. Schleiermacher, *Brief Outline on the Study of Theology,* trans. Terrence N. Tice (Richmond: John Knox Press, 1966), §6, p. 20.

4. Brian A. Gerrish, *A Prince of the Church: Schleiermacher and the Beginnings of Modern Theology* (Philadelphia: Fortress Press, 1984). See also Gerrish's chapter "Continuity and Change: Friedrich Schleiermacher on the Task of Theology," in his *Tradition and the Modern World: Reformed Theology in the Nineteenth Century* (Chicago: Univ. of Chicago Press, 1978). Much background on this and other topics is given in Martin Redeker's *Schleiermacher: Life and Thought,* trans. John Wallhausser (Philadelphia: Fortress Press, 1973).

5. John D. Godsey, "Portrait of Barth," in Karl Barth's *How I Changed My Mind,* trans. John D. Godsey (Richmond: John Knox Press, 1966), 27. A more detailed account is given in Eberhard Busch's *Karl Barth: His Life from Letters and Autobiographical Texts,* trans. John W. Bowden (Philadelphia: Fortress Press, 1975).

6. See Karl Barth's *Protestant Theology in the Nineteenth Century: Its Background and History,* trans. Brian Cozens, John W. Bowden, et al. (London: SCM Press, 1972), where Barth's idea of the task of church dogmatics reflects Schleiermacher's discussion of the same in the *Brief Outline.*

7. For our purposes it must suffice to say that at about the time of the appearance of *Die christliche Dogmatik in Entwurf, vol. 1, Die Lehre vom Worte Gottes* (1927), Barth's thinking began to move in new directions. This turn from

the stark "dialectical" polemic of his 2d ed. of *The Epistle to the Romans* to more constructive concerns was symbolized in the appearance in 1931 of his *Anselm: Fides Quaerens Intellectum*. For the details of this crucial turn, which paved the way to the *Church Dogmatics*, see, e.g., T. F. Torrance, *Karl Barth: An Introduction to His Early Theology, 1910–1931* (London: SCM Press, 1962), 182; Hans W. Frei, "Niebuhr's Theological Background," in *Faith and Ethics: The Theology of H. Richard Niebuhr*, ed. Paul Ramsey (New York: Harper & Bros., 1957), 41, as well as n. 37; and Hans Urs von Balthasar, *The Theology of Karl Barth*, trans. John Drury (New York: Holt, Rinehart and Winston, 1971), 48–81.

8. von Balthasar, *Theology of Karl Barth*, 32.

9. As we saw in n. 7, the year 1931 marked the transition of Barth to more constructive dogmatic concerns. Examples of his criticism in passing may be seen in his "Evangelical Theology in the Nineteenth Century," in *The Humanity of God*, trans. Thomas Wieser and John Newton Thomas (Richmond: John Knox Press, 1960), 14 (here he repudiated the theology and ethics of Schleiermacher and his successors after most of Barth's teachers had signed a declaration of support for the Kaiser at the outbreak of World War I); in his "The Strange New World of the Bible," in *The Word of God and the Word of Man*, trans. Douglas Horton (New York: Harper & Bros., 1957), 45 (here he repudiated the "human standpoint" of Schleiermacher and neo-Protestantism); and in his "The Word of God and the Task of the Ministry," in *The Word of God and the Word of Man*, 195–97 (here he read Schleiermacher out of the "ancestral line" of authentic response to biblical revelation, running "back through *Kierkegaard* to *Luther* and *Calvin*, and so to *Paul* and *Jeremiah*," and made a criticism of Schleiermacher's correlation of sin and grace that will be touched on in the essay of Robert F. Streetman). Most of the essays in *The Theology of Schleiermacher* were published only in 1978; thus their greatest impact has been reserved for our own generation.

10. Paul Tillich, "Two Types of Philosophy of Religion," in his *Theology of Culture*, ed. Robert C. Kimball (New York: Oxford Univ. Press, 1959), 10.

11. Torrance, *Karl Barth*, 83–84. Torrance cites T. E. Hulme's *Speculations* (London, 1924) on this concept.

12. F. D. E. Schleiermacher, *The Christian Faith*, trans. H. R. Mackintosh and J. S. Stewart (Edinburgh: T. & T. Clark, 1928), §4, p. 12.

13. Samuel Terrien, *Job: Poet of Existence* (New York: Bobbs-Merrill, 1957), 236.

14. Ibid., 239.

15. H. R. Mackintosh, *Types of Modern Theology: Schleiermacher to Barth* (London: James Nisbet & Co., 1954), 267.

16. Barth, *Theology of Schleiermacher*, xi.

REOPENING
THE
DEBATE

Part

1

Barth's Early Interpretation of Schleiermacher

1

JOHN E. THIEL

Karl Barth's persistent critical interest in Friedrich Schleiermacher's work has often tempted us to think of this hermeneutical encounter as Barth's "lifelong dialogue" with Schleiermacher. If the image of dialogue as applied to the interpretation of past texts suggests at least that the interpreter conducts his business judiciously and sympathetically, then Barth's dialogue with Schleiermacher was not lifelong but began with his essay on Schleiermacher in *Protestant Theology in the Nineteenth Century* (1947).[1] Though severely critical in that essay of Schleiermacher's theology, Barth made every effort to understand Schleiermacher in context. He thus departed from the one-sided, thoroughly polemical, and even ahistorical approach that characterized his preoccupation with Schleiermacher during the 1920s.[2] It would be more in keeping with the content and tone of Barth's early Schleiermacher interpretation to speak of it as a monologue on Schleiermacher's thought. Monologue does not seek nuanced understanding but rejects the possibility of dialogue with a flurry of sweeping accusations and condemnations.

The fact that Barth's early hermeneutical encounter with Schleiermacher took the form of a monologue is itself unusual. I can think of no other instance in the history of theology in which a theological interpreter understood himself to stand in such sharp opposition to—and conducted a "running battle"[3] with—a theological predecessor.[4] In controversies of this sort, a contemporary opponent usually provides the challenge that raises the proponent's theological hackles. Figures from the past are rarely sufficiently threatening to generate the urgent, and even angry, commitment that produces and sustains the interpreter's monologue. But Barth's early interpretation of Schleiermacher provides an example of exactly that rarity.

How does one account for this anomaly in the conduct of theological debate? I think that the most cogent answer is that Barth—dare I use the next word?—experienced Schleiermacher as a contemporary. Henri Bouillard made this same observation of the relationship between Barth and Schleiermacher, though for him it described the judicious and more appreciative evaluation of Schleiermacher in Barth's history of nineteenth-century Protestant theology.[5] But as Barth initiated his dialogue with Schleiermacher in that work, he did not meet Schleiermacher as a contemporary but rather made himself an intellectual contemporary of Schleiermacher's. He understood Schleiermacher in historical, intellectual, and emotional context. Barth's monological approach to Schleiermacher in the 1920s originated from his encountering Schleiermacher as a threatening contemporary, as a formidable adversary against whom he struggled and yet on whom he was oddly dependent for the formation of his theological self-understanding.[6] This aspect of Barth's early Schleiermacher interpretation is well worth understanding, not because it helps us come to grips with Schleiermacher but because it sheds light on Barth, who of the two, I believe, has given clearer definition to our own theological identities.

Until recently, the published writings that substantially constituted Barth's early interpretation of Schleiermacher were three essays and one review that originally appeared between 1924 and 1927. The three essays, later collected with others under the title *Theology and Church* (1938), are "Schleiermacher's Celebration of Christmas" (1924), "Schleiermacher" (1926), and "The Word in Theology from Schleiermacher to Ritschl" (1927). Barth's review of Emil Brunner's anti-Schleiermacher polemic *Die Mystik und das Wort* appeared in a 1924 issue of *Zwischen den Zeiten*. With the publication in 1978 of Barth's first university lectures on Schleiermacher, delivered at Göttingen in the winter semester of 1923–24, we have in our possession for the first time the architectonic of Barth's early Schleiermacher interpretation. Let us first consider the contribution these lectures make to our understanding of Barth's monologue on Schleiermacher.

THE THEME OF PEACE IN
THE GÖTTINGEN LECTURES AND THE
PUBLISHED ESSAYS

At the outset of the Göttingen lectures, Barth announced his plan to examine Schleiermacher as a preacher, a professor of theology, and a philosopher. Because of limitations of time, Barth omitted analysis of Schleiermacher's philosophical work except for the *Speeches on Religion,* which he ranked under the subject matter of this discipline. Dietrich Ritschl, the editor of the Göttingen lectures, divides Barth's notes into two sections entitled "Die Predigt" and "Die Wissenschaft." In order to focus my interest in these lectures, permit me to express an opinion about each of these two sections. Barth's treatment of "Die Wissenschaft," which comprised the theological encyclopedia, hermeneutics, dogmatics, and the *Speeches,* is a tedious exposition of Schleiermacher by way of Schleiermacher, with an occasional caustic comment, raised eyebrow, or cluck of the tongue on Barth's part. Barth's examination of Schleiermacher's scientific works is disappointingly unoriginal. This, however, is not surprising. Barth exhibits all the traits of a professor offering a new course early in his career. He is plodding as he finds his way for the first time; he subjects his students to details he must learn, which when synthesized would excite future students but which could only bore those of the winter semester of 1923–24.

What professor, though, exhibits genius in his first interpretation of a seminal figure? But Barth himself did in his treatment of Schleiermacher's sermons. Barth was aware of his originality and, looking back on that semester in the last year of his life, observed that "no one either before or since [the Göttingen lectures] has attempted to interpret Schleiermacher in the light of his sermons."[7]

Barth began his examination of the homiletic literature by suggesting that the "characteristic lines of Schleiermacher's thinking and utterance" be analyzed in a "short sequence of his sermons,"[8] and after assuring his audience that his choice of material was purely at random, settled on the last six sermons Schleiermacher preached, beginning with the New Year's Day sermon of 1834. Despite Barth's disclaimer that any vested interest influenced his choice of subject matter, one cannot help noticing how foundational that New Year's Day sermon was for Barth's early interpretation of Schleiermacher.

The text for New Year's Day 1834 was John 20:19: "Jesus said to them, 'Peace be with you.'" Schleiermacher's exposition of this Gospel passage addresses the reception of the Redeemer's peace at all levels of social life, by the nations, Christian communions, the universities, and Christian homes. His treatment of this theme is thoroughly Romantic, sensitive, and full of optimistic expectation. Here one meets the personal hopes and heartfelt wishes of a man who spent his career, indeed his mature life, in search of peace in all its elusive manifestations. I hope that it would not be too Romantic of me to say that Schleiermacher's sermon is touching. And yet Barth's reading of this sermon might be likened to a foxhound yapping at the heels of its quarry. Why of all possible Schleiermacher texts did Barth choose this one as a paradigm of all that he found wrong with the theologian, and why did a Schleiermacher sermon on peace, of all things, excite his critical ire? In order to answer these questions, let us hear Barth's objections to the New Year's Day sermon.

According to Barth, this sermon's theme of peace "characterizes all Schleiermacher's teaching in these years (and perhaps not in these alone)."[9] Barth continues,

> Not so much the disposition of the preacher [commends this peace], for in many places, especially in the early sermons, this is critical and polemical almost to the point of a certain irritability, but rather in the purpose and intellectual content of his proclamation. The uniting of what is divided, the reconciling of what is opposed, communion between those that differ—this seems to be (in a very general sense) the concern which ultimately motivates him.[10]

This ultimately motivating concern of peace, Barth maintains, is the "secret of Schleiermacher's genius."[11]

Barth urges the theme of peace upon his Göttingen audience as an interpretive key to Schleiermacher's thought. Schleiermacher's concept of peace, Barth claims, "always means the overcoming of antitheses in a higher *third thing*, the achieving of a balance between the two arms of the great scales of life."[12] Barth recognizes that this "higher third thing" is not the consummating moment in a dynamic Hegelian type of dialectic. For Schleiermacher, the resolution of antitheses lies within, not beyond, their scope. It is the life of equanimity, the life beyond turmoil and anxiety, in Schleiermacher's own theological terminology, the life of blessedness.

Barth recognizes Schleiermacher's ostensible concern that the Christian life of peace be christologically founded but judges his effort in this regard a failure. Barth charges that Schleiermacher reduces Christ to a mere exemplification of the ideally balanced Christian life. The Christ of Schleiermacher's last sermons becomes for Barth the experience of peace itself. Once this interpretation is suggested, Barth's conclusion is an expected finale to his relentless pursuit: "It was clear that even Schleiermacher could not self-evidently find his Christ, the Christ of synthesis, in the Bible."[13]

In the Göttingen lectures, Barth sees Schleiermacher's preoccupation with peace as a misguided yearning for the harmony of Christianity and culture which accommodated the gospel to secular life. Even when he admires Schleiermacher's openness of vision and powerful voice,[14] Barth ultimately rails against the inadequacy of what he takes to be Schleiermacher's theological complacency, his sacralization of bourgeois achievement, and his obeisance to the expectations of culture. In other words, what Barth finds objectionable is Schleiermacher's inability to employ theology as a critical tool turned in the direction of human nature and its social setting. As Barth states forcefully in the following passage, Schleiermacher could only be a critic of schismatic criticism:

> Schleiermacher strives against all strife, against all that might come from it or lead to it; he allows himself the liberty of being cross with all who are cross and sharp; he fights zealously for peace and harmony; he is filled with a passion for mediation, agreement, and the quenching of all passion.[15]

We find quite similar condemnations of this "Schleiermacherian heaven of peace"[16] in Barth's examination of Schleiermacher's christological festival sermons and the household sermons of 1818. It is hardly surprising, therefore, that Barth finds the theme of peace indispensable as he continues his monologue in his published Schleiermacher essays.

The most famous of Barth's published Schleiermacher essays from this period is the text entitled simply "Schleiermacher," which appeared in 1926. In this general and rather desultory writing, Barth reaffirms his commitment to the theme of peace as the unifying category in Schleiermacher's thought. Here, however, Barth elaborates this theme under the rubric of the "principle of the center." This image, with its suggestion of the middle point of a circle, is a direct assault on the image of the ellipse which Schleiermacher had offered as the correct portraiture of his thinking.[17] The "principle of the center," posed by Barth as an alternative metaphor, denies the dialectical polarity of Schleiermacher's thinking and indicates what to Barth's mind is the quiescent goal of peace toward which Schleiermacher's thinking is inclined. According to the 1926 essay, this "centre beyond all contradiction, this One which absorbs every two into itself, is the deeper sense of Schleiermacher's concept of union. It is this which he meant when he preached peace."[18]

Barth argues throughout the 1926 essay that the theme of the center appears in virtually every aspect of Schleiermacher's work. In the *Dialektik* it takes the form of the presupposed ground of thinking and being; in the *Speeches* it is the immediate consciousness defined by the passivity of intuition and the activity of feeling; in *The Christian Faith* the center appears as the God-consciousness that transcends thinking and doing, relative dependence and relative freedom. Standing above the self-world antithesis in Schleiermacher's thought is what Barth calls a "Schleiermacherian Unity, a peace in relation to which this contradiction is relative and evanescent."[19]

Barth understands the principle of the center in this essay just as he understands the theme of peace in Schleiermacher's later sermons. In fact, the principle of the center is simply an image for the Schleiermacherian peace that preoccupied Barth in the Göttingen lectures. The center is the untroubled experience of the harmonious life with which Barth identifies Schleiermacher's understanding of religion. It is the goal of the religious quest, the x binding all particularities into the unity of the whole. It is the heart of human culture, the coincidence of the natural and supernatural to which all human potential aspires and in which human achievement rests in the appreciation of historical fulfillment.

This same quarrel, or if you please monologue, is continued in the other two Schleiermacher essays Barth published in the 1920s. Although Barth does not make specific appeal to the theme of peace in these writings as he did in the Göttingen lectures and the essay of 1926, he adopts the same critical standpoint. In the essay "Schleiermacher's Celebration of Christmas" (1924), Barth judges Schleiermacher's 1806 dialogue *Die Weihnachtsfeier* to be misguided in its interpretation of the incarnation as a symbol of the integrated human life.[20] Barth argues that this universal truth of the Christ event—the peaceful unity of the God-consciousness so worthy of imitation—overwhelms Schleiermacher to the extent that he overlooks the historical particularity of Christmas. Barth observes that Schleiermacher employs two recurring images in his dialogue to represent the completed and fulfilled, that is, peaceful, human life: motherly love (which Schleiermacher develops as the relationship between Ernestine and Sophie)[21] and the healing power of music (with which Schleiermacher has his company end their at times testy dialogue precisely because, Barth maintains, it is finally in a "musical Christianity" that the words and concepts that lead to dissension are left behind in the peace that is the "genuine miracle of Christmas").[22] In its own way, Barth's essay "The Word in Theology from Schleiermacher to Ritschl" (1927) very briefly makes this same point in its insistence that Schleiermacher denies the objective authority of

Scripture in order to affirm the corporate subjectivity of the Christian community grounded in the untroubled blessedness of the Redeemer.[23]

Perhaps Barth's consistent appeal to such images as these can be summarized by way of a judgment we find in the 1926 Schleiermacher essay. Speaking of Schleiermacher's preoccupation with the theme of peace, Barth observes with his customary élan that the "great X which Schleiermacher had in mind was not so much the Christian revelation as the modern pagan feeling for life."[24] An exaggeration? Certainly! This sort of statement is the very thing for which Barth excoriated Emil Brunner in his 1924 review of *Die Mystik und das Wort.* And yet our recognition of Barth's unfairness should not prevent us from understanding this sweeping, inflated judgment that so sharply punctuates Barth's monologue. Why did Barth label Schleiermacher's notion of the peaceful and harmonious Christian existence the modern (notice, modern) pagan feeling for life?

SCHLEIERMACHER AS CONTEMPORARY: THE DIALECTICS OF PEACE AND STRIFE

One can find the beginnings of an answer to this question in the writing that heralded Barth's early theological position, the *Epistle to the Romans* in its second edition (1922). This work was Barth's manifesto against the liberal theological tradition that, he believed, Schleiermacher had fathered. Through the concepts of paradox and crisis, Barth employed a rigorous dialectical method to assess the integrity of a theological climate that had lasted an entire century. According to his often-stated conclusion, the culture-Protestantism of the preceding century had reduced the gospel to the themes of subjectivity and religion, talk about God to talk about human existence, the strife of God's Word to the peace of human experience and its cultural expression.

It is interesting that the three times Barth mentions Schleiermacher by name in the *Epistle to the Romans,* he does so in the context of his discussion of the "last human possibility," namely, religion. In these three examples, which I quote at length, I call the reader's attention to the dialectic Barth constructs between peace and strife:

> The Gospel of Christ is a shattering disturbance. . . . For this reason, nothing is so meaningless as the attempt to construct a religion out of the Gospel, and to set it as one human possibility in the midst of others. Since Schleiermacher, this attempt has been undertaken more consciously than ever before in Protestant theology—and it is the betrayal of Christ. The

man under grace is engaged unconditionally in a conflict. This conflict is a war of life and death, a war in which there can be no armistice, no agreement—and no peace.[25]

The second example is less direct but consistent in its use of imagery:

The romantic psychologist may make many attempts to hush . . . up [sin's triumph in religion]: he may represent religion as that human capacity by which "all human occurrences are thought of as divine actions"; he may define it as "the solemn music which accompanies all human experience" (Schleiermacher). Against such representations, however, religion is always on its guard. . . . Religion, so far from being the place where the healthy harmony of human life is lauded, is instead the place where it appears diseased, discordant, and disrupted.[26]

The third example is most pointed:

Religion spells disruption, discord, and the absence of peace. . . . It is almost incredible that, on the day when Schleiermacher finished writing his "Lectures about Religion," his joy in creation, apparently suddenly, was crossed by the fear of death. "What a shame it would be," he said, "were I to die to-night!" One would have supposed that, whilst writing so many beautiful and moving words "about religion" (!) he would have been faced continually by the fact of death. Is it possible to recommend religion to men who long sincerely and simply for peace?[27]

A rhetorical question to which Barth expects the retort of a loud, Brunnerian no! Simply put, Barth found in Schleiermacher's theology the antithesis of his own. Barth's dialectical theology recognizes the inescapability of conflict as human possibility is confronted by the actuality of the eternal, as the words generated by reason confront their inadequacy in the Word of God received in faith. As Barth put it in his Göttingen lectures, "In this battle against all religious excitement, against every either-or, Schleiermacher finally attacks all real *tensions*, all *crisis*."[28]

Barth objected to Schleiermacher's treatment of the theme of peace on the grounds that the harmony Schleiermacher sought through his mediating approach was a chimera. For Barth, the Schleiermacherian understanding of peace was the consummate expression of the self-satisfaction accompanying all religiosity, the human tendency to invert the self-God relationship.[29] This "peace," in Barth's view, did not describe a state of affairs among nations or Christian communions, in the universities or Christian homes. It described an experience that, to his mind, was nothing but the sinful condition that permeated fallen human nature and that his theological generation celebrated as the center of Christian life at the expense of the gospel. Seeing Schleiermacher's understanding of peace in this way led Barth to describe it as the "modern pagan feeling for life."

I would like to conclude by considering this phrase one last time. It is odd, I think, for anyone to describe peace in this way, but perhaps Barth's early Schleiermacher interpretation has made his histrionics more understandable. For Barth, the Schleiermacherian peace is a "feeling for life" because it is human nature itself. It is "pagan" in its ignorance of the gospel message. But what is "modern" about the "modern pagan feeling for life"? In light of my earlier claim that Barth regarded Schleiermacher as a threatening contemporary, I might rephrase this question by asking what, in Barth's own experience, this illusory Schleiermacherian peace was, this thin mask of harmony that disguised the unavoidable conflict of time and eternity in the human condition. Most generally, Barth encountered the illusion of peace as the glorified complacency of the status quo which, I would like to suggest, he met in three principal dimensions of his theological existence: the pulpit, the factory, and the university.

That Barth settled on Schleiermacher's sermons as an entry to his theology tells us much more about Barth than it does about Schleiermacher. Barth found Schleiermacher to be the sort of preacher who skirted the challenge of the pulpit, preaching comfort and tranquillity while avoiding the strife and turmoil of the gospel message. No doubt, Barth encountered his representation of Schleiermacher as the preacher of peace—whether fair or not—not only in the homiletic activity of his colleagues but also as a constant temptation as he carried out his own pastoral duties.

Closely related to this first dimension of Schleiermacher's contemporaneousness is the content of Barth's preaching in his early years as a pastor in Safenwil. Without entering the debate as to when and to what degree Barth was a socialist, I believe there is sufficient evidence to claim that the young Barth saw entrepreneurial capitalism as an aspect of the status quo which brought the illusion of economic peace to a few at the expense of the many.[30]

Finally, Schleiermacher's contemporaneousness manifested itself to Barth in the setting of the academy, as nearly all his theological teachers gave their support to the militaristic policies of Kaiser Wilhelm II. Barth regarded this action as a sign of the ethical failure of the liberal theological tradition, for its proponents' nationalistic commitment was so confused that it could find an untroubled self-righteousness in the prospect of an unjustified war.[31]

If Barth did experience Schleiermacher as a contemporary in the early years of his career, he experienced his threatening vitality in those who cried, "Peace!" where there was none. And if one at all accepts the premise that Barth was correct in his theological assessment of the nineteenth century, then perhaps only by the abrasiveness of the monologue could one expect to inject the dissonance of the gospel into the great chorus of liberal voices singing the harmony of religion to the peaceful status quo of contemporary culture. Is it not ironic that Barth could write playfully in his last year of his "eschatological peace with Schleiermacher" to be enjoyed as they continued their discussion in the kingdom of heaven?[32] As Barth never tired of reminding us, eternity and time are not the same, and evidently neither are the forms of discourse one speaks in the two realms.

NOTES

1. Karl Barth, *Die protestantische Theologie im 19. Jahrhundert* (Zollikon: Evangelischer Verlag, 1947); ET: *Protestant Theology in the Nineteenth Century*, trans. Brian Cozens and John Bowden (London: SCM Press, 1972).

2. Several commentators have noted Barth's more appreciative assessment of Schleiermacher in this essay. See, e.g., Henri Bouillard, *Karl Barth: Genèse et evolution de la théologie dialectique*, vol. 1 (Aubier: Editions Montaigne, 1957), 153–54; and Paul Seifert, *Die Theologie des jungen Schleiermacher* (Gütersloh: Gerd Mohn, 1960), 11.

3. Karl Barth, "Schleiermacher" (1926), in *Theology and Church: Shorter Writings, 1920–1928*, trans. Louise Pettibone Smith (London: SCM Press, 1962), 199.

4. One possible exception is Emil Brunner, whose book *Die Mystik und das Wort* (1924) is a thoroughly polemical assault upon Schleiermacher's thought. As different as Brunner's Schleiermacher criticism is from Barth's at the level of detail, its principles are deeply indebted to Barth's theological standpoint. As history has demonstrated, it is Barth's challenge to Schleiermacher that is memorable precisely because its vision is unique.

5. Bouillard, *Karl Barth*, 153.

6. Interestingly, Barth noticed this aspect of Brunner's relationship to Schleiermacher while failing to recognize it of his own. See Karl Barth, "Brunners Schleiermacherbuch," *Zwischen den Zeiten* 8 (1924): 52.

7. Karl Barth, "Nachwort," in *Schleiermacher-Auswahl*, ed. Heinz Bolli (Munich: Siebenstern Taschenbuch Verlag, 1968); ET: "Concluding Unscientific Postscript on Schleiermacher," trans. George Hunsinger, in *Studies in Religion/Sciences religieuses* 7 (1978): 122.

8. Karl Barth, *Die Theologie Schleiermachers*, in *Karl Barth Gesamtausgabe*, vol. 5/2 (Zurich: Theologischer Verlag, 1978); ET: *The Theology of Schleiermacher: Lectures at Göttingen, Winter Semester of 1923/24*, ed. Dietrich Ritschl, trans. Geoffrey W. Bromiley (Grand Rapids: Wm. B. Eerdmans, 1982), 3–4.

9. Ibid. (ET), 10–11.

10. Ibid., 11.

11. Ibid., 24.

12. Ibid., 12.

13. Ibid., 16.

14. Ibid., 39.

15. Ibid., 39.

16. Karl Barth, "The Paradoxical Nature of the 'Positive Paradox': Answers and Questions to Paul Tillich" (1923), in *The Beginnings of Dialectic Theology*, vol. 1, ed. James M. Robinson, trans. Keith R. Crim (Richmond: John Knox Press, 1968), 145.

17. The well-known example is in Schleiermacher's letter to the philosopher Jacobi. See Friedrich Schleiermacher, *Aus Schleiermachers Leben: In Briefen*, vol. 2, ed. Ludwig Jonas and Wilhelm Dilthey (Berlin: Georg Reimer, 1860; Berlin: Walter de Gruyter, 1974), 349–53.

18. Barth, "Schleiermacher" (1926), 167.

19. Ibid., 173.

20. Karl Barth, "Schleiermacher's Celebration of Christmas" (1924), in *Theology and Church*, 137–38.

21. Ibid., 146.

22. Ibid., 157.

23. Karl Barth, "The Word in Theology from Schleiermacher to Ritschl" (1927), in *Theology and Church*, 202–3.

24. Barth, "Schleiermacher" (1926), 191.

25. Karl Barth, *Der Römerbrief*, 2d edition, (Munich: Chr. Kaiser, 1922); ET: *The Epistle to the Romans*, trans. Edwyn C. Hoskyns (New York: Oxford Univ. Press, 1933), 225.

26. Ibid. (ET), 257–58.

27. Ibid., 266–67.

28. Barth, *Theology of Schleiermacher*, 43. The theme of peace served as an excellent contrast to Barth's portrayal of the human condition as *diastasis* during the 1920s. As Barth changed theological direction late in the decade, his interpretation of Schleiermacher by way of the theme of peace was left behind.

29. For a discussion of Barth's treatment of the category of "religion" in *Der Römerbrief*, see Gérard Vallée, "Foi et religion dans le commentaire de l'épître aux romains de Karl Barth," *Science et esprit* 32 (1980): 331–46.

30. For a compilation of the important texts and articles, see *Karl Barth and Radical Politics*, ed. and trans. George Hunsinger (Philadelphia: Westminster Press, 1976).

31. Although I agree with Wilfried Härle's position that Barth's break with liberal theology cannot be dated, following Barth's later recollections, with the

October 1914 declaration *An die Kulturwelt!*, by the ninety-three intellectuals, I find it difficult to minimize the significance of this event at the time in Barth's theological odyssey to the degree that Härle does. The absence of mention of this incident in Barth's Thurneysen correspondence rightly merits suspicion about the claim that this event was crucial to Barth's development, but equally deserving of suspicion is Härle's tendency thoroughly to minimize the impact of this event, especially in light of the fact that he dates the beginnings of Barth's break with the liberal tradition from the year 1911. It is difficult to imagine that a personal theological agenda three years old would have missed the significance of such an occurrence. See Wilfried Härle, "Der Aufruf der 93 Intellektuellen und Karl Barths Bruch mit der liberalen Theologie," *Zeitschrift für Theologie und Kirche* 72 (1975): 207–24.

32. Barth, "Concluding Unscientific Postscript," 133–34.

Christ, Nature, and Consciousness: Reflections on Schleiermacher in the Light of Barth's Early Criticisms

2

RICHARD R. NIEBUHR

In the course of his epoch-making and often polemical career, Karl Barth issued not just one or two but a virtual spate of critical responses to Friedrich Schleiermacher. These frequent returns to Schleiermacher suggest that within his deep opposition to the foremost German theologian of the nineteenth century something like an irrepressible affinity repeatedly drew Barth's thoughts back to the Berlin preacher, church statesman, and university professor with whom at one point he announced himself to be at war.[1] In the stairwell of Barth's house in Basel, a portrait of Schleiermacher hung in a preeminent position, second only to the place occupied by a likeness of "Father Kant," and in an informal conversation one evening in 1958, Barth spoke of Schleiermacher at length and in warm terms, praising him for his fidelity to the vocation of preacher and for his Christocentrism.

The best known of Barth's critical engagements with Schleiermacher appears in his volume on nineteenth-century Protestant theology published in 1947, by which time Barth had become the dominant voice in Protestant theology.[2] That essay and a number of others he devoted to the same subject did much to kindle the interest of readers of Barth's works in the theologian he evidently took so seriously.[3] Now we have a published translation of an earlier and much longer critique of Schleiermacher delivered by Barth as a course of lectures at Göttingen in the winter semester of the academic year 1923–24.[4] In this volume's "Concluding Unscientific Postscript on Schleiermacher," dating from 1968, or forty-four years after the lectures were given, Barth explains that a time of decision came in 1914 when he had to turn against Schleiermacher. That turning point was the declaration by a group of German theologians of their support of the war policy of Kaiser Wilhelm II. Many of Barth's own teachers had been signatories, and Barth reacted by judging "that the entire theology which had unmasked itself in that manifesto . . . was grounded, determined, and influenced decisively by [Schleiermacher]."[5] Barth adds that he remained convinced Schleiermacher himself would not have put his name to this manifesto, but the sentiments he expresses in the "Postscript" confirm that Schleiermacher had become for him something like an omnipresent antagonist whose shadow he detected everywhere he looked—not only in the theology of his teachers but also in the theology of his contemporaries, notably Rudolf Bultmann and the many others who like Bultmann contended that theology had to be "*existential* . . . in a material, technical, and fundamental sense." "Once again," Barth exclaims, referring to this group "the symbiosis of theology and philosophy so characteristic of Schleiermacher! Once again, an anthropologizing of theology, just as in Schleiermacher, who had thereby simultaneously brought the theological learning of the eighteenth century to completion while establishing that of the nineteenth century!"[6]

An "anthropologizing of theology"! Here we have a principal thesis in much of what Barth wrote about Schleiermacher. In this essay, with Barth's criticism in mind, we will first inquire into the structure of Schleiermacher's treatment of the relation between the supernatural and the natural, and then we will reexamine aspects of his "anthropological starting point," that is, aspects of his delineation of the Christian religious consciousness.

CHRIST AND NATURE

Barth's lectures of 1923–24 begin, fittingly enough, with a survey of Schleiermacher's Christmas, Good Friday, and Easter sermons on Christ. A clause in a very early Christmas sermon, preached by Schleiermacher in 1790 or 1791 at the age of twenty-two or twenty-three, expecially attracts Barth's attention: "[Christ] presents to us his own example as the highest triumph of human nature."[7] On the basis of this and similar locutions, Barth infers that according to Schleiermacher there is between Christ and ourselves "only [a] quantitative difference," a difference that can be diminished by our approximating Christ's example.[8] Barth finds this judgment confirmed not only by other sermons but also by *On Religion: Speeches to Its Cultured Despisers* (1799); by the "dialogue" on Christmas of 1806, *Die Weihnachtsfeier:*

Ein Gespräch;[9] by *The Brief Outline of the Study of Theology* (1811; rev. ed., 1830); and by the theological accomplishment of Schleiermacher's maturity, *The Christian Faith* (1821–22; rev. ed., 1830–31). Hence, when Barth comes to comment on §13 in *The Christian Faith* ("The appearance of the Redeemer in history is, as divine revelation, neither an absolutely supernatural nor an absolutely supra-rational thing"), he does not surprise us when he declares, "Fundamentally there is nothing super*natural* here—Christ, too, is an act of nature, a final development of its spiritual power."[10] Barth is right, of course, about the absence of the "absolutely" supernatural from Schleiermacher's theology, but he is misleading in saying that Schleiermacher's Christ is an act of nature. What he fails to note in his declaration is that the "spiritual power" with which §13 is concerned is a power *divinely* instituted in the divine constitution of human being in its relationships to the whole system of beings governed by God. Schleiermacher is not oblivious of the venerable distinction between the natural and supernatural; rather, he deliberately challenges it. Barth, on the other hand, at the time of his lectures on Schleiermacher in 1923–24 has a great deal invested in the distinction or difference, as his brilliant *Epistle to the Romans*, published a few years earlier, attests. In order to gauge for ourselves the import of the language about the appearance of Christ as being not "absolutely supernatural" in §13 of *The Christian Faith*, we should have in mind several principles Schleiermacher enunciates and at least one of his major "tactical" decisions, a decision reflected in the arrangement of the parts of the book. We will begin by noticing three of these principles and take account of the tactical decision subsequently.

The first of these principles is that theology is a *positive* science. Schleiermacher announces the principle at the outset of his theological encyclopedia, *Brief Outline of the Study of Theology*, and it informs the entirety of *The Christian Faith*. Theology is a positive science in the sense that it distinguishes, describes, and assesses historical and empirical moments of religious faith. Again, it is positive because it arises in response to the needs of a determinate mode of faith or form of God-consciousness. These needs are social needs inasmuch as determinate modes of faith generate and are generated by visible religious communities or churches. The social needs to which theology responds are those of solving practical problems that church communities face.

The second principle concerns the *location* of dogmatic theology. It stands out most forcibly when we consider Schleiermacher's placement of dogmatics in relation to the other branches of theology. Theology as a whole divides into three main parts: philosophical theology, historical theology, and practical theology. Dogmatic theology is a subdivision of historical theology, because it examines and restates a church's inherited faith in that church's *present* historical times. Its task is threefold: (*a*) to set forth a church's mode of faith in doctrinal propositions; (*b*) to judge the greater or lesser normative weight of these doctrines for the community in its present circumstances, making these judgments with a view to the past, to the anticipated future, and to the relations of "antithesis" in which that church stands to other Christian communities; and (*c*) to arrange these doctrines in systematic order. Hence, dogmatic theology is temporally and spatially *situated:* like its sister theologies, it too springs from and contributes to the task of guiding a visible church community through the exigencies of a time and a place. Therefore, no dogmatic theology can pretend to validity for all Christian communities in all times and places. This idea of dogmatic theology as being always situated, even while discharging its various tasks, carries far-reaching consequences.

The third principle is a further specification of the second. To discharge its tasks in a timely way, Christian dogmatic theology executes two operations that require practiced skill. The first of these appears in the maxim that it is living faith, not mere attachment to ecclesiastical antiquity, that endows doctrine with authority. Accordingly, a task of dogmatic theology is to transpose the actual "religious affections" of a determinate or localized Christian mode of faith into doctrinal propositions of a conceptual kind. Propositions that do not express actual religious affections have no dogmatic value. The second operation is the ordering of these propositions into a fruitful, forward-looking systematic whole. Many systems are possible, but to discern which system is forward-looking and productive is taxing indeed. *The Christian Faith* offers evidences of its author's struggles to achieve this effect. *The Christian Faith,* composed to serve the newly formed Evangelical church, a union of the hitherto divided Lutheran and Reformed churches of Prussia which Schleiermacher himself had helped to bring about, is its author's contribution to dogmatic theology in accordance with the foregoing principles. The book presents this church's mode of faith as being (*a*) monotheistic in its wide compass; (*b*) specifically teleological; (*c*) still more specifically Christian; and (*d*) particularly evangelical in the sense just mentioned. Schleiermacher condenses virtually all of these moments into a single proposition:

Christianity is a monotheistic mode of faith, belonging to the teleological type of religion, and is essentially distinguished from other such [modes of faith] by the fact that in it *everything* is related to the redemption accomplished by Jesus of Nazareth. (§11; emphasis added)

In one sense this proposition is admirably clear. In another it is misleading, because such stiff taxonomic language shrouds the fact that modes of faith are forms of social and individual life. Labeling and classifying religions tends to hypostasize them, to turn them into fixities. We need to be on guard, therefore, lest the kind of language §11 features impede our understanding of Schleiermacher's deeper purpose. To be sure, §11 is not a dogmatic statement but a "borrowed proposition"—in this instance borrowed from apologetical theology. Still, in its extraordinary compactness it reflects a perplexity pertaining to order that a dogmatic theology constructed on Schleiermacher's principles must address. How does a dogmatic theology project the path or curve of faith, the multiple loci that faith "occupies" all at one time? With which religious affections does a dogmatic theology begin and with which does it conclude, as it orders its presentation of a living mode of faith into a timely, forward-looking system? Does it begin with the consciousness of simple [absolute] dependence on God and interdependence with everything comprehended in the system of nature, that is, the world? Or with the consciousness of being vivified and transformed by the new life issuing from Christ? Neither option is wholly satisfactory; each exacts a price. No series of propositions can show how the affections they express are all continually modulating one another. But Schleiermacher requires that dogmatics show that the community's faith relation to Christ modulates its relation to the world, to the "system of nature," and that its relation to the "system of nature" modifies its relation to Christ. The task of church guidance demands as much. A theology charged with accomplishing the tasks on which Schleiermacher insists faces a genuine dilemma. He makes a statement in his open letters to Friedrich Lücke, his apologia for *The Christian Faith*, that casts the dilemma in sharp relief. "Christians," he writes, "bear their whole God-consciousness only as a fruit brought forth in them by Christ."[11] The moment that dogmatics goes to work distributing this organic whole into a systematic articulation of scientific propositions, it loses precisely what it wants to present. It is clear then that a *living* determinate mode of faith or form of God-consciousness resists, even defies, reduction to an orderly, linear presentation in dogmatic propositions. We have external evidence that Schleiermacher recognizes as much, at least to a degree, because in his open letters to Lücke he recounts his own debate about which group of doctrines to give first place: the complex of doctrines pertaining to "creation" and "preservation" of the world or the complex pertaining to "fall," "redemption," and "sanctification." Among other things, the conception of nature and the natural is at stake in this debate. As we know, Schleiermacher's compromise is to keep the conventional order, but he does his best to mitigate the consequences.

An inspection of the progression within the book itself alerts us to these difficulties. We can discern them if we examine the arrangement of the main parts of *The Christian Faith* and their corresponding headings:

INTRODUCTION

Chapter 1, Toward a Clarification of Dogmatics
Chapter 2, On the Method of Dogmatics

THE CHRISTIAN FAITH, FIRST PART

Development of the religious self-consciousness as it is always already presupposed by but also always comprehended in every Christian religious affection

THE CHRISTIAN FAITH, SECOND PART

Development of the actual matters [*Tatsachen*] of the religious self-consciousness as they are determined by the antithesis [of sin and grace][12]

Leaving aside the introduction for the moment, we should observe that the three "sections" of the first part all concern the "relation between World and God in so far as that relation appears in *Christian* religious self-consciousness." That which Christian religious affections *presuppose* is also *comprehended* in them. Next, we should observe that the second part continues to set out propositions about the relation of World and God, especially in its "second section," deploying these propositions according to the schematism of the religious self-consciousness as determined by sin and grace. Together, these observations impress on us that Schleiermacher presents dogmatic statements concerning God and World, that is, God and nature or the natural, throughout the entire body of the work. And this entire body of the work, moreover, is a setting-forth of Christian religious affections. A reciprocal of this fact is that *The Christian Faith* does not confine its statements about nature and the natural to any single part of the work.

Returning now to the introduction, we note that in the letters to Lücke, Schleiermacher variously calls the introduction an "ante-chamber" and a "determination of the place (or site)" of the dogmatic theology that follows. The latter phrase is especially striking, since it echoes two of the author's principles that we have already noted: that theology is positive, and that it is situated.[13] He also voices some dismay that readers of the first edition apparently concentrated their attention entirely on the introduction and neglected the substantive exposition of dogma in the first and second parts. (In his 1923–24 lectures, Barth addresses himself only to the introduction and not to the book as a whole.) Proposition 13, for example, which, as we have seen, Barth severely criticizes, falls within the introduction. But since the introduction is no more than the antechamber, it is only reasonable to enter the edifice made up of the first and second parts to discover the actual import of the language of §13. Similarly, when Schleiermacher writes in §13, part 1, that even from the point of view of the highest Christology "the appearance of the Son of God . . . as having become human [*Menschwerden*]" can be regarded "as something natural," readers should consider not only the propositions in the first part concerning the "World" and the "whole system of nature" but also the propositions in the second part concerning the person of Christ and, in the "second section" of the second part, the "Constitution of the World in Relation to Redemption" before they judge what the author means by "natural."

As the headings of the first and second parts announce, each part is a development (*Entwicklung*) of the Christian religious self-consciousness or the affections (*Erregungen*) of that self-consciousness. *Entwicklung* has many senses: development, growth, unfolding, elucidation. Here the biological senses are, if not uppermost, only just beneath the surface of the text. Therefore, these headings underscore the centrality of the question, Where does one begin when presenting a development? With the seed, the sapling, the more mature plant, or the fallen tree decaying back into the earth? (Schleiermacher often compares himself to a tree— a tree bearing many buds or one shaken and stripped by storms.) Schleiermacher knows, of course, that he is presenting this develop-ment from the perspective neither of its beginning nor of its end; rather he is writing from *within* the process of development. This knowledge directly informs the language he uses in the headings of the two parts of the dogmatics. The first part presents what "is always already presupposed by but also always comprehended in every Christian religious affection." The second part presents the affections of the Christian religious self-consciousness "as they are determined by the antithesis" of sin and grace, namely, the experience of being redeemed. The relationship of the two parts appears to be circular, or perhaps spiral would be a better analogy. Inasmuch as Schleiermacher is presenting a living, determinate mode of faith, writing as situated in that very faith, he cannot extract himself from the consciousness of sin and grace or redemption when he is engaged in presenting the doctrines pertaining to creation or the natural order. We can see, then, that not only does the second part "presuppose" the first part but that the first part "presupposes" the second. "Redemption" requires "creation," but theological interest in "creation" presupposes confidence in "redemption." Alternatively, each part derives its meaning from the two parts as making a whole, and the whole from each of the parts. And in fact this is a principle fundamental to all interpretation, according to Schleiermacher, the architect of modern hermeneutics. His letters to Lücke tend to confirm the foregoing construction. In the second of these letters, Schleiermacher says that he seriously considered placing the doctrines of Christ and redemption first in the order of exposition. If he had done so,

> the Father would have first become visible in Christ. The first definite statements about God would have been that [God] had renewed the human race through the sending of Christ and through establishment of his spiritual Kingdom in the race; and the first divine attributes [to be discussed] would have been wisdom and love.[14]

That arrangement might also have better demonstrated to readers the author's conviction that John 1:14 is the foundation text at every point of the entire dogmatics.[15] Schleiermacher valued the Fourth Gospel especially, argued for its priority in time, and drew freely upon Johannine Christology. The Johannine Christ is, of course, eternal life in time: "Before Abraham was, I am." It is not surprising, then, that in his central christological propositions in the second part, he affirms that the appearance of Christ and the creation of humankind are rooted in one and the same divine decree: "Christ even as a human person was ever coming to be simultaneously with the world" (§97, part 2).

A motif of the entire second part is that Christ appears in history as a particular fact or *Tatsache*—to use Schleiermacher's language—and yet is coordinate with the whole divine ordering of the world. When

Schleiermacher comes to expound election as being solely determined by the divine "good-pleasure," he writes in §120, part 3:

> Christ therefore was determined as he was, only because, and in so far as, everything as a whole [*der ganze Zusammenhang*] was determined in a certain way; and conversely, everything as a whole was only so determined, because, and in so far as, Christ was determined in a certain way.

"Faith," he adds, "is itself nothing else than sharing in this divine good-pleasure, which abides in Christ and the salvation grounded in him."

Perhaps now it is time to recapitulate the general argument that the organization of *The Christian Faith* presents. By the time Schleiermacher came to compose the work, he had concluded that the conventional scholastic distinction between the natural and the supernatural is specious and unproductive. Nonetheless, he still uses "nature" and "natural," but the sense of these terms no longer depends upon the contrasting term "supernatural." When, for example, he writes in §13, part 1, that Christ "even regarded as the incarnation of the Son of God ... is a natural fact," he uses "nature" and "natural" to signify the interconnectedness of all beings and events. He means that the appearance of the Redeemer in history must be connected with everything that has happened before and everything that has happened afterward.

We should emphasize here that Schleiermacher uses "world" or *Welt,* "system of nature" or *Naturzusammenhang,* and "everything as a whole" or *ganze Zusammenhang* as equivalent terms. In this connection it is helpful to study carefully the text in part 1 of §34, which comes near the outset of the first part of the system of doctrine in *The Christian Faith.* As we have already noted, this first part is an exposition of the *Christian* religious consciousness of the world in dependence on God, not an exposition of a general or indeterminate religious consciousness of the world.[16] And here, in part 1 of §34, Schleiermacher writes that

> the whole system of nature or the world is co-posited in our self-consciousness, insofar as we are conscious of ourselves as parts of the world. [And] this must be the case in every Christian religious affection by virtue of the fact that the sensible [*sinnliche*] self-consciousness always accompanies [every such Christian religious affection].

Thus Schleiermacher affirms that every Christian religious affection carries as a concomitant a consciousness of being part of a world whole. But the grounds for this affirmation do not appear clearly until we follow Schleiermacher into his exposition of Christ, redemption, and election in the second part of *The Christian Faith.* There, to the sentences concerning election quoted just above, Schleiermacher immediately adds,

> To say this is obviously to take our stand upon the divine good-pleasure, and to say that the determination in both cases is what it is simply through the divine good-pleasure.

Two aspects of Schleiermacher's purpose are, I believe, now clear. First, he wants his primary theological subject matter, namely, the Christian's living relation to Christ or experience of redemption and sanctification, to serve as the "place" or arena in which the religious significance of nature or the world appears. The activity of Christ—and of the Holy Spirit—"shapes" our consciousness of being part of the "system of nature." It is in this way that nature acquires its specific Christian theological meaning. Redemption and sanctification make the "lens" through which we read our being in the world. Much as Calvin made the Bible a pair of spectacles through which we might recognize the Creator of the universe, Schleiermacher makes the experience of grace overcoming sin such an "optical" aid. Moreover, to state the obvious (but then the obvious is often just what needs stating), the experience of grace or of being vivified by the life that Christ imparts is through and through social; it transpires in embodied self-consciousness that always entails consciousness of being in relation; it transpires in the community that is the church. Second, Schleiermacher can effect this intention only by firmly anchoring Christ and the church and the system of nature as well in the eternal divine good-pleasure or the electing activity of God.

This way of reading Schleiermacher may not be the customary way but is more plausible than Barth's way. It is, in a manner of speaking theocentric, theocentric in the following sense. The divine good-pleasure determines all things. That is what the Christ-shaped religious consciousness discovers in itself. But *what* is so discovered is not to be confused with the action of discovering. The action of discovering requires that we engage in scrutinizing our consciousness as it is informed by all with which we stand in relation, as that system of relations is being transformed by the redemption wrought in Christ. In the action of discovering, we begin with no private self but with genuine self-consciousness, that is, with consciousness of ourselves in relation, *and the center of our relatedness is the relation Schleiermacher describes as our simple dependence on God.* He is, then, theocentric in something like, but not exactly like, Calvin's way of being theocentric. "True and substantial wisdom principally consists of two parts," Calvin writes, "the knowledge of God, and the knowledge of ourselves." And we can know God, Calvin repeatedly declares, *only* as God is related to ourselves. Similarly, Schleiermacher reminds the reader in the introduction to the dogmatic body of his work: "Any communication [*Kundmachung*] of God which is to be effective on and in us can only express God in his relation to us; and this is not an infrahuman ignorance concerning God but the essence of human limitedness in relation to him" (§10, postscript). On this score one significant difference between Calvin and Schleiermacher is that the latter offers no discussion of a forfeited original revelation of God in the fabric of the world, while Calvin does. Another significant difference is that Schleiermacher declines the doctrine of double election, because double election would violate our Christian religious sense of being related to all other beings.

In sum, we have grounds to believe that Schleiermacher hoped to work out an idea of nature within his theologizing on the Redeemer and redemption. The large idea of nature with which he worked is one that we associate with Romanticism and with the cultural shift from the root metaphor of the machine to the root metaphor of the living organism. The being in which Schleiermacher is really interested is *living* being; he rejects the expression "nature mechanism" as one that is not appropriate to his subject matter.[17] As attentive readers of Schleiermacher know, his true theological interest in the natural is *human nature*, human nature in society, in friendships, in families, in religious communities. Unlike Calvin, Schleiermacher spends little time in marveling at the signatures of God in the canopy of the heavens. Correspondingly, he brings his discussion of the world as created to its culmination in *The Christian Faith* with an exposition of the "original perfection of man." The "original perfection of the world" lies wholly in its suitability for human development; if we look for anthropocentrism in Schleiermacher, it is here that we find it: the center of the cosmos is in *anthropos* and *polis*.

Given the special circumstances of our times, we are aware in a different way than was Barth's generation of the potentially fateful consequences of the idea of nature with which a theology works either implicitly or explicitly. Schleiermacher accepted this responsibility explicitly. Nevertheless, had he yielded to his inclination to reverse the order of doctrine, the structure of his theological thinking, as distinguished from the order of his exposition, would be much clearer to the reader.

It seems evident, then, that the theology embodied in *The Christian Faith* is a theology rooted in a religious consciousness inwardly and outwardly determined by the redemptive activity of Christ—or God through Christ. It is a theology of grace and sanctification, of *life* within the "kingdom" of grace or the Spirit-filled church.[18]

Readers familiar with Barth's *Church Dogmatics* may recall that Barth also characterizes Christ as the "goal" and the "beginning," the "beginning" and the "goal," of creation.[19] Barth makes this statement in the context of his exposition of creation and covenant, but the embracing context is his doctrine of revelation. Schleiermacher shies from the word "revelation" in *The Christian Faith*. One reason, he tells us in the postscript to §10, is that "revelation" carries the connotation of a cognitive operation and too easily lends itself to the reductive meaning associated with "doctrine." We could retain the term, Schleiermacher allows; if we did, then we might say that revelation "signifies the originality [underivability] of the real fact [*Tatsache*] which lies at the foundation of a religious communion." In the case of Christianity this *Tatsache* is Jesus of Nazareth and the redemption accomplished through him. But Schleiermacher abandons the term as too imprecise. It is the whole unique existence of Christ and the communication of that whole existence, or life, to others that constitutes the basis on which dogmatics is possible. Doctrine or dogma is a description of that life as it manifests itself in Christian religious consciousness.

Barth, for his part, in *Church Dogmatics* also wants to guard against the misconception that revelation is a gift assimilable to our general cognitive capacities as human beings. His motive, however, is to maintain the integrity and the priority of revelation. Revelation occurs *within* the godhead, as God's knowledge of God. Revelation works a metamorphosis in us. Within God's knowledge of God, we no longer are subjects constituting an object by our action of knowing; rather, God's self-knowing constitutes us as subjects as we participate in it.[20]

Of course, in his 1923–24 lectures, Barth has not yet reached this way of formulating his position. But he distrusts Schleiermacher's emphasis on *life:* "How can [Schleiermacher's theology] really be reconciled with confidence in Protestantism's power of truth?" he asks.[21] Schleiermacher's theology is cellular and biotic. "It is a bit of the cosmos. . . . *Living* systematics [however] is the Word . . . in its difference from life and supremacy over it."[22]

No more need now be said about Christ and the natural order as

Schleiermacher and Barth conceive them, and we may turn to consider Schleiermacher's "anthropological starting point."

SOVEREIGN CONSCIOUSNESS

In the "Concluding Unscientific Postscript on Schleiermacher" appended to his 1923–24 lectures, Barth asks,

> In Schleiermacher's theology or philosophy, do persons feel, think, and speak . . . in relationship to an indispensable . . . Other . . . superior to their own being, feeling, perceiving, willing, and acting? . . . Or [do they] feel, think, and speak . . . in and from a sovereign consciousness that their own beings are conjoined, and are indeed essentially *united*, with everything which might possibly come into question as something or even someone distinct from them?[23]

I wish briefly to pursue here the issue of this "sovereign consciousness" about which Barth asks. Is human religious consciousness, as Schleiermacher describes it, indeed sovereign in the sense that Barth implies? Has Schleiermacher made it the substantive center and hence effective deity of his theology? It is a commonplace to attribute to Schleiermacher a theology of the supremacy of human consciousness. In that way interpreters make him responsible for preparing the way for Feuerbach. Indeed, he may have done just that in some inadvertent way; but leaving aside the complex matter of the historical life of ideas, I ask once more what Schleiermacher is evidently intending to accomplish in his various delineations of the economy of the religious consciousness, with the special roles they assign to feeling or *Gefühl*.

In order to read Schleiermacher's intentions, we have to begin with the premise from which he starts out, the premise he most explicitly sets forth in his *Ethik* and *Dialektik* but that is also present (less explicitly, perhaps) in the *Speeches* and *The Christian Faith*.[24] This premise is that we have access to no consciousness save earthly, historical consciousness in which being is present. Both in ourselves and in others we apprehend only embodied consciousness, and we cannot prescind from that polarity. From this point on, it seems to me, there are principally two different ways it is feasible to interpret Schleiermacher.

The first proceeds by emphasizing the fact that *Gefühl* constitutes the unity that Schleiermacher believes to be indispensable to consciousness; it is the locus of the inalienable personality [*Eigenthümlichkeit*] of each human being. Without it our thinking and our acting would be merely two parallel series, incapable of modifying each other, and we correspondingly would not be selves, in the modern sense of that term, but would be mere fortuitous catenations of perceptions, ideas, and deeds. The question then arises, How much strength in its own right—how much independent strength—are we to attribute to this unity of consciousness, for which *Gefühl* is the linguistic symbol?

Taking Schleiermacher's own highly architectonic mentality into account, particularly as it exhibits itself in the *Brief Outline of the Study of Theology* and in *The Christian Faith*, we have persuasive reasons to interpret the unity of which he speaks as being very strong indeed. For example, the latter work systematically excludes all material of a "mythological" nature (such as creation ex nihilo, resurrection, and "last things") from the purview of dogmatic theology, on the grounds that nothing answering to such doctrines appears in Christian religious consciousness—at least in the Christian religious consciousness Schleiermacher purports to describe. This judgment scarcely commends itself as convincing, to present-day readers at any rate. In fact, Schleiermacher also appeals to the criterion of "scientific value" in making these exclusions, largely on the grounds that figurative language lacks clarity and stands in the way of achieving maximum internal theological consistency. This must be one of the most dubious features of Schleiermacher's entire enterprise. One wonders what kind of personal intelligence, otherwise so amply endowed with sophistication, would engage in such wholesale expunging of mythic themes. Perhaps, only someone grown weak in the *Phantasie* that the *Speeches* so much extolled? Or perhaps someone who overestimates or mistakes what unity of consciousness means? Barth is well justified in calling attention to a certain continuity between Schleiermacher and Rudolf Bultmann, who attempted to present modern consciousness in a similar way. Does Schleiermacher suppose that flesh-and-blood beings live in only one symbolic or imaginative world? Such stringent reductionism hardly seems consistent with the personal genius of a man who prided himself on his ability to "divine" the minds of others. "I project myself into a thousand different likenesses in order to behold my own more clearly."[25] Is his own sense of identity never shaken by these excursions into other personalities? Does he never recognize the fragility of the boundary between what is self and what is not self, the "merely momentary discrepancy"—as William James puts it—that separates him at any given instant from what he might otherwise be? To Eleanore Grunow he writes, "Our mode of viewing each person as a whole, . . . of believing in . . . dissonances in human nature but not in incongruities, and not in total transformations but only in development and improvement, . . . is undoubtedly correct."[26] Indeed, his entire theology does appear to be developmental in much the sense these words to Grunow imply. Hence, there is a good deal to suggest that Schleiermacher does repose, if not precisely in a sovereign consciousness, nevertheless in a consciousness well fortified with confidence, a consciousness that rises serenely above all chance happenings, stable and invincible in its own exalted state. Ought we then to conclude that Barth is right? The temperament pervading Schleiermacher's theology appears to be that of one who is secure in the faith that all things are in fact essentially and harmoniously united to the well-being of the devout personality. And certainly temperament does count for a great deal in any author. Yet we should not suppose that Schleiermacher never knew what it is to be shaken to the roots. His letters from his exile in Stolpe are ample evidence of that fact; and if they are not enough, the sermon he preached at the grave of his son Nathaniel should surely suffice to convince us.[27]

But to say only this much is to leave too much unsaid, and we need, therefore, to seek out another way of reading Schleiermacher to serve as a complement and corrective of this first way.

The second way of reading Schleiermacher that I propose proceeds by emphasizing the loci in which he speaks of *Gefühl* not only as an internal principle of unity but also as an *active receptivity*, as "free self-surrender" and as "will to be affected," *Affiziert-sein-Wollen*.[28] The import of these phrases is that in the heart of consciousness, in *Gefühl* itself, there is something amounting to what we might call a neediness for that which is other, that which is not self. An absolute passivity of feeling or *Gefühl* would amount to a negation of human being. *Gefühl* symbolizes, then, not an utter sovereignty of consciousness but rather its insufficiency if taken by itself. As Schleiermacher writes in the 1799 edition of the *Speeches*, "Religion is sense and taste for the infinite";[29] and in the second edition of 1806 he adds, "If man is not one with the *Universum* in the immediate unity of intuition and feeling, then he remains forever separated from it, in the [merely] derivative [unity] of his own consciousness."[30] In this estrangement, personal consciousness deprives itself of the source of its life.

Other passages point in this direction also. For example, in §3 in the second edition of *The Christian Faith*, where Schleiermacher characterizes *Gefühl* as an "abiding in self," we find that "abiding in self" contrasts markedly with the more explicitly active "passing beyond self" that especially characterizes acting or *Tun*, but also knowing or *Erkennen*, since knowing is also a species of acting. Yet this feeling is not a pure passivity, which would amount to inertness; we might call it an *active patience*, which perhaps may be construed as an indigenous need or want. Again, in his 1822 lectures on dialectic, Schleiermacher draws a parallel between "religious feeling" and perception: "Religious feeling [is the means by which] the *Urgrund* is posited in us, just as in perception [*Wahrnehmung*] things are posited in us."[31] We know that Schleiermacher holds perception to be a primitive mode of the relation of consciousness to being, a mode of relating to what is *other*, which is entirely fundamental to every endeavor to know; as such it is an indispensable form of *appropriation*, of becoming related, in which consciousness rises to thought and to self-consciousness. Hence, we may infer that "religious feeling" is also an *appropriative* relation, though that with which religious consciousness comes into relation is more than simply other beings: it comes into relation to, or receives its relation to, the ground of the whole *Naturzusammenhang*. The motif of love as the impetus to move into such relation to what is "other" lies in the background here, in muted form.[32]

Language connoting active receptivity of this order is particularly evident in the *Speeches*. In the second edition he writes,

> To receive [*aufnehmen*] everything individual as a part of the whole, everything limited as a presentation [*Darstellung*] of the Infinite in our lives, and to allow ourselves to be moved by it, that is religion.[33]

Another passage in the same vicinity in the second edition amplifies the foregoing:

> Your feeling is piety insofar as you *have* the individual moments [of the being and life of the *Universum*] as the working of God in you.[34]

Religious feeling is, then, patient responsiveness to the activity of the infinite, in and through the finite, in and through other selves as well as our own selves.

There is little doubt that even though Schleiermacher dampened the frequency with which "intuition," or *Anschauung*, appears in the later editions of the *Speeches*, *Gefühl* takes over part of the work that *Anschauung* performed in the 1799 edition. *Gefühl*, in other words, comes to carry connotations of noesis. Though it is not capable of an act of cognition, and though it does not conceptualize, it is a species of sensibility. This is very apparent in the most famous passage of the *Speeches*—a passage Schleiermacher never significantly altered:

I lie on the bossom of the infinite world: in this moment I am its soul, for I *feel* all its powers and its infinite life as my own; in this moment it is my body, for I permeate its muscles and its members as my own, and its innermost nerves move themselves according to my mind and my presentiment as do my own.[35]

This passage does lend support to Barth's "suspicion" that Schleiermacher emphasizes the unity of consciousness with the other. But that is not the sole lesson we learn from it. Another equally significant import of the passage is that consciousness has no life of its own apart from the larger whole in which it exists. Feeling is the medium through which life communicates itself to each person. We can put the same thought in a complementary way by saying that the life we give is the life we receive as dependent beings. In the second edition, Schleiermacher adds here, "In this way [viz., in the immediacy of feeling] is first created the reception of everything living in each sphere of your life, hence also in [the sphere of] religion."[36]

The mistake we can too easily make in reading *The Christian Faith* is to take the account of *Gefühl* given in the introduction as sufficient in itself. Barth does this in his 1923–24 lectures.[37] But the introduction is no more than a sketch of the topography in which the dogmatics is situated, and the dogmatic body of the work gives the substance of what the introduction only outlines. It is in the body of the work that we find that the "feeling of simple [or absolute] dependence" is the obverse of the simple or undivided activity [productivity, *Ursächlichkeit*] of God (see §51). Consciousness, which again is always embodied consciousness, is the effect of this timeless productivity. Since Schleiermacher does not allow for any distinction between creation ex nihilo and the preservation of all that exists, the direct implication is that consciousness—including, of course, religious consciousness—is being continuously created. The feeling of simple dependence is the registration of the fact that selves exist only on the "margins of the field" of God.

We could follow out this line of thought almost indefinitely. But we have seen enough, perhaps, to realize that we cannot justly speak of consciousness as "sovereign" in Schleiermacher's theology. Schleiermacher may indeed employ an "anthropological" point of departure, but we have seen that the *anthropos* with which he is concerned is embedded in a plenitude of being. Persons in relation—in relation to communities, to natural phenomena, to the eternal—constitute the real point of departure. If that is an anthropological starting point, so be it.

In any case, points of departure for thinking are one thing; the lines drawn from them contain many other points as well. These other points deserve as serious consideration as the first. If the undivided whole or the pure productivity that is God does not precisely merge with consciousness, nonetheless it permeates consciousness while constantly sustaining it. It is that sustaining presence of God in the field of human consciousness that religion and its daughter, theology, seek to clarify.

In this sense, which of course would not satisfy Barth's reservations, persons do indeed "feel, think, and speak . . . in relation to an indispensable . . . Other," according to Schleiermacher.

NOTES

1. Karl Barth, *Die Theologie und die Kirche: Gesammelte Vorträge* (Zurich: Evangelischer Verlag, n.d.), 2:189.

2. *Die protestantische Theologie im 19. Jahrhundert: Ihre Vorgeschichte und Geschichte*, 2d, rev. ed. (Zurich: Evangelischer Verlag, 1952). The ET comprises eleven chaps. of the foregoing: *From Rousseau to Ritschl* (London: SCM Press, 1959).

3. These other essays on Schleiermacher appear in Barth's *Theologie und Kirche*, vol. 2.

4. Karl Barth, *The Theology of Schleiermacher: Lectures at Göttingen, Winter Semester of 1923/24*, ed. Dietrich Ritschl, trans. Geoffrey W. Bromiley (Grand Rapids: Wm. B. Eerdmans, 1982).

5. Ibid., 264.

6. Ibid., 269.

7. Ibid., 52.

8. Ibid., 54.

9. Trans. W. Hastie as *Christmas Eve: A Dialogue on the Celebration of Christmas* (Edinburgh, 1890); retrans. Terrence N. Tice as *Christmas Eve: Dialogue on the Incarnation* (Richmond: John Knox Press, 1967).

10. Barth, *Theology of Schleiermacher*, 241.

11. *Schleiermachers Sendschreiben über seine Glaubenslehre an Lücke*, ed. Hermann Mulert, Studien zur Geschichte des neueren Protestantismus, ed. H. Hoffmann and L. Zscharnack (Giessen: Alfred Töpelmann, 1908), 31. ET: *On the Glaubenslehre: Two Letters to Dr. Lücke*, ed. James A. Massey, trans. James Duke and Francis S. Fiorenza, American Academy of Religion Texts and Translations 3 (Chico, Calif.: Scholars Press, 1981), 55–56.

12. I have drawn the wording of these headings from Martin Redeker's critical ed. of the German text (*Der Christliche Glaube nach den Grundsätzen der evangelischen Kirche im Zusammenhang dargestellt*, 7th ed., 2 vols. [Berlin: Walter de Gruyter, 1960]).

13. The first three groups of propositions in the Introduction are "borrowed" from ethics, philosophy of religion, and apologetics respectively.

14. *Schleiermachers Sendschreiben*, 31 (*On the Glaubenslehre*, 55–56).

15. *Schleiermachers Sendschreiben*, 34 (*On the Glaubenslehre*, 59).

16. In the ET, the first proposition in the first part, i.e., §32, is slightly mistranslated in a way that can lead to misunderstanding. The ET reads, "The immediate feeling of absolute dependence is presupposed and actually contained in every religious and Christian self-consciousness as the only way in which, in general, our own being and the infinite Being of God can be one in self-consciousness." In the German text no "and" appears between "religious" and "Christian," and the order of the two words is reversed: "Christian religious self-consciousness." See *The Christian Faith*, trans. H. R. Mackintosh and J. S. Stewart (Edinburgh: T. & T. Clark, 1948). For the German text, I have used Redeker's critical ed., cited above in n. 12.

17. Schleiermacher, *The Christian Faith*, 191.

18. John Martin Creed made this point many years ago. See his highly perceptive *The Divinity of Jesus Christ: A Study in the History of Christian Doctrine since Kant* (Cambridge: Cambridge Univ. Press, 1938), 73.

19. Karl Barth, *Church Dogmatics* 3/1:232.

20. Barth, *Church Dogmatics* 2/1: "[First] of all and in the heart of the truth in which we know God, God knows himself. . . . This occurrence in God Himself is the essence and strength of our knowledge of God" (p. 49). "[Our knowledge] of God is thus not the relationship of an already existing subject to an object that enters into [our] sphere. . . . On the contrary, this knowledge first of all creates the subject of its knowledge by coming into the picture" (p. 21).

21. Barth, *Theology of Schleiermacher*, 259.

22. Ibid., 171–72.

23. Ibid., 275.

24. *F. D. E. Schleiermacher, Werke: Auswahl in Vier Bänden*, ed. O. Braun and D. J. Bauer (Leipzig: Verlag von Felix Meiner, 1913), 2:533 (vol. 2 is a critical ed. of Schleiermacher's philosophical ethics); and *Friedrich Schleiermachers Dialektik*, ed. R. Odebrecht (Leipzig: J. C. Hinrichs, 1942), 19ff.

25. *Schleiermacher's Soliloquies*, ed. H. L. Friess (Chicago: Open Court Pub. Co., 1926), 33.

26. *The Life of Schleiermacher as Unfolded in His Autobiography and Letters*, 2 vols., trans. Frederic Rowan (London: Smith, Elder & Co., 1860), 1:319.

27. See "Schleiermacher's Sermon at Nathaniel's Grave," trans. and intro. Albert L. Blackwell, *Journal of Religion* 57 (1977): 64ff.

28. *Friedrich Schleiermachers Ästhetik*, ed. R. Odebrecht (Berlin: Walter de Gruyter, 1931), 51. The phrases come from a student notebook. See Odebrecht's explanation of his use of sources in his intro., xxviiiff.

29. *Friedrich Schleiermachers Reden über die Religion*, critical ed., ed. G. B. C. Pünjer (Braunschweig: C. A. Schwetsche & Sohn, 1879), 49. The trans. from the *Reden* are my own. The corresponding passage in John Oman's trans., now published by Harper & Row, appears on p. 39. Oman does not give a critical

apparatus that informs the reader of the alterations Schleiermacher made in the later eds.

30. *Friedrich Schleiermachers Reden,* 52 (Oman, 40).

31. *Friedrich Schleiermachers Dialektik,* 290.

32. See the discussion of Schleiermacher's philosophical ethics and dialectic as the context of his theology in my *Schleiermacher on Christ and Religion* (New York: Charles Scribner's Sons, 1964), esp. 92ff.

33. *Friedrich Schleiermachers Reden,* 59 (Oman, 48).

34. *Friedrich Schleiermachers Reden,* 57 (Oman, 45); emphasis added.

35. *Friedrich Schleiermachers Reden,* 78 (Oman, 43); emphasis added.

36. *Friedrich Schleiermachers Reden,* 55 (Oman, 43–44).

37. Barth, *Theology of Schleiermacher,* 243.

Interviews
with Karl Barth and
Reflections on His Interpretations
of Schleiermacher

3

TERRENCE N. TICE

PROLOGUE

From 1959 to 1965, I had several discussions with Karl Barth on his interpretations of Friedrich Schleiermacher, and one lengthy interview. I was then between ages twenty-seven and thirty-three, and during this time I completed my doctoral studies and, then, after a one-year interlude at Centre College of Kentucky, worked as an ecumenical theologian in Europe. Barth (1886–1968), still vigorous in his seventies, was doing his final teaching and entering retirement. Basel, where the Tices sojourned from September 1959 to January 1961, was chosen as the place to complete an extensive dissertation project for Princeton Theological Seminary on Schleiermacher's theological method, this in the domain of Barth, purportedly Schleiermacher's arch-opponent and on my short list (then and now) of greatest theologians, along with Augustine, Aquinas, Calvin, Luther, and Schleiermacher. I bore great respect for Barth's theology, much of which I had read, though thought of Schleiermacher as in many ways my nearer contemporary.

The research was well under way by 1959. Its contents were to include (important to note for what follows) biographical and critical background on Schleiermacher, his view of religion, the strict churchly and scientific orientation of his dogmatics, the ground and structure of dogmatic propositions, dogmatics as historical theology, methods for ordering the dogmatic material, and the system in its essence and architectonic outline. It continued to be my primary occupation while I was in Basel.[1]

In that period I regularly attended Barth's German and English colloquia and other lectures and seminars by Barth, as well as by the philosophers Heinrich Barth (Karl Barth's brother) and Karl Jaspers. Gradually I came to be in touch with Barth on a personal basis as well. We both came to acknowledge that our friendly, collegial relationship had grown as much out of our common knowledge and "love" of Schleiermacher as out of the fact that I approached Barth's theology in an appreciative yet highly reflective and critical spirit, not as a camp follower or as a hostile, even an overly wary, opponent. During my service as theological secretary of the World Alliance of Reformed Churches/World Presbyterian Alliance (1962–65) in Geneva, we talked further. Our conversation included work on the doctrine of the Holy Spirit that I was doing and the dissertation, which he had read. (As will be seen, the two topics were closely associated, though somewhat differently, in both our minds.)

Presented below is first a report of a lengthy 1960 interview, taken down practically verbatim at the time. Only brief references to our other talks will be given, since this is the crucial one for details of Barth's interpretations not available elsewhere. This report is followed by some historical background for, and a summary of, Barth's pre-1968 interpretations of Schleiermacher. The summary was approved word by word by Barth after slight revisions, exactly as it is given here. An epilogue includes references to his 1923–24 lectures and to his postscript to a selection of Schleiermacher's writings published in 1968, his last—but as he said, by no means "finished"—interpretation.[2]

INTERVIEW OF JULY 27, 1960[3]

First Professor Barth went through my translation of his "Systematic Theology" biographical sketch, pronounced it good with three minor changes of words, and approved its publication in the *Scottish Journal of Theology*.[4]

Then I showed him my outline of the dissertation. He looked it over carefully, halting at each point, where I usually told him briefly what my thesis was. He showed great interest in the biographical introduction. Later, while examining another section, he broke out suddenly and said, "I think you are right about those Landsberg sermons—I have read them: the whole man was there before the *Reden*." When we had gone through the entire outline, he pointed out two sections as of crucial importance: one on philosophy and theology and another on systematic principles—the two parts of *The Christian Faith* and the three forms of dogmatic propositions. He asked how I thought dogmatics could really have a "protective" aim for Schleiermacher. I doubt my answer wholly satisfied him, but he did not reply to it. I referred especially to the confessional orientation of *The Christian Faith* and to Schleiermacher's desire to protect theological language against encroachment of alien ideas.

Barth also tapped at the chapter on dogmatics as historical theology. "Aha! That's a difficult point. How can he really believe theology to be historical, empirical, and the like?" He agreed that *geltend* did not mean merely "current," though he was worried about the relation of dogmatics to church statistics. Since he made a point of stating that *geltend* also means "right" doctrine for Schleiermacher, he evidently saw a considerable problematic in Schleiermacher's thought at this juncture. That is, Schleiermacher is not a purely historical dogmatician, yet does his venture not really end up like this?

He suggested that perhaps I should add a section on Christology within a projected chapter discussing the major characteristics of theological knowledge. I told him that that was to be handled in the introductory chapter, then later in the architectonic, but I think he still believed it should have a place there too. He insisted on nothing, of course, but he was extremely cordial and amiable throughout. He expressed agreement with my procedure over and over again. Except with the questions just indicated, he nodded agreement to my explanations throughout concerning the nature of the man, his intentions of doing dogmatics, and the general lines of his method. We did not discuss these questions in any detail at this time.

Then I gave Barth a copy of the following questions, which he answered at length. The interview lasted two and one-half hours.

1. *TT:* What led you to embrace Schleiermacher's analysis of religion and faith, in particular, in your university days?

   KB: My first attempt to theologize was with Kant. I was a real Kantian! But I couldn't see a way from Kant to theology. I didn't like his theory of religion. Schleiermacher, whom I found on my own, became the way out—or in! He offered a more complete statement of what humanity is, which had a kind of religious a priori in it. I took Schleiermacher to myself, and he became my man.

2. *TT:* What role did Kant play for you then in your understanding of Christian faith? That is, what role as compared with Schleiermacher?

He was startled that I had thought to ask this, since it was this relationship that was of the greatest importance for him at that time. On the way downstairs later, he showed me the pictures on his staircase and noted that Kant was first, then Schleiermacher; the last one upstairs: Harnack!

3. *TT:* When you found yourself unable to accept Ernst Troeltsch's historicism, were you already in process of rejecting Schleiermacher's experiential-historical perspective—as you later came to represent it?

   KB: No. Troeltsch's thinking was pure historicism. I was from the beginning a systematic thinker. Troeltsch was only an onlooker, and not a religious thinker. [Wilhelm] Herrmann was better; and Herrmann and Troeltsch were always at swords' points. Herrmann once said that the *Reden* was the most important event in theology since apostolic times. [*TT* mentioned Herder.] I knew nothing of Herder at that time. No, it was just this opposition between Herrmann and Troeltsch that was involved then. I stuck to Schleiermacher all through this time.

4. *TT:* Can you recall any particular literature which helped you realize the Titanism, Romanticism, naturalism, and culture-oriented theology of Schleiermacher, as you referred to it in the *Römerbrief* of 1921?

   KB: That is hard. But look what my situation was at the time. I was brought up in the environment of *Die Christliche Welt.* The whole circle of people represented by this magazine were more or less influenced by Schleiermacher. They were the actual representatives of Schleiermacher*ism* in my time. [*TT* mentioned Paul Wernle.] Yes, Wernle, to be sure! But also many others, for example, Martin Rade, editor of the magazine. I referred indirectly to all these men in my *Römerbrief,* so that anyone who knew them at the time would recognize the references. It was their Schleiermacher I was opposing. At that time I was not conscious of fighting Schleiermacher himself.

5. *TT:* I find the first evidence of your identification of Schleiermacher's thought as the ripe classic of the *Aufklärung* in your exchange of 1923 with Harnack, in which you refer to Schleiermacher's *Bangemachen vor der "Barbarei"*[5] [he chuckled at that] as the normal way since the eighteenth century. Does this indicate a broadening of your understanding of eighteenth- and nineteenth-century theology between 1921 and 1923?

KB: Not yet.

TT: Why were you able to make this identification now but, apparently, not earlier?

KB: I had not a clear understanding of the eighteenth and nineteenth centuries then. Neither then nor earlier had I yet made this identification.

TT: Did your attention to Franz Overbeck in 1920 have anything to do with it?

KB: Yes, but not only Overbeck. Ah, this was a troublesome time! Dostoevsky had his influence too, and Plato! I was a Platonist. Then I was occasionally opposing Schleiermacher, but I always wanted to remain with him. During and after the writing of the *Römerbrief,* I was always thinking, "Surely the younger Schleiermacher at least would agree with me." This was my feeling all through this period.

6. *TT:* Were you engaged in any public or personal battle with Erich Schaeder in your Göttingen days?

KB: No.

TT: That is, did you debate with him over what constitutes "theocentric" and what constitutes "anthropocentric" theology? As with Georg Wobbermin?

KB: No. I thought at first when I read Schaeder that perhaps he was a man I could follow; then I saw that he and Wobbermin were really alike. This was later on. Schaeder was a "positive theologian," as the group was called at the time, and Wobbermin was a liberal; but essentially they were the same. The same was true of [Adolf von] Harnack, the liberal, and [Reinhold] Seeberg. Wobbermin I did combat. He was at Göttingen then too.

7. *TT:* In your 1926 lecture on Schleiermacher, the only Schleiermacher interpreters you referred to were Heinrich Scholz and Ferdinand Kattenbusch. Does this indicate that they were particularly helpful or corroborative in your attempt to comprehend Schleiermacher's theological method?

KB: Kattenbusch, no. [I think he had not read Kattenbusch's history.]

TT: Was Kattenbusch of any significance to you other than that he published his history of German evangelical theology and that it was readily available for study?

KB: He was very old then—likable, but I had no relation to him. And he was of no importance for my interpretation—only that one incidental reference to Schleiermacher as a *Kunstlertheologe*. But Scholz, definitely yes.

TT: Did you know Scholz before the Anselm seminar in 1931?

KB: Yes. I first met Scholz in 1906, winter term. He was the leader, the senior member of a seminar of Harnack's in church history, sixteen members. I was a youngster, in only my fifth semester. I only knew him from far away: he was too high for me! I had read his Schleiermacher book and his *Religionsphilosophie* before 1926. His ideas and mine about Schleiermacher are much alike. We have in common a great love for Schleiermacher. He had been a systematic-theology professor at Breslau, then changed to philosophy at Kiel, then to Münster. From there he came to Bonn in 1931 to lecture on logic, and it was then that I first actually got to know him.

8. *TT:* Did you read Schleiermacher's *Glaubenslehre* before hearing Herrmann's lectures on dogmatics in 1908?

    KB: I first studied it in 1908, the same year.

9. *TT:* Did you attend any seminar on Schleiermacher with Herrmann?

    KB: No. My first seminar on Schleiermacher was with [Hermann] Lüdemann in Bern, 1907—an unhappy time. I was president of Sophema [sp.?] that year. We wore white caps! The summer term when the seminar was being held I was too busy being president and didn't have time for seminar, so I didn't get anything out of it.

10. *TT:* How largely instrumental was your intensive critical analysis of Herrmann's and Schleiermacher's *Prinzipienlehre* between 1924 and 1926 in your deciding to present your prolegomena of 1927?

    KB: That is hard to say. There was such a complex of problems. It was too quick a decision. I was teaching prolegomena and thought it might be useful for others to read it. But I had to do it all over again. I discovered [Ludwig] Feuerbach for the first time in those years. This is very important. I saw that what Schleiermacher was doing, and the others, really ended in Feuerbach.

11. *TT:* Were your lectures on eighteenth- and nineteenth-century theology given only first in 1929–30, or also previous to that?

    KB: No, that was the first time. But the *Vorgeschichte* was only first done in Bonn. I began with Schleiermacher, then the rest of it. Except for a few minor changes, the manuscript stayed the same. The article *"Das Wort von Schleiermacher zu Ritschl"* [which *TT* mentioned at this point] was of no great importance: that was only from lectures I gave.

TT: Was the 1926 "Schleiermacher" article written before the Schleiermacher chapter?

KB: No. That 1926 article was the same as in my first lecture, in 1929. That lecture was later changed to its present form in *Die evangelische Theologie.* . . . [So that actually the 1926 article was first and the present form of the Schleiermacher chapter came somewhat later, probably in Bonn, and was a revision of the 1926 article.]

12. *TT:* Have you ever given seminars on Schleiermacher?

KB: Not at Göttingen.[6] I'm not sure about Bonn—probably the *Kurze Darstellung* there. But in Basel at least two times on the *Kurze Darstellung;* two terms on the *Glaubenslehre;* two seminars on the *Reden;* and one on the *Weihnachtsfeier.* [On another day he permitted me to study the protocols from the Basel seminars. There were eight in all.]

13. *TT:* Why did you prepare the 1957 article *"Evangelische Theologie im 19. Jahrhundert"*?

KB: This was for a conference in Hanover. I was asked to do it. The Goethe Gesellschaft gave a series of lectures on the nineteenth century, and I was asked to do evangelical theology. My position has not changed, but don't you see a softer tone here, less polemic?

14. *TT:* Do you always require your students to study the *Glaubenslehre?*

KB: Certainly I do! I tell them to prepare Luther, Calvin, orthodoxy of the seventeenth century, by way of Schmid and Heppe,[7] and at least Schleiermacher among the moderns. I had the Schleiermacher bust moved into the seminar room from elsewhere, so that we would always have him in our presence. Especially in the Schleiermacher seminars I point to him and say, "See, he is watching us; be careful what you say!"

15. *TT:* Are you aware of any subsequent alteration or relaxing of your original critique of Schleiermacher?

KB: No. But more and more I tried to be a loving student and not an enemy. I always accepted him within the *communio sanctorum,* not as a heretic. True, there is more formal than material agreement. But do you know what [Hans Urs] von Balthasar said of me, that I am always more Schleiermacherian than I know myself? That is possible! My own theology may be looked upon as a complete reversal of his. I try to look from above [he stretched his hands, butts together, fingers outspread over his head], he from below. There is a difference of vantage points. But there is also a together-ness. Schleiermacher and Herrmann have both been in their own manner christocentric theologians; this is one point where we are together and where the line has never been broken!

After this we shared some thoughts about Schleiermacher as a theo-logian. "Look," Barth said, "there has never been a systematician in modern times like Schleiermacher. He knows the beauty of theology. The rest do not." Further: "The 'Humanity of God' essay of 1956 was also a theme given to me, like the 1927 one. There is no change. I was saying this already in the 1930s. [A conference at Aargau was the occasion of the essay.] Tillich came to see me and said, 'Oh, now I can appreciate you. You have finally come around. That is marvelous what you say!' That only proved that he had not read one word of my *Church Dogmatics*." Also: "I did have a first lecture on Schleiermacher in Göttingen, for a whole winter term. That was my first real study of him. Giving four lectures per week, I gave first the Heidelberg Catechism one winter term—I had to work hard; I had been only a pastor all those years—then Calvin (summer), then Zwingli (winter), then Reformed confessions (summer), then a whole term on Schleiermacher. I began especially with the sermons and could only speak briefly on *The Christian Faith* and *Brief Outline*. This was in 1924, the year my Christmas Eve article came out."[8]

Finally, I showed him my summary of his Schleiermacher critique. After he read it over carefully and we talked about various points—he said that Ferdinand Kattenbusch was of no importance and that I should take out the term "aesthetic," which was too much like Emil Brunner's position—he stated that the whole thing was correct. I asked, "Is it a fair treatment?" He replied, "Not completely. It is correct, but I don't like the impression it leaves. It makes me look like a lawyer accusing him, doesn't show that I love him as my neighbor. I should have preferred a kinder view to come across, more respectful. Never have I done such a thing as Brunner did. After his book, I said to him we should get together and study the matter. He said he couldn't [and deep, flushed emotion crept into Barth's face, halfway between tears of sorrow and rage], that he had burned his papers! He was done with him! [A sweep of the arm, a look of extreme disgust.] Imagine! For me, Schleiermacher is present, within the church, my comrade, the finest of them all!"

I then handed him a copy of the last paragraph of his 1926 article (see

p. 53 below) and said that I had not been satisfied to leave the critique where I did either, except that his written critiques had for the most part demanded it. Would this excerpt represent his truest feelings concerning Schleiermacher? "Yes," he said, "it does. I had forgotten I wrote this. It was written against Brunner. This is the spirit in which I approached Schleiermacher then, despite my sharper and sharper criticisms as I moved from the beginning of the essay to the end. This is how I should wish to be represented as to my attitude toward him.'"

BACKGROUND ON BARTH'S CLASH
WITH SCHLEIERMACHER[9]

The enormously influential Albrecht Ritschl (1822–89) acknowledged Schleiermacher's general contribution to theological method, but he was extremely antipathetic on doctrinal details. Moreover, he seems to have relied heavily on at least the spirit of many earlier critiques, notably those of Ferdinand Christian Baur (1792–1860) from the 1820s on, and not to have known Schleiermacher's writings very well. The first extensive overview of Schleiermacher's theological system was provided by the Ritschlian philosophical theologian Wilhelm Bender (1845–1901), whose 1868 dissertation in philosophy had treated Schleiermacher's doctrine of God and who published a two-volume work on his theology (1876–78) at the beginning of his short theological career as professor at Bonn. Although before my own 1961 study he was the only writer to offer a complete picture of Schleiermacher's dogmatics, one based on a perspicuous examination of most available texts and in relation to previous critical literature, and although he was the first to draw attention to the complex, interlocking particulars of his method, Bender's judgments were seriously handicapped by the attempt to represent the whole as a development out of basic philosophical principles. Consequently, his book only served to entrench the traditional view that Schleiermacher grounded his theology in a science of religion (which derived in turn, according to Bender's more sophisticated analysis, from his psychological and ontological analysis of consciousness) or, as Jacob Friedrich Fries (1773–1843) had claimed, that he only presented his philosophy over again under the thin guise of theology.

Relevant to this issue, one of the most significant historical facts of the half-century preceding the appearance of Barth's *Epistle to the Romans* in 1918 was that almost the entire theological literature on Schleiermacher was produced by liberals. A great number of these were students of Ritschl, Herrmann, Harnack, and Troeltsch. While there were more dissertations, articles, and treatises on religion than ever, interests were broadening with the times. Schleiermacher achieved fame not only as the "church father of the nineteenth century" (Christian Lülmann, 1907) but also as one of the great fathers of modern education, politics, aesthetics, and ethics. He was the *Kulturtheologe* par excellence, the ideal of the journal *Die Christliche Welt*, the great aesthete and apologist. After 1870, Wilhelm Dilthey, Rudolf Haym, and Otto Kirn had fastened Romanticism to his title. Others were busily asserting "influences" not only from Kant and Spinoza but also from Leibniz, Lessing, Herder, Goethe, Schelling, and the Herrnhuter Brethren, or making grand comparisons with Fichte, Hegel, Rousseau, Luther, and Melanchthon (but almost never Calvin, Aquinas, Augustine, the early fathers, the classic confessions, John, or Paul). The interest of the age was predominantly cultural, even among theologians.

Accordingly, no one bothered to explore the full churchly and scientific scope of Schleiermacher's dogmatic method, though Scholz wrote a big book purportedly on Schleiermacher's view of Christianity and science, Hermann Süskind wrote one on his view of Christianity and history, Georg Wehrung one on his so-called philosophical-theological method (all in 1911), and Johannes Wendland one on the development of his theories of religion and redemption (1915). During this period only a single student called sharp attention to the centrality of Schleiermacher's Christology for his dogmatic method: Horst Stephan (1901). But apparently nobody listened—perhaps because Stephan did not altogether succeed in showing how or why. Hermann Mulert's dissertation (1907) on Schleiermacher's historical-philosophical standpoint in relation to his theology lacked the fuller perspective too, as did Wehrung's study of his early development (1907).

Barth pursued his own early studies within this atmosphere. Even into the early 1920s, Schleiermacher was still, so to speak, his hero. As was already evident in his first, enthusiastic appraisal of him in 1910, however, his reasons were quite different from those of most of his contemporaries, and they did not keep him from lodging a razor-sharp critique against the traditional Schleiermacher. The theological intentions of Schleiermacher were basically right: *sola fide, solus Christus*. His methods consistently went awry and with them most of the content of his theology. In Barth's view, Schleiermacher had tried to look at the life of faith anthropologically, from the underside up, with an eye to cultural witness. Now the direction had to be turned upside down, so that we begin from above, with the free, eternal Word of God.

If one theme stands out in Barth's entire 1923–24 lecture series at Göttingen, only recently made available (1978 in German, 1982 in English), it is his angry rejection of Schleiermacher's virtually unbroken emphasis on peace (and therefore on liberality, love, holistic perspective, equality, and unity). Temperamentally Barth seemed more readily to find and express his own perspective in opposition to that of others, this alongside a genuine desire to understand, which he shared with Schleiermacher. From first to last, the emphases in Barth's own work are placed on divisions and crises, especially between the divine and the human, the Word of God and the word of man. In his struggle for obedient listening to a distinct, authoritative, confrontive divine Word, these crises and divisions must be underscored first; then they may be thought of as redeemed or reconciled and, in this manner if at all, overcome in Christ. Schleiermacher could be polemical too, though even then his basic temperament was irenic. In sermons and writings alike, however, he unfailingly centered upon the enablement of human beings to share in Christ's reconciling ministry—this in recognition of the limitedness and time-boundedness of mere words and in expectation that the Holy Spirit makes all things new. Thus his interest was preeminently in the actual overcoming of all that unwholesomely separates one spiritual being or group—religious or otherwise—from another.[10]

In his last years, Barth insisted that he had never regarded Schleiermacher as a heretic but had always embraced him as a comrade within the *communio sanctorum,* that even when he had to turn his back on his methods he always deeply loved him as a man and as the one truly great modern theologian. Although his later critiques, in 1957 and 1968, carry a softer, less polemical tone than his earlier ones, even in 1926 he was able to conclude his first article with these words:

> Schleiermacher is a power whom one ought never to suppose himself to have felled, either at the first, or at the second, or at the third stroke. I should rather prefer to consider this moment not as my "final settlement" with him, but as merely an account over my conversation with him at the present time. I believe I am at one with my friend E. Brunner [he says with tongue in cheek] in choosing to apprehend and to carry out our common war against this man as a mobile war.[11]

One can but accept this as a sincere claim. On the other hand, this must not serve to obscure the bold lines of demarcation he has attempted to draw. Early and late, Barth made many positive protestations about Schleiermacher. In all his interpretations, however, he unmistakably showed that it is not merely the Schleiermacher interpreted by nineteenth- and twentieth-century theologians that he was attacking but Schleiermacher himself, his theological method, and the doctrinal details as Barth understood them. In fact, Barth's critiques sometimes went below the level of honest disagreement or cynicism, to harsh, obstreperous, even mean, attack. Overall, his continual dialectical oppositions left Schleiermacher with no solid ground to stand on in Barth's eyes—only a few attractive but merely formal claims.

SUMMARY OF BARTH'S
SCHLEIERMACHER CRITIQUES,
VERIFIED BY BARTH ON JULY 27, 1960

In agreement with Scholz,[12] in direct reaction to the Schleiermacherian theology of his teacher Herrmann,[13] in the appropriated spirit of Overbeck[14] (in which spirit the attitudes of Ritschl and Kattenbusch are also not altogether missing),[15] and in a manner recalling his very early antipathy to the *religionsgeschichtliche* methods of Troeltsch,[16] Barth has continued to hold his early opinion of Schleiermacher as essentially a "culture" theologian.[17] His consistent indictment has been that Schleiermacher's genuine intention of doing church theology has utterly failed,[18] primarily on account of his personal, philosophical, and apologetical compromise with modern culture, a compromise already partially achieved in the equally historicist-experiential outlook of Herder, Schleiermacher's immediate predecessor,[19] but epitomized to this day in the "great ripe classic" of Schleiermacher's own work.[20] Like Brunner, Barth recognizes a strong mystical element in Schleiermacher's ideal for the religious life (and in fact there is scarcely a single negative element in Barth's critique which was not already clearly enunciated in Brunner's book),[21] but he believes, against Brunner,[22] that it is essentially subordinated to and determined by the task of conducting one's life in the world, above all in the world of culture. Thus it is not in a mystical sense of religious experience but in a cultural determination of religious activity that the Word of God has been subverted by Schleiermacher and in fact by the whole dominant but esoteric tradition of the eighteenth and nineteenth centuries,[23] and this gives modern theology, both Protestant and Roman, a distinctly apologetical cast,[24] taking mediation rather than real proclamation to be its proper task.[25] The human being is left master and subject even of theology.[26] Christ is only a "predicate,"[27] a "foreign body,"[28] a correlate of experience;[29] God is wordless, "ineffable,"[30] "mysterious,"[31] nonobjective,[32] *nuda essentia*,[33] heartless,[34] a "neuter," "an *x*";[35] and thus, since there is no independent Word, there is also no true theology of the Holy Spirit.[36] Consequently, in Barth's eyes, Schleiermacher's whole theological endeavor is subjected to a fundamental pervasiveness of humanistic, pantheistic naturalism[37] and his enlightened program is reduced to a cultural, apologetical, and only covertly pietistic philosophy of life.

EPILOGUE

Some twenty-five years ago, my own extensive analysis of Schleiermacher's works led me to the conviction that Barth's critique was seriously mistaken at every juncture, and I told him so more than once, explaining in some detail. Although there are fundamental differences not only in temperament but also in both method and doctrine between Barth and Schleiermacher, many of the widely accepted, positive contributions of Barth actually constitute a revival of the genuine Schleiermacher—especially the renewed understanding of the church orientation of dogmatics and of its radical grounding in the personal Word of God spoken by grace in Christ. Likewise, some dogmatic elements proposed by Barth that are less generally palpable—for example, several aspects of his doctrine of grace and election and his interpretation of the covenant community—are actually more nearly proximate to Schleiermacher's view than to that of almost any other modern theologian before Barth. Nevertheless, true contradictions do appear in the preliminary doctrines of revelation that govern the dogmatic production of these two men. These contradictions are especially evident in their particular attitudes toward scriptural authority, the divine attributes or perfections, the classical two-natures doctrine of the person of Christ, and the trinitarian formulation of doctrine; and here some may be led to conclude, as I have, that not all promise lies on the side of Barth.

One day after I had returned to Switzerland (1962–65), we had been talking for some time in his study. I told him that despite the differences and what I regarded to be his serious misreadings, he of all the theologians since Schleiermacher was Schleiermacher's truest heir and had overall been the most faithful to what Schleiermacher was trying to do. At this, he rocked back and forth in his chair and for some minutes loudly laughed and laughed. After a thoughtful pause he said, with great earnestness, "I would wish that to be true, I hope it is." Then he spoke again of his love for Schleiermacher, of his having viewed him dialectically in light of modern trends traced to him, of his regrets, of his critical position's having become softer in tone, of his wishing for a chance to talk it all out with him in heaven, and of its being perhaps too late to go back and try again, that others must do that.

Barth had other complaints about Schleiermacher's thought that have not been directly noted above. For example, he did not favor what he took to be a blind, fatal belief in the progress of civilization. He was troubled by the priority given to community over the mere individual. He asked, "Can *real* pneumatic authority be delegated to such a relative and fluctuating construct as the fellowship of the Christian church?"[38] Yet at other times he held that for Schleiermacher the individual is the true agent of the kingdom of God (= supreme good).[39] He tended to perceive Schleiermacher's discourse as a sometimes banal culturalization of Moravian Brethren piety, as evolutionistic idealism, historicist relativism, Goethean cultural sentiment, as spiritualized empiricism and feeling-centeredness, all played out in an obfuscating theological language. Barth wanted absolute truth claims instead, whereas Schleiermacher felt he could not offer them. Barth believed that Schleiermacher therefore offered "no external givenness of God," that his was not a theology that relied on the "truth of Christian revelation."[40] Did Barth himself perhaps have a tendency to make theology and Christianity a philosophy, comprising true propositions, rather than a witness? Schleiermacher, at any rate, did not, or tried hard not to, though he used philosophical tools and concepts to clarify the witness, which itself in turn profoundly influenced his philosophical ideas from early on.[41]

On the other hand, Barth did recognize a saving grace in Schleiermacher's regard for church tradition and saw that in this way he was "subject to the compulsion of the matter itself."[42] He admitted, "I regard Schleiermacher as not just an outstandingly clever person but also as a sincerely devout Christian."[43]

Barth's profound ambivalence about Schleiermacher forcefully appears in the 1968 "Postscript," where he said of his 1923–24 study, "I also learned to appreciate from afar certain matters where I stood (or again came?) much closer to him theologically than I had ever supposed could be the case after 1916," in view of his teachers' wrenchingly disappointing support of the Kaiser's war effort in 1914 and the considerable new, anti-Schleiermacher influence of Eduard Thurneysen, yet spoke of a "conscious distancing of myself from him which could no longer be reversed."[44] Barth has admitted in print, as in private, that there is much of Schleiermacher that he had not read. A further difficulty lay in his tending not to inquire into the questions he raised, in his not going back to the texts for more careful study. Or perhaps more accurately put, he did do this in several seminars but brought to the texts a template so firmly formed that he was not likely to change perspective. He was not even sufficiently bothered by his occasionally self-conscious inability to understand, for this to make him inquire further. And yet he could not leave Schleiermacher alone. Despite his brusque, sometimes impertinent attacks, he still loved the man and was drawn to his thought. He was drawn even to the point of wanting to protect Schleiermacher from others' neglect, as he spoke of wanting passionately, vengefully to do in his own father's behalf in the early years after his death in 1912.[45]

I am inclined to think that, with some necessary corrections in formulation, the four sets of imagined positive interpretations of Schleiermacher which Barth in the 1968 "Postscript" said would bring him into "profound agreement" are correct. I felt such a rush of recognition upon reading each of them that I could not help but wonder whether I might have had some influence on Barth's thinking, for we discussed all these points. This thought was all the more persuasive in that he immediately suggested for the next agenda a "theology of the Third Article," a "theology of which Schleiermacher was scarcely conscious [?!], but which might actually have been the legitimate concern dominating even his theological activity." This latter claim I had also definitely set forth in our conversations, though it is also important to note that in his last years of teaching, Barth had been trying to form a doctrine of the Holy Spirit and finally (how much like Aquinas?) gave it up as something he could not manage. (My own *Come, Creator Spirit!* was among current new efforts; it was published in several languages by the World Alliance of Reformed Churches in 1963. Barth read and liked it, but he would not have seen the influence of Schleiermacher implicit within it, since this was not explicit in its language and it was written very much with a Reformed context in mind, in preparation for an Alliance World Assembly in 1964.)

I believe that if Barth had been able to convince himself of these quite positive, largely correct theses, he would indeed have been able to approach Schleiermacher's texts quite differently. He would thus have been spared his "great, and for me very painful, perplexity" about Schleiermacher's "basic standpoint."[46]

NOTES

1. Of this, only my revised *Schleiermacher Bibliography* (Princeton: Princeton Univ. Press [for Princeton Theol. Sem.], 1966) is so far published. Recently, two additions by me have also appeared: *Schleiermacher Bibliography (1784–1984): Updating and Commentary* (Princeton: Princeton Univ. Press [for Princeton Theol. Sem.], 1985) and *Schleiermacher Bibliography: Corrections, New Information, and Comments* (Princeton: Princeton Theol. Sem., 1985). My translations of *Brief Outline on the Study of Theology* (Richmond: John Knox Press, 1966), *Christmas Eve* (Richmond: John Knox Press, 1967), and *On Religion* (Richmond: John Knox Press, 1969) all carry forward but are largely consistent with this earlier study, which employed both historical-critical and conceptual analyses. See also my "Schleiermacher's Conception of Religion: 1799 to 1831," in *Schleiermacher*, ed. Marco M. Olivetti (Padua: CEDAM, 1984), 332–56.

2. Karl Barth, *The Theology of Schleiermacher: Lectures at Göttingen, Winter Semester of 1923/24*, ed. Dietrich Ritschl, trans. Geoffrey W. Bromiley (Grand Rapids: Wm. B. Eerdmans, 1982).

3. Modern thinkers referred to here include a leading contemporary Roman Catholic interpreter of Barth, Hans Urs von Balthasar; the Reformed theologian Emil Brunner (1889–1966), of Zurich, whose trenchant Schleiermacher critique was first issued in 1924 (Barth had read it in manuscript); the left-wing Hegelian philosopher Ludwig Feuerbach (1804–72), who wrote several highly critical works on religion and Christianity, esp. in the 1840s; Barth's teacher, the great church historian Adolf von Harnack (1851–1930), of Berlin; Ritschlian systematic and apologetic theologian Wilhelm Herrmann (1846–1922), of Marburg; Enlightenment philosopher Immanuel Kant (1724–1804); Ritschlian systematic theologian Ferdinand Kattenbusch (1851–1935), then at Göttingen; Hermann Lüdemann (1842–1933), of Bern, Barth's first dogmatics teacher; the New Testament scholar Franz Overbeck (1837–1905), of Basel; the systematic theologian Martin Rade (1857–1940), of Marburg, editor of *Die Christliche Welt* from 1886 to 1931; the theologian Albrecht Ritschl (1822–89), of Göttingen; Erich Schaeder (1861–1936), of Breslau after 1918, an outspoken advocate of a "theocentric" theology; the philosopher and onetime theologian Heinrich Scholz (1884–1956), whose 1909 Berlin dissertation was on Schleiermacher's *The Christian Faith;* the Lutheran church historian Erich Seeberg (1888–1945); the philosophical theologian Paul Tillich (1886–1965), in the United States from 1933 on; the philosophical and historical theologian Ernst Troeltsch (1865–1923), who was successor to the noted "human science" philosopher Wilhelm Dilthey in Berlin; Paul Wernle (1872–1939), Eduard Thurneysen's teacher at Basel, who issued a well-known introduction to theological study in 1911 and a small book on Melanchthon and Schleiermacher in 1921; and the systematic theologian Georg Wobbermin (1869–1943), in Göttingen from 1922 to 1935 and a frequent writer on Schleiermacher.

4. Karl Barth, "On Systematic Theology," trans. Terrence N. Tice, *Scottish Journal of Theology* 14 (1961): 225–28.

5. "Intimidated by the Cultural 'Barbarians.'"

6. See his correction below, referring to the 1923–24 lectures cited in n. 2 above.

7. Collections of Lutheran and Reformed post-Reformation orthodox theology.

8. Among Barth's concluding remarks in his 1923–24 lectures are these: "For me the results of this study are fairly shattering. When I embarked with you on this material, which I had not examined closely for many years, I was prepared for something bad. But I was not prepared to find that the *distortion* of Protestant theology—and we have to speak of such in view of the historical importance of the man—was as deep, extensive, and palpable as it has shown itself to be. . . . Schleiermacher's achievement fills me with *respect* and *admiration*. I now know better than I did before that he was a great and gifted and pious man, that among all who came after him, whether they followed in his tracks or tried to kick against the pricks, there was and is none to hold a candle to him. Protestantism has not in fact had any greater theologian since the days of the reformers. But this theologian has led us all into this *dead end!* This is an oppressive and almost intolerable thought," he added, then shortly thereafter stated, "The only possibility that remains—and I do not see how one can avoid this—is obviously that of a *theological revolution*, a basic No to the whole of Schleiermacher's doctrine of religion and Christianity, and an attempted reconstruction at the *very* point which we have constantly seen him hurry past with astonishing stubbornness, skill, and audacity. . . . Schleiermacher undoubtedly did a good job. It is not enough to know that another job has to be done; what is needed is the ability to do it at least as well as he did his" (*Theology of Schleiermacher*, 259–60). Barth's article "Schleiermachers 'Weihnachtsfeier' " is an only slightly revised version of his November 1923 lectures. It first appeared in *Zwischen den Zeiten* 3 (1925): 38–61; then in *Die Theologie und die Kirche* (Munich, 1928) and its ET (*Theology and Church: Shorter Writings, 1920–1928,* trans. Louise Pettibone Smith [London: SCM Press, 1962]).

9. In his 1923–24 lectures, Barth referred to twelve of the authors mentioned in n. 3 above: Brunner, Dilthey, Feuerbach, Harnack, Kant, Kattenbusch, Rade, Ritschl, Scholz, Troeltsch, Wernle, and Wobbermin. He also referred to, among others, the Schleiermacher commentators Baur, Bender, Fries, Haym, Hegel, Lülmann, Mulert, and Wendland, all mentioned below.

10. In his 1923–24 lectures, Barth was disturbed by his (misshapen) view that Schleiermacher is an "open enemy of all excitement, of all that is crude and sudden and direct in the Christian life" (*Theology of Schleiermacher*, 41) and is "against every either-or, . . . all real tensions, all crisis" (p. 43). "There is no expectation of a decided Yes or a decided No" (p. 164), he says, "no sharp margins and contrasts or questions and answers" (p. 171). Much later in life Barth appreciatively acknowledged Schleiermacher's irenic temperament

("Concluding Unscientific Postscript on Schleiermacher," trans. George Hunsinger, in *Theology of Schleiermacher*, 272).

11. Karl Barth, "Schleiermacher," *Zwischen den Zeiten* 5 (1927): 422–24. This paper was written in the summer of 1926 and also appeared in *Die Theologie und die Kirche* in 1928 and in its ET, *Theology and Church*. Brunner seemed really to consider himself done with Schleiermacher at the time. Kattenbusch had claimed that his day was gone forever. On Barth's explicitly warlike intentions from 1921 on, see Dietrich Ritschl's preface to *Theology of Schleiermacher*.

12. In Barth's 1932 lecture on Schleiermacher, first published in 1947 in his *Die protestantische Theologie im 19. Jahrhundert: Ihre Vorgeschichte und Geschichte*, 2d, rev. ed. (Zurich: Evangelischer Verlag, 1952); ET in *From Rousseau to Ritschl* (London: SCM Press, 1959), 327. For his first lectures on nineteenth-century theology, in 1929–30, he used the 1926 essay. The new manuscript used in Bonn in 1932, including the eighteenth-century material, remained virtually unchanged for the 1947 publication. [Further on Scholz, see *Theology of Schleiermacher*, 262. Bracketed material in this and subsequent nn. was added by me in 1984; the rest is what Barth saw in 1960.]

13. The "quintessence" of both theologies, Barth wrote in 1925, is contained in the first, introductory part of their systems ("Die dogmatische Prinzipienlehre bei W. Herrmann," in *Die Theologie und die Kirche*, 242). Cf. Barth's *Church Dogmatics* 2/2:520, 543–44, 3/2:446. A sensitive analysis, "K. Barth and W. Herrmann: Pupil and Teacher," by A. A. Jagnow (*Journal of Religion* 16 [1936]: 300–316), rightly reflects the radicality of Barth's departure from Herrmann.

14. Barth's "Unerledigte Anfragen an die heutige Theologie" (1920), in *Die Theologie und die Kirche*.

15. In his 1926 "Schleiermacher" essay, reprinted in *Die Theologie und die Kirche*, Barth agrees with Kattenbusch that Schleiermacher is a *Künstlertheologe* (p. 139). This apparently does not so much imply, however, that his approach was aesthetic (as Kattenbusch claimed it was) as that he approached the business of theology as a craftsman—perhaps too much so. Once Barth had developed an architectonic of his own, he was particularly inclined to recognize Schleiermacher's profound sense for the beauty in theology.

16. Karl Barth, "Systematische Theologie," in *Lehre und Forschung an der Universität Basel, dargestellt von Dozenten der Universität Basel* (Basel, 1960), 36 (for ET, see n. 4). Cf. his article in *Schweizerische Theologische Zeitschrift*, 1910. This, of course, continued in *The Word of God and the Word of Man* (New York: Harper Torchbooks, 1947), 2; *Church Dogmatics* 4/1:383.

17. In 1926, Barth referred to this culture theology as "realistic" and "positivistic" rather than idealistic (*Die Theologie und die Kirche*, 161), but also as "aesthetic" (p. 187), despite his own general intentions to the contrary over against Brunner. In his 1932 lecture he followed the same themes (*From Rousseau to Ritschl*, 317ff.).

18. The restatement of Barth's view in "Evangelische Theologie im 19.

Jahrhundert," *Theologische Studien* 49 (1957), revealed no alteration of his earlier position even in details, though his attitude is certainly less abrupt than in the *Römerbrief* period (see *Word of God*, 195–96).

19. Regarding Schleiermacher's inheritance of Herder's historicist-experiential outlook, see Barth's 1932 lecture (*From Rousseau to Ritschl*, 200, 227–28, 214), as well as *Church Dogmatics* 1/1:219, 1/2:526, [4/4:255n]. The importance of these two factors in Barth's critique cannot be overemphasized (*Die Theologie und die Kirche*, 141, 159–80; *From Rousseau to Ritschl*, 338–54; later in *Church Dogmatics* 1/1:219, 2/1:74). Already from 1891 on, Dilthey had indicated *innere Erfahrung* and *kritische Geschichte* as the two basic elements of the "new theology" begun at the time of the Reformation (see his *Weltanschauung und Analyse des Menschen seit der Renaissance und Reformation* [1914], 42).

20. Barth, *Church Dogmatics* 1/1:38.

21. [Barth had already read the manuscript of Brunner's book in 1923 or 1924. In the 1923–24 lectures he only begins to refer to him directly in February 1924. See esp. *Theology of Schleiermacher,* 266.]

22. Barth, *Die Theologie und die Kirche*, 181; and idem, *From Rousseau to Ritschl*, 317–18.

23. Barth, *Die Theologie und die Kirche*, 136–44; and idem, *From Rousseau to Ritschl*, 335, 352; and idem, *Church Dogmatics* 1/2:799, 813, 2/2:127ff., 3/2:9, 3/4:516. Cf. idem, *Word of God*, 195–96. In "Das Wort in der Theologie von Schleiermacher bis Ritschl" (1927), Barth's identification is more qualified, even to the point of showing that Schleiermacher's neo-Protestant successors improved on him at various points.

24. This element was particularly stressed by Barth in 1932 (*From Rousseau to Ritschl*, 321–31) and later, e.g., in *Church Dogmatics*, 2/1:347–48, 2/2:520, 541, 3/2:79.

25. Barth, *Die Theologie und die Kirche*, 137, 144–59; and idem, *From Rousseau to Ritschl*, 331–38, 346ff., 294–95.

26. This was a constant point of the early essays (as of his first attempt at prolegomena in 1927) and was dramatically climaxed in Barth's interpretation of Feuerbach's anthropological theology as the extreme logical result of Schleiermacher's method. In the end, all that is left is a dead God (*Church Dogmatics* 2/1:494). And his view of religion is ultimately "inhuman" (*Church Dogmatics* 2/2:553–54), contrary to the reality of both religion and revelation (cf. *Epistle to the Romans* [Oxford, 1933], 530–31). Barth's "Introductory Essay" to the Harper Torchbook ed. of Feuerbach's *The Essence of Christianity* ([New York, 1957], x–xxxii) is from his 1926 lecture published in *Die Theologie und die Kirche*. The same antianthropological criticism is regularly thrown up in *Church Dogmatics:* 1/1:39, 68, 144, 2/1:185, 339, 3/2:446, 4/1:153 [or according to his later preference, "christianocentric"; *Church Dogmatics* 4/3:498].

27. Barth, *From Rousseau to Ritschl*, 354. [Also thirty years later, opposing what Schleiermacher "in his own brilliant fashion understood and explained"; *Church Dogmatics* 4/3:754.]

28. Barth, *Die Theologie und die Kirche*, 179.

29. Barth, *From Rousseau to Ritschl*, 345–46. [In *Church Dogmatics* 4/3:553, he saw the Christocentrism of Schleiermacher ("also of the Reformed tradition"), for which he often then gave him credit in conversation and teaching, as a "distant and, of course, severely distorted echo" of a "basic Calvinist proposition," the union with Christ. See also *Church Dogmatics* 4/4:118.]

30. Barth, *Die Theologie und die Kirche*, 139, 159–60; and idem, *From Rousseau to Ritschl*, 335.

31. Barth, *Church Dogmatics* 2/1:270.

32. Barth, *Die Theologie und die Kirche*, 165; and idem, *From Rousseau to Ritschl*, 336.

33. Barth, *Church Dogmatics* 2/1:327.

34. Ibid., 370.

35. Barth, *Die Theologie und die Kirche*, 159–60. [Also, very late, in *Church Dogmatics* 4/4:57, 103, 243, a view that for Barth can lead only to self-help, renewed volition.]

36. Barth, *From Rousseau to Ritschl*, 352. [See also *Church Dogmatics* 4/4:27, 4/3:754.]

37. Barth, *Die Theologie und die Kirche*, 148, 162, 165–66; and idem, *From Rousseau to Ritschl*, 348ff.; also in idem, *Church Dogmatics* 2/1:339, 3/3:117.

38. In Barth's *Theology of Schleiermacher*, 117; see 27ff. See also *Church Dogmatics* 4/3:772, where Barth pits his "strictly theological" approach to "the Christian community in world-occurrence" against Schleiermacher's. Despite what Schleiermacher did "in his own brilliant fashion," "it is seriously to be doubted, however, whether there can be even an approach on these lines to that which constitutes the particularity of the Christian community." In *Church Dogmatics* 4/3:743, he states, "The existence of the people of God cannot be subsumed under the concept of religion," despite Schleiermacher's having "finely expounded" the notion to its cultured despisers.

39. E.g., ibid., 138. See this same point in Barth's *Church Dogmatics* 4/4:243.

40. Barth, *Theology of Schleiermacher*, 217, 173.

41. Ibid., 151, 163.

42. E.g., ibid., 105–6.

43. Ibid.

44. Ibid., 267.

45. Ibid., 265.

46. Ibid., 277.

EXPLORING POINTS OF DIALOGUE

Part
2

Barth and Schleiermacher: Divergence and Convergence

4

HANS W. FREI

DIVERGENCE

When Karl Barth lectured on Friedrich Schleiermacher in Göttingen in the winter semester 1923–24,[1] he declared that he did not want to act the part of a theological historian. He eschewed, then and later, any lengthy account of Schleiermacher's development, and he referred only peripherally to his precursor's cultural context. Having been Schleiermacher's disciple once and rebelled against him, he wanted to keep coming to grips with him directly in his works. It was as though he were looking for a common context in which he and Schleiermacher both lived and in which they were both accountable for what they wrote. In 1923, the footprints of the second edition of the Romans commentary were still fresh in the sands of time, and the deliberate and significant change in title from the abortive *Christliche Dogmatik* to *Kirchliche Dogmatik* lay some years ahead. In one of the prefaces to the *Römerbrief*, Barth had poured out his wrath over those *wissenschaftliche* scholars who, once done with their spadework of philological, cultural, and historical commentary, called it quits and with obvious condescension turned the last volume of the series over to the practical theologians, the "Niebergalls" of this world. Just when *real* explication of the text should have begun! It was a denigration of both explicative and applicative labor—in other words, of the very heart of conceptual exploration. Barth shared Hegel's contempt for those scholars who substituted historical explanation for *Anstrengung des Begriffs*. Schleiermacher was far too important to him for any other treatment than that curious combination of exposition and interpretation (some would say exegesis and eisegesis) of the text that one accords to an equal—a person with whom one shares a common platform, subject, and audience.

Schleiermacher as Apologist

Commentators have expressed surprise and disappointment that the Göttingen lectures were so thoroughly expository rather than interpretive, but with the twenty-twenty vision of hindsight we can say that that is just what one ought to have expected after the *Römerbrief* prefaces. In order to understand an author one must above all understand the author's text, and to understand the text is to think with the author, in agreement, disagreement, and constant reconceptualization. Understanding means using the text to treat the author as an equal. Historical understanding of the author, which can only be either propaedeutic to textual understanding or consequent upon it, achieves this equality only rarely and with great difficulty.

Barth's interpretation of Schleiermacher in the Göttingen lectures consists in shaping certain dominant themes, to the repetition of which we become accustomed; indeed, some of them, like the image of "peace" or the peaceful middle between extremes, or of "meditation," tend to become tiresome. But since, as John Updike has observed, martial images proliferate in the writings of our feisty author, the contrasting rhetoric of his nineteenth-century precursor and conversation partner might indeed have struck him profoundly. The theme of mysticism also tends to be repeated, especially in the wake of Emil Brunner's book on Schleiermacher, *Die Mystik und das Wort*, but right from the start Barth is hesitant about the appropriateness of that theme to Schleiermacher's thought. Much clearer and more continuous is the theme of Schleiermacher as Christian apologist, which is later heavily emphasized in Barth's long, sustained effort to come to grips with him in his essay on Schleiermacher in *Protestant Theology in the Nineteenth Century.*[2] In contrast to apologetics, "mysticism" seemed to Barth an inadequate denotative category for that transcendence of the subject-object duality which he thought Schleiermacher shared with his Idealist philosophical contemporaries but which, unlike them, he posited *theologically* rather than philosophically, setting it in the relation between the feeling of absolute dependence—not the intuitive or discursive intellect—on the one hand, and God as Spirit, on the other. The place of this notion in Schleiermacher's thought is central for Barth, especially in the long essay just referred to, not only in its own right—just where or how does the intercourse *(Verkehr)* between God and human beings, to use Wilhelm Herrmann's term, take place and does it involve a kind of coinherence of divine human apprehension?—but because it has immediate logical implications for other crucial topics, particularly faith and Christology. And so Barth will return to it but, as we shall note, rather differently and less programmatically, in his last comments on Schleiermacher some thirty-five years later. At any rate, "mysticism" is for Barth at best an awkward term for what is at stake in Schleiermacher's interpretation of the transcendence of the subject-object dialectic. If Schleiermacher is a "mystic"—at least in the way the word has usually been bandied about in Protestant polemics against other religions and parts of the Roman Catholic tradition—the place of Christology in his system becomes moot or at best secondary. Jesus Christ would be Redeemer only in a thoroughly instrumental and dispensable sense, an occasion for the realization of a divine-human communion in principle achievable without him. But Barth realized that Schleiermacher's whole system was directed toward arguing the indispensability of Jesus Christ to the meaning of Christian faith and that, successfully or otherwise, this is what he wanted to show to believers and unbelievers alike.

By contrast, then, to calling Schleiermacher a mystic, Barth has no problem in characterizing him as an apologetical theologian. His definition of apologetics in the large Schleiermacher essay has become famous:

> Apologetics is an attempt to show by means of thought and speech that the determining principles of philosophy and of historical and natural research at some given point in time certainly do not preclude, even if they do not require, the tenets of theology, which are founded upon revelation and upon faith respectively. A bold apologetics proves to a particular generation the intellectual necessity of the theological principles taken from the Bible or from church dogma or from both; a more cautious apologetics proves at least their intellectual possibility.[3]

The natural context of this definition is the relation of theology to other *Wissenschaften*, especially to philosophy as *Wissenschaft*. The crucial operative terms in the definition are *Denknotwendigkeit* and *Denkmöglichkeit*, precisely the terms that are at issue between Hegelian-Idealist theology and a Schleiermacherian-mediating theology. For the former there is no conceptual possibility of theology unless it implies conceptual necessity; for the latter the two are logically discontinuous and although theology is a philosophical, that is, conceptual, possibility, the compelling claim to truth and even to meaningfulness of its subject matter rests on other grounds than those of conceptual necessity. For himself, Barth describes those other grounds as "revelation," a concept that plays a dominant part in his thought throughout the twenties, climaxing in the program of an internal prolegomena to dogmatics in *Church Dogmatics* 1/1 and 1/2, in which he unfolds the concept of revelation descriptively rather than constructing an argument for its conceptual possibility (in contrast to the external prolegomena to Schleiermacher's *The Christian Faith*). The concern about the epistemic or epistemological status of dogmatic theology evinced by the use of concepts such as revelation or faith—the latter being seen in polar relation to the former—is stronger in the Barth of this period than it ever was in Schleiermacher. The communion of the Christian with God is, for Barth, the Christian's *knowledge* (however problematical) of God, and sometimes he faults Schleiermacher for two contrasting things at the same time: too close a relation between philosophy and theology, on the one hand, and the denial of the cognitive character of theological statements, on the other.

Schleiermacher was the mediating theologian par excellence, so that Barth's preoccupation with the theme of apologetics in Schleiermacher was appropriate. But what Schleiermacher's apologetical theology mediated between were a large number of different things, of which theology and philosophy, or theology and the more limited sciences— historical and physical—were only examples. There was, at least potentially, also a correlation between Christianity and the other religions, between Christian forms of living and other forms, between Christianity in its specific essence and culture as historically developing reality, and finally, between the church as a community and the civic community represented by the state, cultural associations, and the family. Clearly, whatever may be the case in some other writings, the Barthian Schleiermacher who dominates the essay in *Protestant Theology in the Nineteenth Century* is the apologist who mediates between *Wissenschaftslehre* (transcendental philosophy) and dogmatic theology, and the dominant note is that the test case for the success of this enterprise is Christology, which Barth takes to be the defining instance of the concept of revelation.

Barth's Reproach

We might put Barth's question to Schleiermacher like this: Are statements about the uniqueness and absoluteness of Jesus as the revelation of God intelligible and plausible in a broader, trans-Christian conceptual, philosophical-cultural context? Early on in the essay Barth indicates the answer:

> Christology is the great disturbing element in Schleiermacher's *Glaubenslehre*. . . . Jesus of Nazareth fits desperately badly into this theology of the historical "composite life" of humanity, a "composite life" which is really . . . self-sufficient. . . . But nevertheless he is in fact there.[4]

And then, toward the end, we listen to the same strain when he says that the Reformation correlation between Word of God or Jesus Christ, and faith becomes equated with the correlation between history and experience as the two foci of an ellipse for Schleiermacher. This is a favorite Barthian (if not exactly Ritschlian) metaphor for the reproach that divine grace or prevenience and human possibility are simply synergistically related in this theology, nullifying the central thrust of the Reformation, for which not only can "Word of God" and "faith" not be exchanged for any other terms but their "correlation" takes place only in the absolute priority of Word to faith. This is again a way of criticizing Schleiermacher's theology for its dual and interconnected christological and epistemic deficiency.

Only at the end, and as a brief afterthought, does Barth take note of the basic *soteriological* rather than epistemic arrangement of Schleiermacher's whole christological enterprise, namely, the organization of the whole of *The Christian Faith* into the division between consciousness of sin and consciousness of grace, and the location of the christological topics under the latter. Even then he does so in effect only to illustrate the previous point—that in this case too Schleiermacher moves toward a synergism or relativization in which there is no untranscendable "juxtaposition [*Gegenüberstellung:* the translation "opposition" is wrong] between God and man, between Christ and the Christian."[5] And the viewpoint from which this antisynergistic polemic is launched is, as I said, the epistemological one—a revelation Christology and revelation trinitarianism that is logically prior to soteriologial considerations.

In short, the agenda of this large Schleiermacher essay appears to parallel that of *Church Dogmatics* 1/1. Barth asks whether Schleiermacher's theology presupposes the deity of the Logos (the content of revelation) as seriously as the Reformers presupposed that of the Holy Spirit.[6] He doubts it; he suggests that the seriousness of the Reformers' mutual juxtaposition (*Gegenüberstellung*) of the Second and Third Persons of the Trinity prevented either or both from being regarded as—or collapsed into—a mode or predicate (as Barth liked to say) of human cognition: both are equally "moments of the divine revelation."[7] There are no adequate safeguards of this sort in Schleiermacher's theology, and that is of course the basic threat not only to his pneumatology but to his Christology as well.

Barth wanted to bring together four questions or critiques of Schleiermacher: (1) On the assumption that Schleiermacher's mediating theology is basically one of religious consciousness and therefore at least potentially a theology of the Spirit, he asks whether it really is a theology of the Holy Spirit or instead one of relational or even purely monistic spirituality. Is the latter, he asks, what the feeling of absolute dependence is really about? (2) He asks whether this theology can be a theology of the Holy Spirit short of a far stronger correlation between pneumatology and Christology than Schleiermacher's mediating procedure can provide, and he implies that the answer must be negative. That is, for Barth the correlation between Christ and the Spirit present now in and to faith, or between the Second and Third Persons of the Trinity, must be absolutely prior to and something much more than the communal spirit—identical with the church—that provides the continuity between the Redeemer or history and present experience. (3) He asks whether Schleiermacher's apologetical or correlationist motif will allow for a strong enough doctrine of *revelation*, in which God and creatures are untranscendably and therefore unconfusedly juxtaposed to each other, even in faith. (4) He asks whether Schleiermacher's apologetical or correlationist motif will allow for a strong enough doctrine of *prevenient grace* to assure that faith is the work of divine forgiveness and not merely a cooperative enterprise between grace and repentant faith.

Barth was looking for ways to show that the correlation of distinctive Christian concepts with concepts derived from general human experience inevitably leads in the direction of the reduction of Christian concepts. Mediating theology is an unstable compromise between a christocentric theology properly at risk because stripped of all external foundational support, on the one hand, and a theology that has put itself at the mercy of consistent conceptual "demythologization," on the other. Mediating or apologetical theology has a superior standpoint from which to mediate between these two extremes on even and harmonious terms—Schleiermacher's "peaceful center"—but of course Barth thought that it was a place that did not, or should not, really exist. Right theology is a *theologia viatorum* that has no secure earthly resting place, and that includes the lack of a secure philosophical, experiential, or cultural home.

In the process, Barth conflated the two issues expressed in the third and fourth questions (about adequate doctrines of revelation and prevenient grace), arguing that the issues were in effect two aspects of one and the same more basic problem, that of the untranscendable objectivity of the divine-human juxtaposition in Christian faith. But they were not two aspects of that issue, certainly not historically and probably not logically. They may well, of course, have been aspects of some other, more basic problem, but that would have meant that Schleiermacher's *basic* correlation was not the theological one between revelation and the universal character of the feeling of absolute dependence. Barth did not consider that possibility in this essay.

In fact, the first of the two issues (that of the third question) is about the communication of divine truth through a privileged historical event that is its indispensable channel. Is such a thing either conceivable or, if conceivable, likely? It is the problem of Lessing's ugly ditch, of accidental truths of history being able or unable to furnish proof for eternal truths of reason by means of miracle, prophecy, and inspiration or—in Schleiermacher's case—to furnish meaningfulness, though not proof, for them by means of religious experience. This is the problem of the conceivability of revelation.

The second problem (that of the fourth question) is whether the experience of sin, or something like it, is a universal phenomenon that is at least *to some extent,* even if not wholly, intelligible apart from the understanding of particular historical redemption in Christ. Here the meaningfulness of the concept of Christ is (again, to some extent at least) logically dependent on the meaningfulness of sin as a universal rather than a specifically Christian concept. This is the problem of the universal meaningfulness of redemption or reconciliation through a particular, historical Savior. The most powerful modern endeavor to combine the topics of revelation and reconciliation systematically and conceptually was mounted in the theologies of the German classical period, Hegel's and Schleiermacher's at the forefront. But apart from such systematic combinations, revelation and reconciliation are at least logically two different conceptual issues, and in each case "correlation" with nontheological conceptions can be carried out differently.

Christian Theology as Practice

We cannot pursue these topics here, but as Barth's *Dogmatics* developed past the prolegomena, it is clear that the concept of revelation tended to recede in significance and the doctrine of reconciliation became more important. In the process, the doctrines of the person and work of Christ, Christology and soteriology, moved closer to each other, the bond between them being a concept of personhood as self-enacted agency or performative project rather than the epistemic notion of revelation as existentially imparted and appropriated knowledge or understanding. In that sense and that alone, one can say that Barth became a "narrative" theologian: Jesus was what he did and underwent, and not simply his understanding or self-understanding. He was an agent in a narrative plot, in his particular narratable plot, that is, the restoration of the broken covenant which is also the realization of the aim of divine creation. It is more accurate to say that the meaning of the theological doctrines or conceptual redescriptions is the *story* of which they are (partial) redescriptions, rather than conversely, that the meaning of the story is the doctrines. The unity of Christology and soteriology is their unity in the narrative rather than a *conceptual* unity in which the two concepts "person" and "work" become perfectly integrated. As for our *appropriation* of person and work, it receives no systematic but only a dogmatic correlation in Barth's later work. Its logical possibility in a church-dogmatic context is based strictly on the actual, once-for-all accomplishment of Christ's work on our behalf, and not even partially on a native, inherent capacity—or for that matter incapacity—of ours for responding. Schleiermacher would not have found it a very congenial view.

These developments in Barth's theology would surely serve, however, to circumvent his earlier endeavor to see the problems of revelationally founded Christology and of soteriology in Schleiermacher as together *simply* aspects of the more basic, in fact the *most* basic, issue of the "untranscendable over-againstness" of God and humankind, and thus to see the relation between the problems solely in epistemic terms— even if the knowledge is "practical" rather than "theoretical." Not that this issue would be eliminated, but it would now be relativized and come up—together with the character of Schleiermacher's theology as one of the Spirit—as *one* question rather than as *the* test case for judging the adequacy of Schleiermacher's theology.

The recession of the restrictively epistemic character of Barth's earlier views makes him more relaxed about the practical character of Christian theology. The tension between the "indirect objectivity" or constative quality of Christian statements, and their appropriative, that is, illocutionary and perlocutionary performative character—the latter the emphasis of pietists and existentialists—becomes not solved but simply relaxed in Barth's later work. The affirmation of the practical aspect and aim of theology had always been there for him anyway: right from the beginning he knew that theology was there to serve preaching and the Christian life in Christian as well as civil community. But later on, the emphasis was less problematical: in a proper theological hermeneutics, explication, reflective understanding, and application simply go together. Likewise, for any proper theology, faith is a coherence of knowledge with acknowledgment and obedience. More than that cannot and need not be said.

In Barth's 1923–24 lectures, Schleiermacher's *Brief Outline of the Study of Theology* had received extensive treatment.[8] Never again; and Barth neglected two important aspects of it thereafter in his treatment of Schleiermacher in the late 1920s and 1930s: (1) To a somewhat lesser degree, he neglected the strong emphasis on the *ecclesiastical aim* of theological training and its influence on Schleiermacher's theology. He repeated it often but drew relatively few material consequences from it for his evaluation of Schleiermacher's theology. (2) To a greater extent, he neglected Schleiermacher's cognate emphasis on the *practical* character and aim of theology. And yet his own theology became not only more "practical" in basic sensibility, as we have mentioned, but increasingly *kirchlich* rather than simply *christlich*. Not only was that in a subtle manner contextually, psychologically, and existentially important but, I believe, it made an increasingly important conceptual difference in his writing as he grew older: concepts are social skills, theological concepts are ecclesiastical and ecclesiological skills. In turn, I believe, this development made a basic difference for his treatment of fundamental and broad methodological issues such as those concerning the relation between philosophy and theology when he finally looked at Schleiermacher for the last time shortly before his death. It allowed him, without receding for a moment from his own christological concentration in theology, not to make Christology the immediate and explicit touchstone for agreement or disagreement with Schleiermacher's mediating theology. Instead, he could take a fresh look at the conceptual differences that Schleiermacher's ecclesiastical aim and practical intentions might have made in his theology and in the way he correlated philosophy and theology.

CONVERGENCE

The subtitle of this part of the essay might well be "Journey to Dullsville," for unlike the first section, this part involves one of those minute clarifying operations that could perhaps pay off handsomely, but only if one could push it considerably further than I can on the present occasion. The line along which the convergent movement either takes place or turns out to be a mirage continues to be that which traces the character of theology and its relation to other disciplines, particularly philosophy. But the focus of that relation will no longer be confined so explicitly to Christology and revelation. The question I want to ask is, What would have to be the character of theology for there to be such a convergence—no more, and certainly not agreement—between these two theologians? My claims, you will note, are not only modest, they are entirely in the subjunctive mood. Still, there might be important consequences, if only time, patience, and skill were available in equal measure. I will now spend more time on Schleiermacher, but I will again begin with Barth and end with him.

A Hypothesis

We must now look at Barth's "Concluding Unscientific Postscript on Schleiermacher,"[9] in which he recounts three stages of his relation to his theological forebear. First, he was Schleiermacher's disciple during his youthful liberal days. Then he distanced himself from Schleiermacher in his dialectical and postdialectical days, with greater acerbity at first than later on. This was the period of Barth's Schleiermacher lectures and essays, of which we have taken note. But now Barth, in his last year, distances himself from, without abandoning, his earlier self-distancing from Schleiermacher's theological outlook.[10] Barth now raises five questions, each with first a positive and then a negative edge: (1) Is Schleiermacher's enterprise intrinsically concerned with theology and accidentally with philosophy, or vice versa? And note that Barth speaks of intrinsic or authentic Christian theology as the kind that is "oriented toward worship, preaching, instruction, and pastoral care."[11] (2) Is Schleiermacher talking about a religious (my term, not Barth's) relationship to an untranscendable *other* toward whom "adoration, gratitude, repentance, and supplication are concretely possible and even imperative"? Or is he talking about a relation that is essentially one of *unity* between human consciousness and that which transcends it? (3) For Schleiermacher, are human beings primarily related to a *particular* and concrete reality, or is the reverse the case? (4) "Is the spirit which moves feeling, speaking, and thinking persons an absolutely *particular* and specific Spirit" to be distinguished from all others and called "Holy"? Or is that spirit a universally effective spiritual power that is basically diffuse? (5) And finally (and admirably put), are these the right questions for further conversation about Schleiermacher's intentions? (Note the absence of Christology as a *special* topic.)

Even if we respond yes to the last query, the others are put in that shorthand or summary fashion which comes from a tradition's long-standing use of the same technical philosophical and theological language applied to the same technical issues. Let me reword them a little, just to make them a little more accessible. They concern respectively (*a*) the relation of theology, the enterprise of a specific religious community, to philosophy, the self-grounded and coherent set of formal rules and universal criteria for intelligibility, meaningfulness, and truth for all fields of reflection, and perhaps (debatably!) the material science informative of the structures of reality; (*b*) the "objective" God of the "classical" tradition vs. the God of the transcendence of the "subject-object schema"; (*c*) the place of the "scandal of particularity" in Christian theology (presumably Christology and reconciliation in particular) vs. the hermeneutical priority of the "meaning context" requisite for the epistemological and religious significance of Christology, etc.; and (*d*) the especially German and Idealistic inquiry into the apparently disjunctive alternative of the unity of the Holy Spirit either with the "objectivity" of divine grace or else with the creative spontaneity of universal human subjectivity or "spirit"—the inquiry into which of these two is the source of the possibility of "spiritual" community between the divine and the human. The parallels between these questions and the topics covered in the large, earlier Schleiermacher essay are striking. But so is their open-endedness and less integrated or systematic character.

We will have to enter into this conversation on its own terms. If, in answer to the fifth question, we say that Barth's questions point at least in the right direction, part of what we are buying is (*a*) the common *philosophical* heritage between the two theologians which permits them common ground for agreement and disagreement about philosophy, and (*b*) the possibility that there is more than one way of relating that philosophical heritage with the theological heritage, if in fact the two disciplines are not identical. About (*a*) there can be little doubt, even if Barth's philosophical sounds are a bit like Hegel's, while Schleiermacher makes noises more reminiscent of Schelling. About (*b*) there is at the very least a lively possibility that Schleiermacher, like Barth, thinks that philosophy and theology are generically different enterprises. Given the rather vague area of agreement between the two theologians, a genuine convergence of their views would entail for Schleiermacher a vigorous emphasis on the radical difference rather than the compatibility between the two disciplines; for Barth, conversely, it would mean stressing strongly that radical difference means incomparability rather than incompatibility. Let us explore this two-sided possibility, all the while bearing in mind the hypothetical character of this enterprise, and therefore the prejudicial, highly selective character of my choice of texts, especially from Schleiermacher. In effect, I am confining myself to Barth's first question, viewing it as a central topic between the two theologies that may be disentangled, without at the same time arguing the question of priority between Christology and soteriology, or the relation of both to the character of revelation or our knowledge of God—important as all these issues are for discussion between the two men.

Theology as a Christian Skill

In his important book *Theologia*,[12] Edward Farley traces the history not only of theological education but of the concept of theology itself. We learn that from the High Middle Ages until the beginnings of the Enlightenment a distinction was made between theology as a cognitive state or *habitus*, usually though not always of practical kind, a "state or disposition of the soul which has the character of knowledge,"[13] and theology as a science or discipline. Farley goes on to say that, especially from the days of Pietism and the Enlightenment on, the notion of theology, particularly as a technical discipline, has become determined by the disposition of clergy education into a set of distinct "sciences" (I suppose one might say "skills") for study, destroying a previous unity and forcing to the fore the question of their interrelation.[14] From being a unitary discipline, second-order theology went to being an aggregate of specialties, while first-order theology changed from "sapiential habitus" to practical know-how. This new outlook grew out of several changes, prominent among them the Pietist treatment of theology (*Gottesgelahrtheit*) as a means to an end, namely, the exercise of the Christian life or Christian piety (*Gottseligkeit*). The climax of this development, both in theological method and ministerial education—characterized by a series of writings called "theological encyclopedia"—is Schleiermacher's *Brief Outline of Theological Study* (finished in 1810),[15] written about the same time as his essay *Gelegentliche Gedanken über Universitäten in deutschem Sinn* (1808; written in connection with the founding of the University of Berlin and in response to essays on the relation of the faculties in universities and on the method of academic study by Kant, Fichte, and Schelling).[16] Farley draws attention to both of Schleiermacher's essays. Schleiermacher, according to Farley, sees theology as a means to an end of professional education for the ministry. Theology is a practical or "positive" skill rather than a pure science. Like law and medicine—and the faculties in which they are taught— theology provides the cognitive skills for a social practice: the governance of a religious community. "Theology is unified by the social situation of clerical praxis external to the university and the faculty of theology."[17] But Schleiermacher also proposes a second and "material" rather than "teleological" unity for the three theological disciplines— practical, philosophical, and historical theology—in which he appeals to the distinctive "essence" of Christianity. This appeal involves the conception that Christianity belongs to a religious and religious-communal genre that must be distinguishable from other areas of culture and their study, and the affirmation that the student is to develop internal or participative (my term) access to Christianity's historical shape and, along that route, also to its reality and truth as a universal reality—faith—in one particular cultural form.[18]

The question I want to focus on is to what extent the first or "clerical paradigm" for theology, as Farley calls it, provides not only the *aim* (as Farley seems to think) but part of the very *essence* of theology, as well as of its pedagogic structure, for Schleiermacher. Is it not only in aim but in procedure "oriented toward worship, preaching, instruction, and pastoral care," as Barth asked in his first question? An answer satisfying Barth would obviously have to include the "practical" aspect of theology, on which Schleiermacher lays such strong stress in the third part of the *Brief Outline*. But more than that, the "philosophical" and "historical" aspects would also have to indicate signs of strong ties to the practical aspect and aim of theology—and so would "dogmatic," as part of historical theology. That, in turn, would mean (negatively) that in two senses the philosophical aspect of theology *cannot* unequivocally set the criteria for the meaningfulness, meaning, and truth of theological statements: (1) Any purely formal, universal canon of reason which adjudicates the coherence, consistency, and intelligibility of the "method" governing a particular field of study cannot do so in this case. (2) There cannot be a priority to theology of any specific (material) philosophical scheme—whether of a rationalist, transcendent (a priori), empiricist (a posteriori), or transcendental kind—that would assert that theological descriptions and claims must be subsumed under it. In short, neither formally nor materially can philosophy be a foundational discipline for theology.

We know from Schleiermacher's constantly reiterated assertions that he denied that theology is an aspect of philosophy in the *material* sense, that its content—for example, its notion of God—is identical with philosophical "ideas." The consistency of this disavowal might perhaps best be tested by an intensive investigation of that most difficult of his unfinished works, the *Dialektik*. But certainly he reiterates it constantly in his theological works, while at the same time affirming the compatibility, indeed the convergence, of the two disciplines. By consensus, the hard question is the relation of his theology to philosophy in the more *formal* sense, that is, to philosophy as universal *Wissenschaftslehre*. Here the *Gelegentliche Gedanken über Universitäten in deutschem Sinn* (rather similar to the *Dialektik* but with a different immediate purpose in mind) are very useful. In this essay he clearly associates *Wissenschaft* with transcendental philosophy qua foundational, formal structure for knowledge rather than qua compelling ontological system. The business of *Wissenschaft* is not only to constitute the basic character of the "academy of the sciences" but to provide the idea, if not the reality, of the university. The business of the university is to teach youths to see everything from the point of view of "science"—"to see everything particular not for itself but in its nearest scientific relations and insert it into a wide common frame, in steady relation to the unity and total comprehensiveness [*Allheit*] of knowledge [*Erkenntnis*], so that they may learn in all thinking to become conscious of the basic laws of *Wissenschaft*."[19] But this cannot be done by "mere wraithlike transcendental philosophy," but requires the association of philosophy with real knowledge *(reales Wissen)* "so that from the start the supposed opposition between reason [*Vernunft*] and experience . . . can be annihilated" and the "large realms of nature and history be opened up."[20]

There is for Schleiermacher a *parallel* between the relation of formal *Wissenschaftslehre* and individual empirical fields of study, on the one hand, and religion in general and positive, cultural forms of religion, on the other. In both arenas the status of what is general is transcendental, the formal condition of a possibility inhering solely in the actuality of what is positive, empirical, or particular. But there is also an important *difference*, so that the parallel is at best imperfect. For the three faculties of law, theology, and medicine are not part of the "idea" of a university founded on a *wissenschaftliche* basis. Their subjects are therefore not related to "science" qua formal philosophical structure in the way that a particular content is related to formal, general possibility. These three faculties have their original *raison d'être* prior to or outside the university understood as a scientific construct. They are *Specialschulen* "that the state has either founded or at least, because they relate to its essential needs, taken under early and privileged protection. . . . The positive faculties originated individually through the need of founding with sureness an indispensable practice *(Praxis)* through theory, through a tradition of *Kenntnisse*."[21] In the context, it appears to me at least likely that *Kenntnisse* here means something like the "abilities" or "cognitive skills" requisite for carrying out the given practical work, and that the awkward expression "through theory . . ." means that becoming acquainted through well-accustomed use with the *tradition* of these *Kenntnisse* is pretty much what "theory" amounts to in the "positive" areas governed by these three faculties. "Theory" here does not function foundationally in a strong sense but functions more nearly as a set of grammatical remarks in the use of this particular language (to appropriate the terms of the later Wittgenstein and his little flock).

"The theological faculty was shaped in the church in order to preserve the wisdom of the fathers, in order to distinguish truth from error—as already in the past—and not allow it to be lost to the future, in order to provide a historical basis, a sure and certain direction, and a common spirit for the further development of doctrine and of the church."[22] So far, then, this "positive" enterprise is neither transcendental philosophy nor specific method based on a universal, philosophical foundation but the acquisition and impartation of a developing tradition that is in a broad, nonscientific sense historical (*geschichtlich* rather than *historisch*, to make use of that unpleasant but at times helpful distinction which became onerous only when it was elevated to rigid and absolute status). One could say that theology is part of the heritable social currency of a specific religious community, the Christian church. It is its self-critical inquiry into the use of its language for purposes of applying it and handing it on for use by the same developing and changing community in the future. It presupposes connection to another, more elemental use of the same communal language, that is, the constant transition from the Christian religious affections to their kerygmatic, poetic, rhetorical, and finally their descriptively didactic linguistic shape.[23]

The Functions of Philosophy

From what I have said it should be evident that were there to be a convergence between Schleiermacher's theology and Barth's views underlying his questions of 1968, it would depend on our being able to take Schleiermacher's "teleological" and practical outlook on theology and ministerial pedagogy as more than a final cause or *telos*—that in addition we would have to be able to see the outlook as part of the material cause, the very substance, of his procedure. This is the possibility I have been suggesting. The governing principle is that theology as a practical skill is not simply the application of logically prior philosophical and historical theological insight to logically subsequent and practical matters of church leadership, such as the cure of souls.[24] Theology is a practical discipline as a whole and not merely a theoretical or scientific enterprise—either of a transcendental or of an empirical character—with an as it were external aim. (This *may* be the bearing of *Brief Outline*, §§257–63.) This does not, of course, question the fact that it is *also* a scientific enterprise.[25]

Now Farley, we recall, also spoke of a "material unity" in Schleiermacher's theology provided by the "idea" or "essence" of Christianity. Something like this is indeed the case, even if "material" may be a bit misleading, and the "essence" of Christianity may be one of several contexts in which this second outlook surfaces. Let us recall the important additions Schleiermacher made in the second edition of *The Christian Faith*, additions completely in tune with the *Brief Outline*. He had suggested that dogmatic theology—itself part of historical theology—is founded not on "general principles" but solely in association with the concepts of church and Christian church. The particular character of the Christian church can "neither be comprehended and deduced by purely scientific methods nor be grasped by mere empirical methods."[26] So far this is what we would expect. How do we then grasp the concepts of church and Christian church? By propositions *(Lehnsätze)* "borrowed from" ethics, philosophy of religion, and apologetics. These headings are new and intended for clarification.[27] We are moving in concentric circles toward the essence of Christianity with the help of a group of narrowing specifications, all of them properly *wissenschaftlich* and applicable to empirical, cultural phenomena or data. "Ethics" is the broadest category (its counterpart is "physics," the study of nature) and designates the systematic study of culture and/or history. I think we may safely say that it is Schleiermacher's equivalent of social science, and embraces what came to be the university disciplines of sociology and cultural anthropology, but of course, since he was a German Idealist, in *geisteswissenschaftliche* manner. The "conception of the church" is properly speaking sociology or anthropology of religion and has for its subject matter the distinctive structure of religious communities. Given his orientation toward a view of human being as basically self-conscious *(Geist)*, that structure will not be described in socioscientific terms (which were not then developed, anyway) of social structures or institutions but in terms of what Schleiermacher thought to be the basic, preconceptual, prelinguistic awareness that all people hold in common and that is therefore the bond of communal existence. He calls it "feeling" or "immediate self-consciousness."

While "immediate self-consciousness" in relation to the other human capacities of knowing and willing is part of an elaborate anthropology, its own content is not. That content consists simply of "affective receptivity," or the "feeling of dependence," and "spontaneous activity," or the "feeling of freedom," and Schleiermacher says that "to these propositions assent can be unconditionally demanded." How so? we ask, and his reply is, "No one will deny them who is capable of a little introspection and can find interest in the real subject of our present inquiries."[28] No phenomenological reduction, no elaborate and philosophically founded technical phenomenology, but *a common-sense instrument ("a little introspection") for bringing together a* wissenschaftlich *pursuit, the description or analysis of religious community as a cultural phenomenon, on the one hand, and the Christian-religious conceptual skill of orienting oneself within the church, on the other.* What enables them to come together in self-consciousness cannot be shown straightforwardly by a methodological procedure. For on the one hand, the scientific aspect of the inquiry proceeds on principles that are "borrowed" and thus cannot be applied as though they were on their own terrain: as soon as they *are* applied in strict rather than "borrowed" fashion, it is no longer theology that is being done.[29] But on the other hand, the feeling of absolute dependence is the—empirical? quasi-empirical? transcendental? all of the above?—common basic descriptive content of self individually as well as in community and does allow a family resemblance (even if it is not systematically specifiable) between "scientific" and Christian-participative, practical description of the same community, the church, and of its life and language. In other words, even though "borrowed," the "propositions of ethics" are not inapplicable or inappropriate. And then, in narrowing concentric circles, neither are the further, increasingly focused discriminations of propositions borrowed from the philosophy of religion, rendering for us a scheme for comparing actually existing religious outlooks and traditions, or finally the narrowest and most central discriminations of apologetics, in which "science" and the participative self-description of Christian cognitive skills join most closely. Propositions borrowed from apologetics set forth the specific essence of Christianity, that is, the coherence of redemption, on the one hand, with the specific person of Jesus, on the other. From cultural community we move to religious-cultural and then to specifically Christian community in a journey of reflection that is participative but also quasi-scientific. *If* this hypothetical description of a single procedure in which two logically disparate but not contradictory capacities—positive skill (together with its "grammar") and *wissenschaftliche* understanding—are focused on or correlated by means of the one common phenomenon of immediate self-consciousness is indeed Schleiermacher's path, three consequences are entailed: (1) There is no formal, transcendental scheme under which the two can be unified, the cognitive skills involved in Christian-pious membership in the Christian community—especially its leadership—on the one hand, and the scientific understanding, in which a particular empirical religious content is made intelligible by a method derived from general principles, on the other. *Their unity is a matter of application alone, of direct correlation that allows no further or all-embracing justification of its possibility or intelligibility.* (2) Hence, the introduction to *The Christian Faith* is in fact not an actual theological or dogmatic exercise (and it certainly is not "philosophy") but a preliminary orientation or location,[30] quasi-external and quasi-internal, of the character of theology as scientific discipline and ecclesiastical skill. The introduction functions as an invitation to the cultured reader to exercise Christian understanding, by moving the reader toward it through a sort of indirect communication or maieutic guidance (description by means of concentric, increasingly focused *borrowed* propositions), so that there may be an ability to follow and perhaps even to carry out that skill in the form of a dogmatic system. (3) Hence the system itself has no further or actual systematic principle apart from the preliminary, quasi-scientific yet common-sensical one of the introduction: the feeling of absolute dependence. Beyond that, the persuasiveness, coherence, and completeness of the system consist solely in its actual performance, in the convincing aptness and completeness of its formal organization—perhaps rather like an aesthetic whole. (That formal organization in turn must therefore always be subject to revision.)[31]

In sum, the relation between theology and philosophy as a material system of true ideas virtually does not exist for this hypothetical Schleiermacher as a teacher in the church, except as a purely formal appropriation of the language of various philosophical systems for dogmatic purposes.[32] The relation between the notion of theology as Christian conceptual skill and the notion of it as science in the sense of the specific application of a system of formal, general principles (*Wissenschaftslehre*) is one of direct—that is, not further or transcendentally founded—correlation between independent equals. The correlation takes place by "borrowing" the general principles and applying them to immediate self-consciousness, which not only is the center of selfhood but also as a concept comes closest to specifying the focus or continuing center of the Christian community.

The Integrity of Theology

This hypothetical Schleiermacher and Barth are agreed that theology is the critical self-examination by the church of its own specific language under a norm furnished within that pious linguistic community.[33] There would be a real convergence between them here, because the implication for both is the irreducible specificity of this communal language, which is not even (except in a "borrowed" sense) an instance of a general class called religious-communal language. For Barth the question would be whether the *correlation* of this language on a level of equality with the scientific understanding of religious-communal language as a general class does not already serve to give away the independence and practical aim of the church's critical self-description of its language. The focal, though not the only, problem would be that the feeling of absolute dependence might well, on the correlationist assumption, become a far stronger or more comprehensive integrating factor between the two kinds of skill or procedure than my hypothetical Schleiermacher has suggested and that in consequence it would also become a far stronger systematic focus for interpreting *dogmatic* as distinct from prolegomenal statements. Barth in 1968 seemed to think that something like this was the risk though not the certain consequence of Schleiermacher's policy of correlation. He had already posed this very issue of the independence of theology from the "sciences" with which it may be correlated, or one strongly resembling it, in his Göttingen lectures in connection with the convergence of Schleiermacher's *Brief Outline*, Schleiermacher's critique of Schelling's "Über die Methode des akademischen Studiums," and Schleiermacher's essay on the nature of the university. Is it possible, Barth had asked, that Schleiermacher maintained that so far as science or speculative philosophy go, theology is actually poised in mid-air?[34] In that case "correlation" would obviously not be nearly as nefarious as if it were a stronger systematic and integrating principle. But then Barth expresses his skepticism that this is Schleiermacher's real intention and backs off,[35] never (to the best of my knowledge) to pose the issues between Schleiermacher and himself primarily in these terms again. But in 1968, the possibility appeared on the horizon once more.

As we all know, Barth decided that the formal structure of an independent *Wissenschaftslehre* (to say nothing of a strong transcendental version of it) is not even in "borrowed" fashion a criterion for the meaning of dogmatic language. Not that dogmatics can do without such a structure, but it is subordinate to, rather than an independent correlate of, the rules governing or implied by the church's use of language. Even less than for Schleiermacher, formal reason is simply not a single, demonstrably self-identical transcendental reality or potency for Barth which could by virtue of its apodictic and universal status provide the rules for every language game. And thus, dogmatic prolegomena are an internal part of dogmatics, formal rules of dogmatic reasoning adduced from the dogmatic use itself.[36] Subordination, however, is not necessarily denial. Even if he does not give them transcendental, that is, independent a priori status, Barth never denies that such categories or criteria as coherence, and distinctions such as that between meaning and reference, and even the law of contradiction, are indispensable formal tools for the theologian. But in application they are fragmentary and incomplete this side of the grave or eschaton. We simply do not know, for example, *how* the principle of noncontradiction applies to the doctrine of the incarnation, but we believe that since it does for God (who has neither created an irrational universe nor redeemed it irrationally), we need not resort to evasive substitute and general categories such as "paradox."

Surprisingly, Barth's subordination of *Wissenschaftslehre* to the rules inherent in critical Christian self-description allows him much greater freedom than Schleiermacher to use what he wishes from a variety of *material* philosophical systems or conceptual schemes—for example, medieval realism or Hegelian Idealism.[37] Not being a correlationist, especially not of the transcendental Idealistic kind, Barth does not have to use, as Schleiermacher does, anthropology (whether of immediate self-consciousness or any other kind) as the focus for integrating two independent types of conceptual skills or understandings. So although he agrees with Schleiermacher that no material philosophical system has an intrinsic relation to dogmatics and that any such scheme ought always to be used formally in theology, still he acknowledges that many schemes may be at least as fit, unsystematically, to serve the purpose of dogmatic articulation as non- or pretheological anthropology is. In fact, such schemes are indispensable tools that may be, if we are careful, firmly governed by dogmatic reflection.

Now, my hypothetical Schleiermacher might want to ask some questions of his own about a possible convergence between himself and Barth. There are obvious and not very telling remarks, such as those about Barth's "revelation positivism," his "Christomonism," his "exclusivism," his "obscure conceptuality," or his "objectification" of theology, that I suspect Schleiermacher would leave to others. The maximization of the difference between *Wissenschaftslehre* and theology Barth and Schleiermacher might well (on this account of a possible Schleiermacher) have in common. But Schleiermacher might want to ask Barth whether, despite himself, he has not turned maximum difference into incompatibility through the instrument of the subordination of *Wissenschaftslehre* to Christian-communal critical self-description of the community's language. Without the constant, continuing *practice* of correlation (although surely it must be without a comprehensive principle of correlation), do not all criteria for intelligibility except the minimal, formal rules of grammar and syntax in fact go out the window for Christian theology? Do not principles like that of noncontradiction become not eschatological but Pickwickian if they have no clear theology-independent status in their application to theology? Does not Christian theology threaten to turn into the in-group talk of one isolated community among others, with no ground rules for mutual discourse among them all?

Finally, what about the sympathetic observer to this possible convergence between the two men on the relation between Christian theology and philosophy? Perhaps one's final comment has to be that on this topic or issue any theologian of integrity has to cut his or her philosophical losses, and it is perhaps simply a matter of how it is done. One way results in one kind of loss, the other in another. You simply have to make your choice about what is most important to you in this respect and what is less important and therefore can be allowed to remain more problematical. *Correlating*, for example, the moral life of the church and the problematic requirements of culture, or the Jesus of historical-critical, *wissenschaftlich* reconstruction and the Lord and Savior of the sinful people of God, or the conceptually objectified dogmatic articulation of Christian faith and the general principles of religious-language use, will give you one kind of result, *subordinating* one to the other a different kind. Cutting one's philosophical losses is an occupation that is theologically disastrous only if it means *either* a complete elimination of philosophy as an issue and a means for reflection in Christian theology *or* a pathetic obeisance to philosophy as the master key to certainty about all reason and certainty and therefore to the shape or possibility of Christian theology.

NOTES

1. Karl Barth, *Die Theologie Schleiermachers*, ed. Dietrich Ritschl (Zurich: Theologischer Verlag, 1978).

2. Karl Barth, *Die protestantische Theologie im 19. Jahrhundert: Ihre Vorgeschichte und Geschichte*, 2d, rev. ed. (Zurich: Evangelischer Verlag, 1952). ET of essay is in *Protestant Thought: From Rousseau to Ritschl*, trans. Brian Cozens (New York: Harper & Bros., 1959), 306–54.

3. Ibid. (ET), 320ff.

4. Ibid., 313.

5. Ibid., 354.

6. Ibid., 343.

7. Ibid.

8. In fact, Barth's painstakingly thorough examination of this brief work, together with Schleiermacher's nearly contemporary essay on the concept of a university (we shall tackle its significance for the theological approach of the two men below), is most remarkable. He unerringly poses at least the *possibility* that Christian theology may be without *wissenschaftlich* foundation for Schleiermacher. That is surely different from the then-customary view of Schleiermacher, including Barth's own! But nothing really comes of it, either then or in the large essay in *Protestant Theology in the Nineteenth Century*.

9. *Schleiermacher-Auswahl*, ed. Heinz Bolli, afterword by Karl Barth (Munich: Siebenstern Taschenbuch Verlag, 1968), 293ff.

10. Dietrich Ritschl's contrary judgment in his ed. of Barth's 1923–24 Schleiermacher lectures in Göttingen, that the shift was one of tone only (*Die Theologie Schleiermachers*, viii), is unpersuasive in the absence of substantiating argument.

11. *Schleiermacher-Auswahl*, ed. Bolli, 307.

12. Edward Farley, *Theologia: The Fragmentation and Unity of Theological Education* (Philadelphia: Fortress Press, 1983).

13. Ibid., 35.

14. Ibid., 49–50.

15. Friedrich Schleiermacher, *Brief Outline on the Study of Theology*, trans. Terrence N. Tice (Richmond: John Knox Press, 1966).

16. Friedrich Schleiermacher, "Gelegentliche Gedanken über Universitäten

im deutschen Sinn," *Sämmtliche Werke*, vol. 3/1 (Berlin: G. Reimer, 1, 535–644.

17. Farley, *Theologia*, 84.

18. See ibid., 92–93.

19. Schleiermacher, *Gegentliche Gedanken*, 558.

20. Ibid., 572–73.

21. Ibid., 581.

22. Ibid., 582.

23. Friedrich Schleiermacher, *The Christian Faith*, trans. H. R. Mackintosh and J. S. Stewart (Edinburgh: T. & T. Clark, 1948), §§15, 16.

24. Schleiermacher, *Brief Outline*, §263.

25. The most powerful contrary argument, claiming historical *Wissenschaft* to be the constitutive character of theology for Schleiermacher and therefore straightforwardly to govern theology's practical aspect for him can be found in the excellent chap. on Schleiermacher in B. A. Gerrish's *Tradition and the Modern World* (Chicago: Univ. of Chicago Press, 1983). See chap. 1, esp. pp. 39ff. For perceptive discussions of Schleiermacher's views which are closer to this essay, see S. W. Sykes, "Theological Study: The Nineteenth Century and After," in *The Philosophical Frontiers of Christian Theology: Essays Presented to D. M. Mackinnon*, ed. Brian Hebblethwaite and Stewart Sutherland (Cambridge: Cambridge Univ. Press, 1982), 95–118, esp. 103–8; and idem, *The Identity of Christianity* (Philadelphia: Fortress Press, 1984), chap. 4, esp. 87–88.

26. Schleiermacher, *The Christian Faith*, §1.2.

27. Friedrich Schleiermacher, *On the Glaubenslehre: Two Letters to Dr. Lücke*, ed. James A. Massey, trans. James Duke and Francis S. Fiorenza (Chico, Calif.: Scholars Press, 1981), 80.

28. Schleiermacher, *The Christian Faith*, §4, p. 13.

29. Cf. Schleiermacher, *Brief Outline*, §6.

30. Schleiermacher, *On the Glaubenslehre*, 2d letter, pp. 56, 76ff.

31. Ibid., 69–70.

32. Ibid., 62ff.

33. Karl Barth, *Kirchliche Dogmatik* 1/1:1ff.

34. Barth, *Die Theologie Schleiermachers*, 256.

35. Ibid., 263–64, 274, 283, 292–93, 308ff.

36. Barth, *Kirchliche Dogmatik* 1/1:5ff., 24ff.

37. Ibid., 1/2:816–25.

Schleiermacher and Barth on the Essence of Christianity— an Instructive Disagreement

5

It is in truth somewhat strange that until comparatively recently the theological significance of attempts to define the essence of Christianity has received little attention.[1] That there is a history of such attempts is obvious enough, and historians of the concept have frequently made suggestions as to its interpretation. Carl Heinz Ratschow, contributing in 1957 the article "Wesen des Christentums" to *Die Religion in Geschichte und Gegenwart,* wrote of the apparent disappearance of the problem in existentialist theology's emphasis on the decision of faith but of its reappearance as the question of the continuity of Christian existence and Christian life in the world.[2] Rolf Schäfer's careful analysis of the point of the concept concluded that it retained its usefulness at a time of acute specialization of the subdepartments of theology as a way of holding the disciplines together.[3] Hans Wagenhammer, in the first extended Roman Catholic study of the prehistory and history of essence definition, emphasized its importance as a perennial resource for resisting the absolutizing of a particular historical form of Christianity.[4]

In my study of the nineteenth- and twentieth-century arguments about the essence of Christianity, I have attempted to lay out a somewhat deeper and also somewhat simpler analysis of the roots of the problem.[5] It is, of course, true that when Friedrich Schleiermacher and Karl Barth respectively endorse and refuse the task of determining Christianity's essence, their stances can be understood as part and parcel of their attitudes to religion, revelation, faith, knowledge, and so forth. This is how the specialist literature on Schleiermacher's and Barth's massive theological achievements has so far handled the matter.

But it should also be enlightening to review the matters from the standpoint of a broader theological perspective on what the definition of the essence of Christianity appears to be about. That is to say, we should ask the question, Where do Schleiermacher and Barth fit in the parameters of the problem which gave rise to the long, fascinating, but inconclusive history of attempts at essence definition? This is by no means an alternative method to seeking to relate their stances on this matter to their fundamental attitudes toward philosophy, ethics, and dogmatics, as does Hans Frei most illuminatingly in this volume. But on the assumption that certain problems have a habit of reappearing in Christian theology over the centuries, and that it is pertinent to ask of theologians of the past, questions which they may not overtly ask of themselves, the method of this paper is to interrogate Schleiermacher and Barth on their attitudes toward the fundamental motives that have led to the chronic disputes about Christian identity.

CHALLENGE, CONFLICT, AND IDENTITY

In the first place we need to disabuse ourselves of a prevalent misconception about definitions of the essence of Christianity: that they are attempted only by Protestants. This view was stated classically by Ernst Troeltsch in his study of the methodology of essence definition:

> The definition of the essence does not only involve an imaginative abstraction, but also with it and as part of it a criticism grounded on personal, ethical judgement, which measures the manifestations against the essence. For this reason it is only possible for protestantism, which is based precisely upon the principle that personal insight into what is essential in Christianity is able to evaluate selectively the mass of actual historical manifestations.[6]

It should not be forgotten that these words were written in 1903. On December 16, 1902, five of Alfred Loisy's books had been put on the Index: on January 17, 1903, *L'évangile et l'église* had been condemned by Cardinal Richard; and on February 3 of the same year, Loisy formally repudiated the errors that might be deduced from the book. In discussing Loisy quite appreciatively, Troeltsch nonetheless distances himself from a Catholic developmental notion of essence. It is only Protestantism, rooted as it is in a catastrophic break from Catholicism, that he claims has the necessary objectivity to achieve a historical and critical attitude toward the contradictory phenomena of Christian history. For Catholics, on the other hand, Christianity is simply the church.

Most Protestant commentators have agreed with this. As Schäfer maintains, "The concept 'essence of Christianity' presupposes the Protestant distinction between Christianity and church: *Catholic* thought is at pains to identify the two."[7] Until Wagenhammer, most Roman Catholic writers accepted this verdict.[8] Karl Rahner's dictionary article in *Sacramentum Mundi* (1968) is to a degree nuanced and ambiguous, naturally endorsing the Roman Catholic church's right of self-definition but also allowing to a certain extent both the inclusion of heresies within the legitimate compass of a definition of Christianity and an apologetic grasp of Christianity "from outside" in phenomenology, general history, and sociology.[9] The situation has changed with Wagenhammer's exceptionally painstaking research into the prehistory of essence definition. This has shown how the Neoplatonic and gnostic-hermetic origins of the notion of essence have been a kind of constant resource for those unable to identify Christian religion with any of the particular historical forms. At one stroke, Wagenhammer has undercut the supposition that only Protestants can make use of the concept but also builds into "normal" Catholicism the permanent possibility of critical distance. "Measuring the manifestations against the essence," to use Troeltsch's own words, is indeed the major function of essence definition, but it is not restricted to Protestants.

In the history of attempts to determine Christianity's essence, therefore, we are confronted with a phenomenon inherent in the very problem of the realization of Christianity's identity. This has opened out the possibility, indeed necessity, of asking why it should be that the Christian religion gives rise to dispute about its identity. Only if this prior question is answered do we begin to achieve a perspective on the essence dispute as a whole.

I have argued that the essence problem has two major roots, and one major consequence.[10] As roots, I have identified the inescapability of internal conflict and the nature of Christian theological anthropology; and as a major consequence, the inevitable involvement of theology and theologians in the internal power struggles that have characterized the Christian churches from the first. A further word must be said about each of these.

With regard to the fact of *internal conflict*, it is plain from modern historical study of the early Christian movement not merely that there were as a matter of fact different, and to some extent conflicting, versions of the Christian gospel but also that the very preaching of these versions gave rise to a diversity of understandings and to internal conflict requiring solutions.[11] The danger of misinterpretation was taken with very great seriousness, as Paul's anguished letters to the churches of Galatia and Corinth eloquently testify. Inherent, therefore, in the church's existence was a problem-solving requirement essential to the preservation of its coherence as a movement. The story of the development in the church of a speaking authority is a complex one and at present very far from any agreed conclusions. But the long-overdue application of sociological methods to the interpretation of this history has at least delivered us from the stultifying alternative of either, with Protestants, seeing the canonical—especially Pauline—texts as normative or, with Roman Catholics, accepting what happened as simply providential. Both traditions characteristically discussed the phenomenon of conflict as marginal, a mere occurrence that elicited the normative response. The newer techniques enable the historian to perceive that conflict, decision-making structures, and solutions are integral to one another, and have been both in the past and in the present. Conflict, accordingly, inheres in the realization of Christian identity. Unity means, and has only ever meant, the preservation of conflict within reasonable bounds.

The reason that this conflict cannot, in principle, be eliminated has to do, second, with the *problem of the Christian account of the human person*. The longstanding tradition of emphasis upon interiority which Jesus and early Christian teaching inherited from deeply laid strands in Judaism guaranteed that no resolution of any conflict would ever be permanently protected against the outbreak of further conflict. By interiority, I mean the belief that the disposition of each member of the church is governed by an interior transformation, the work of the Holy Spirit in the heart. No participation in an external ritual, no formal repetition of orthodox belief or performance of prescribed duties could be proof against false or distorted intentions. Orthodoxy always insisted upon the necessary dispositional accompaniment of rites, professed belief, and good works. But in so doing it proclaimed from within the inherent limitations of its solutions to conflict.

Consequently it is characteristic of Christian history that a series of critical challenges have been thrown up, sometimes within the very heart of the church, sometimes on its borders, denying the validity of the church's apparent reliance upon its external qualifications. Of these challenges, Luther's celebrated distinction between external and internal Christendom and his attack on an *ex opere operato* view of the sacraments are classic instances. But there are many others both before and after the Reformation, and Wagenhammer rightly emphasizes the potential of an alliance of Christian doctrine with Platonism for conveying these challenges. And it is important to appreciate that "resolutions" of such disputes, whether in authoritative declarations or punishments of various kinds, in principle leave the matter unresolved.

As a corollary of this state of affairs in Christian history, one must note the way in which theology gets drawn into *internal power struggles.* It is pertinent to observe that the Christian movement, though supported from the first by conspicuously intelligent persons, became a theological religion. This was not, of course, a sudden development. But it had to do with the problem it confronted in the phenomenon of Gnosticism, a series of schools purporting to resolve some of the very pressing speculative questions to which the immediate tradition had no very sophisticated answers. In refusing the gnostic option of resort to special revelations, the Christian intellectual, of whom Origen is the most impressive example, launched the church into the world of scholarship, setting formidable standards of textual study, painstaking exegesis, and philosophical training. It is no accident that Origen fell foul of the episcopate in his lifetime and subsequently incurred the charge of heresy. Theology, insofar as one of its main functions is clarification of meaning by verbal precision, inevitably gets drawn into the conflict-solving procedures of the church's speaking authority. A tension accordingly grows between its usefulness in apologetic argument with outsiders and its necessity as a resource for church leaders in dealing with internal conflict. The contemporary confrontation between two Tübingen Roman Catholic professors of theology, Hans Küng and (now Cardinal) Joseph Ratzinger, classically illustrates the tension in which the discipline is caught. There is an inevitable power connotation in the theologian's work, especially when that work relates to the resolution of the inescapable conflicts into which Christian theology is drawn.

These, on my analysis, are the necessary explanations of why it is that the Christian religion gives rise to dispute about its own identity, and what the implications of these disagreements are for the practice of theology. This background provides us with some new questions to apply to Schleiermacher's and Barth's handling of the theme of the essence of Christianity.

WHAT IS ESSENTIAL FOR SCHLEIERMACHER AND BARTH?

We can ask, first of all, Where do Schleiermacher and Barth respectively locate the unity and coherence of Christianity? In the case of

Schleiermacher the answer lies quite readily for us on the page. One of the major themes of the speeches *On Religion* is the fact, as he sees it, that every religion, Christianity included, has what he calls a fundamental intuition *(Grundanschauung)*, essence *(Wesen)*, or idea *(Idee)* which is to be distinguished both from its phenomenal unity *(Einheit als Schule)* and from the singularity of its historical origin.[12] The essence of a religion is its principle of coherence *(Anzeihungsprinzip)*. He uses this idea to explain one of the episodes of conflict recorded in the New Testament, the imperfect assimilation of the disciples of John the Baptist into the Christian movement. These, he asserts, "were only very imperfectly initiated into the essence of Christianity."[13] Imperfection of grasp upon the essence results in external disunity.

The concept of essence is also deployed so as to make some sense out of the chronic disputes in eighteenth-century Protestantism to which the deployment of scholastic metaphysics had given rise and which the burgeoning Romantic movement had challenged. No one, he argues, can speak properly about religion who has not penetrated to its essence; endless wrangling is all that attends those who misidentify its inner reality. He sees his theory of religion, based on an act of penetration into its secret heart, as having the potential for the restoration of lost peace and harmony. This reconciliation, he believes, coincides with the actual substance of Christianity's fundamental idea, the divine reconciliation of the innate hostility and resistance of all finite things to the unity of the whole. Christianity, from one point of view merely one religion among others, is at the same time in a position to interpret the whole divine economy of the religious life of humanity:

> It manipulates religion itself as a matter for religion. It is thus a higher power of religion [*eine hohere Potenz derselben*], and this most distinguishes its character and determines its whole form.[14]

Finally one notes that, in passing, Schleiermacher advances a suggestion to account for the phenomenon of conflict in Christianity. It is, he says, precisely because the Christian religion recognizes the fact that the finite mind is attached to its finitude in hostility and resistance to the unity of the whole, that at its most characteristic the church is restlessly critical of the tendency to deviation within its own life. It expects corruption and degeneration to occur and is correspondingly fierce with its own failings. This suggestion is subsequently incorporated into Schleiermacher's systematic presentation of the tasks of theology as the discipline of polemics—or the attack upon "diseased deviations" occurring within Christianity.[15]

Schleiermacher's theory of Christianity is, therefore, double sided. On the one hand, it accounts for the history of conflict, but on the other, it does so on the basis of an intuitive grasp of its inner coherence. The obvious questions to ask are, How does he *know* that religions have this source of internal cohesiveness? and, How does he *know* that Christianity has the essence he ascribes to it? It is a little tempting to suppose that, because Schleiermacher holds that religions embody a fundamental intuition, this suggestion is itself an intuition, standing or falling in the light of its own luminosity. But there is supporting argumentation, and it is the character of these arguments which establishes what he designates the "critical" character of essence definition.[16] From this "critical" method, Schleiermacher distinguishes the "empirical," the reading-off of the essence of Christianity directly from its history, and the "speculative," the abstract imposition of philosophical categories upon the substance of Christianity. Plainly, as so often with Schleiermacher, the preferred solution is a via media.

In the *Brief Outline,* the critical method is said to consist in the operation of an interlocking series of disciplines:

1. Ethics or the "science of the principles of history," which establishes how and why religious organizations (churches) are a necessary part of human culture.
2. Philosophy of religion, which shows how religions differ from one another.
3. Philosophical theology, which builds on the previous two disciplines but shows from the standpoint of Christianity itself what its own distinctive essence is.
4. Historical theology, which traces the various exigencies of the essence of Christianity from its earliest beginnings to the present, including the contemporary presentation of Christianity's doctrinal substance.
5. Practical theology, which holds the various practical concerns of the Christian church together and seeks to realize its ultimate purposes in a culture.

These disciplines are not conceived as being studied in a rigid sequence but as interpenetrating. For example, the pivotal third discipline of philosophical theology is carried out *along with* the study of historical theology. In *The Christian Faith,* the well-known discussion of the "natural heresies" illuminates the method rather well. The inquiry into the heretical is said to supplement the inquiry into the essence of Christianity. It is not a matter of accepting the traditional distinction between orthodoxy and heresy but a matter of a study of church history which simultaneously verifies that what has been set up hypothetically (*problematisch*) as of the essence and as heretical is indeed what is encountered in history.[17]

But criticism also entails the "scientific" criterion of ensuring the utility of dogmatics for its intrinsic purposes. Schleiermacher's conception of what theology is about is governed by his sense of the practical orientation of the faculties of theology, medicine, and law.[18] In §17 of *The Christian Faith*, where he maintains that dogmatic propositions must have both an ecclesiastical and a scientific value, Schleiermacher insists that

> dogmatic propositions are the more perfect the more their scientific character gives them an outstanding ecclesiastical value, and also the more their scientific content bears traces of having proceeded from the ecclesiastical interest.[19]

"Scientific value" consists not just in the clarity and coherence of the dogmatic vocabulary but in the fitness of the propositions for the practical tasks faced in the contemporary performance of Christianity. Clarity, coherence, and the performance of those tasks inhere in one another.

If, therefore, we confront Schleiermacher's deployment of the essence of Christianity in his theological labors with the question about Christianity's internal coherence amid conflict, the result is plainly impressive and sophisticated. We find, in fact, that he has provided a theory of why there is conflict in Christianity and that he has proposed a way of assessing this theory by reference to the history of Christianity. Moreover, his understanding of the purpose of dogmatics illustrates quite clearly the kind of "interest" the church has in the success of theological scholarship and education. The essence of Christianity is the comprehensive symbol for these concerns.

If we turn to Barth's discussion of this approach in *Church Dogmatics* §24, "Dogmatics as a Function of the Teaching Church," we are immediately struck by the fact that the perspective has been determined by a sardonic view of the plurality and pretentiousness of the rival approaches toward essence definition. The sequence of authors to whom Barth refers stretches from C. E. Luthardt, a conservative writer who published his dogmatics in 1865, to Ernst Troeltsch, whose posthumous *Glaubenslehre* appeared in 1925. These writers span the period in which essence talk was at its height. But, Barth asks, by what right are their "assumptions" to be made the bases of the systematic exposition of dogmatics?[20]

The point is a serious one. It is by no means implausible to suppose that theologians can come to interpret success in terms of their capacity to impose their own characteristic vocabulary on others. Schools or systems are constituted precisely by their special use of terms and even their creation of neologisms. Single-line definitions of the essence of Christianity are intentionally memorable and lend themselves to deployment as slogans. Barth's objection to this is radical. There can be no summary of what is signified by the Word of God:

> It can only be reported concretely, i.e. in relation to what is at any given time the most recent stage of the process or action or sovereign act of which it is the occurrence. And this report cannot be made the business and function of the object of dogmatics.[21]

Barth proceeds to offer a brief history of the pathway by which Protestantism developed its preoccupation with essence definition. He sees the danger already in the work of the orthodox seventeenth-century Lutheran and Calvinist divines, who made extensive use of the distinction between "fundamental" and "nonfundamental" articles. We should note that Barth's precise objection is to the fact that what François Turrettini (1623–87) called the *fundamentum dogmaticum,* the first part of doctrine, not referable to any other doctrine as its basis and on which all other doctrine depends, had elevated what is essentially a confession to the status of an inflexible law:

> Although it certainly cannot be without a confession, dogmatics as such is not a confession either of the Church or of an individual. Its function is to confront Church proclamation with the Word of God, and in doing this it must not substitute for the Word of God the confession either of a Church or of an individual. If it does, it cannot with complete authority call the Church either to hearing or teaching: it will be only the function of a self-centred and self-occupied Church. The establishment of specific, irrevocable, fundamental articles will block the onward course of the Word of God within the Church. . . . In dogmatics, therefore, traditional notions as to what is fundamental or not, central or peripheral, more or less important, have to be suspended, so that they can become a matter for vital new decision by the Word of God itself.[22]

Although as a matter of fact theologians have to make distinctions and choices, they cannot allow themselves simply to inherit fundamental articles as the church's traditional confession. Protestant high orthodoxy, in repeating the creed of the post-Reformation churches, did not err grievously, but in principle the procedure was wrong "because it involved a definition, limitation and restriction of the Word of God."[23] We do not even need to observe that as a matter of fact the precise determination of fundamental articles was impractical.

How then does Barth propose to solve the problem of a dogmatic method? He would like, of course, to be able to say *methodus est arbitraria*, provided that by "arbitrary" is meant a decision taken after the most careful search.[24] But in the event, he decides to signify what is entailed in this search by the image of a wheel with an opening in its center. The opening stands for the openness of the theologian, unwilling to impose his or her own system upon the material and confident in the power of the object of theology to disclose its own inherent rationality. "Dogmatic method," he affirms, "consists essentially in the expectation that there will eventually be this purification and the consequent emergence of the essence of Christianity."[25] This is Barth's only positive use of the phrase, and it is ineluctably future-oriented. We do not possess this essence. We may not guess at it, nor hypothesize about it; if we leave it genuinely open, then God will confirm or refine what we have done. To adopt the open center of a dogmatics means, simply, that the dogmatician honors, fears, and loves the work of God in God's Word above everything else.

Underneath the tensions and nuances of this fascinating section of the *Dogmatics* there are, if my approach to this topic has any validity at all, some theses about conflict in the church struggling for articulation. Barth at all costs wishes to avoid the arbitrariness characteristic, he believes, of neo-Protestantism's celebration of the creative freedom of the individual theologian. There is, he holds, a qualitative difference between that and the serious responsibilities with which Calvin invested the scholar-pastor, a difference between arbitrary choice and obedient decision. Barth knows perfectly well that even theology carried out in the latter mode will contain differences and contradictions. Furthermore he explicitly recognizes that a theologian's claim that his or her theology has been written in obedience to the Word of God can only be received by another person as "a challenge, a suggestion, a *consilium*, not an ultimately and absolutely binding command."[26]

We have, therefore, to ask of Barth not just how he knows that Christian doctrine is what he says it is but also how *we* can know whether what he says is true. Barth's own answer to the latter question is perfectly plain. We are supposed, as members of the "brotherly [*sic*] christocracy"[27] that constitutes the church, to evaluate it with prayerful openness to the ever-contemporary Word of God. Although Barth does not, any more than Calvin, offer an account of how it can come about that even those who adopt his method of appraisal can disagree with one another, the status of his proposal is remarkably similar to Schleiermacher's. Neither believes that church confessions or the theologies of theologians of the past in any sense bind the present. Both regard the history of Christianity as open to constant reevaluation. Both see the task of constructive statement as a creative endeavor by which the integrity of the church's contemporary performance of its witness is to be held up to scrutiny in a judgment that is strictly provisional. Even the contrasting acceptance and rejection of the definition of the essence of Christianity as a means for articulating the sense of the contemporary church's coherence conceals a more fundamental agreement that such decisions are nonbinding and provisional. The gulf between the "arbitrary choice" of the neo-Protestant and the "obedient decision" of the neo-orthodox closes de facto, and we are left with the necessarily more indeterminate criterion of a sense of seriousness, or conscientious openness, with which to find our way among the inevitably conflicting *consilia* of the theologians. The unity and coherence of Christianity is the concern of the theologian, but it is not an objective fact to be read off their pages.

THE INTERIORITY THESIS

The second question we may want to put to Schleiermacher and Barth in the light of the method we have adopted concerns what I have termed the "tradition of interiority." What impact has this tradition had upon their respective attitudes toward the solution of the problem of Christianity's identity? In Schleiermacher's case this is readily answered from the speeches *On Religion*, whose philosophical and social psychology is an attempt to articulate precisely the inclination of the heart toward the transcendent All. The essence of Christianity cannot, therefore, be for him in the first instance a teaching but must be a mood, tone, or yearning communicated more readily nonverbally in the concrete life of the church. Barth's strictures against the "thin formulae by which later neo-Protestantism thought it could grasp the so-called 'essence of Christianity' "[28] hardly apply to Schleiermacher, who had no time for *formulas* as such. Here the confusion seems to be caused by Barth's erroneous history of the origins of the "essence" idea. It is not the case, as Barth supposes it to be, that the "fundamental articles" tradition is the immediate precursor of neo-Protestant essence definition. As Wagenhammer has shown, there is a longer standing tradition of distinguishing between the essence and the overt, public manifestation of Christianity, and it is on this that the Pietists, who were Schleiermacher's true precursors in this matter, drew.

Where then does Barth stand in relation to this tradition of interiority? The opening at the center of a wheel, to which reference has already been made, is a vivid metaphor for the theologian's inability to express the controlling center of theology in a formula or a single doctrine. "In dogmatics laying the foundation means recollection that the foundation is already laid."[29] Barth's language here is, as so often, rhetorically provocative. By evoking 1 Cor. 3:1, he reminds his reader that the Word of God is not subject to human control. But at the same time the endorsement of the notion of a foundation requires Barth to acknowledge the possibility of the "eventual confirmation" of a systematic certainty by that very Word. The result of this procedure is the simultaneous claim for objectivity in dogmatics and for the fact that the object of dogmatics escapes our comprehension.

My suggestion is that we construe this argument as a more radical version of the interiority thesis, legitimated by the evocation of the divine control, the control in fact of the Holy Spirit, over the whole process of writing dogmatics. As evidence one can cite a passage of *Church Dogmatics*, in the section on dogmatic method. In speaking of the theologian's decision made in obedience, Barth says,

> It is the gift of grace and of the Holy Spirit which must come from God, so that man can take it into account only as a presupposition for which he must pray.[30]

Again in speaking of the way dogmatics must take the dangerous transitional step from *explicatio* to *applicatio*, Barth returns to the claim that the autonomy of dogmatics is a function of the theonomy that is the foundation of the whole church:

> The autonomy of dogmatic thinking, in which we must venture to decide for a particular dogmatic method as we have now done, implies, denotes and signifies (like its heteronomy, of which we spoke in the last section) the autonomy of the Holy Spirit.[31]

As further evidence of Barth's belonging to the most radical version of the interiority tradition, one might also consider the discussion of the outer and inner text of Scripture and the credo of the church in the Anselm book,[32] and the tantalizing "dream" with which Barth closes his final essay on Schleiermacher, with speculation of construing all

Schleiermacher's theological work as an example of Third Article theology.[33]

This construction upon Barth's relationship to the interiority thesis makes his rejection of the essence of Christianity more intelligible. Believing, as he does, that it derives from the era of dogmatic orthodoxy, he misinterprets it as an assertion of human and arbitrary control over the substance of dogmatics. But seen in relation to its origins in the interiority tradition, of which Barth is a radical exponent, it becomes appropriate to ask what in Barth's case actually performs the function of the essence of Christianity. The answer is, plainly, obedience to the Word of God. There is, indeed, every reason why one should say that for Barth the essence of Christianity is obedience to the Word of God. Of this essence the dogmatic correlate is, as it was for Schleiermacher, the redemption. One could further speculate that on closer inspection the radical qualitative difference that Barth loudly proclaims between his and Schleiermacher's accounts of redemption would need to be progressively qualified.

THEOLOGIANS IN THE LIFE
OF THE CHURCH

The third question that our understanding of the roots of the essence dilemma proposes concerns the position of theology and of theologians in the life of the church. In the *Brief Outline*, Schleiermacher had observed that the development of a structured form of church leadership and the rise to prominence of theology occurred at the same time and conditioned each other.[34] Furthermore, he observed that with the church's spread into new linguistic and cultural areas, it was increasingly obliged to develop its theological activity. The observations are historically correct and sociologically acute. Although there is little stomach in the contemporary church for the realistic interpretation of the behavior of its elites, it cannot be seriously doubted that theological learning is one of the major resources of the articulate leader. It is not, of course, the sole source of articulacy, nor are all theologically learned persons articulate. But it has always been the case that immersion in the rhetoric of Christianity by means of theological education has facilitated and attended the rise to the kind of power that church leaders exercise.

Recently Edward Farley has advanced the view that Schleiermacher's contribution to the history of theological education is notable in two respects: in the development of what he terms the "clerical paradigm" and the "essence of Christianity motif."[35] The first is the justification of the place of theology in a university on the practical grounds of its production of clergy to serve the state; the second is the achievement of a unified and comprehensive grasp of the entire range of theological activities under the heading of insight into the distinctiveness of Christianity. These he regards as two quite different ways of conceiving the unity of theology and of theological study. Now, since Farley's avowed aim is to deplore what subsequently is called the "clericalization of theology," this beguiling slogan needs to be handled with some caution. First it must be emphasized that by clergy *(Klerus)* Schleiermacher understands simply "those who participate in church leadership," lay or ordained.[36] Such participation refers simply to "deliberative leadership," the fact that certain persons attain a position of prominence in the community which enables them to influence and direct its life. Such persons, Schleiermacher affirms, should be possessed of both a "scientific" and an "ecclesial" interest. He goes out of his way in the *Brief Outline* not to specify any one system of church government. The so-called clerical paradigm in Schleiermacher's work is not the equivalent of training for the ordained ministry.

Second, as I have attempted to show, Schleiermacher's use of the essence of Christianity, which predates his involvement as a teacher of theology, has in view the endemic Christian problem of internal conflict. Its deployment, therefore, as a unifying factor in a program of theological education for a new university is far from surprising. Nor is it in any way an alternative to conceiving theological education in universities in relation to the practical ends of the state.

Finally, it should be noted that in his remarks on university education, which appeared two years before the *Brief Outline*, Schleiermacher made clear that he regarded it as imperative that those who lectured in the specialized practical faculties of theology, law, and medicine should do so only if they were capable of first lecturing in the philosophical faculty. Participation in that faculty's program ought to form, he argued, the basis of all university education.[37]

Although Schleiermacher's work on theological education has had a profound impact, as Farley shows, upon subsequent patterns, the reason his reflection on the need for an educated leadership occurs in the context of consideration of the essence of Christianity is more intelligible on the hypothesis of this study. The essence of Christianity is a consideration arising out of the fact of conflict in the church, which itself focuses attention on decision-making procedures. Schleiermacher's context, that of the Enlightenment, was one of acute controversy, and he believed that the problem of Christianity's future direction could be resolved only by those who had laid hold of its essence:

> The tasks of any person who is to exert influence of a genuine deliberative character arise out of the way in which he appraises the actual condition of the Church at the present time, according to his conception of the essence of Christianity and of his own particular Church community.[38]

Schleiermacher rightly saw theological education as the acquisition of potential power in the church and expected church leaders to take with full seriousness their need to have a "scientific" as well as an "ecclesial" interest.

It has often been pointed out that Barth's grasp of the same problem is at least analogous. Dogmatics he sees as poised between exegesis, on the one hand, and practical theology. Its task is to ensure the purity of the church's proclamation. By proclamation, Barth means everything to which the church testifies in every aspect of its life. But a central aspect of that proclamation is the preaching of the minister of the Word of God. Thus, "the question of the Church's ministry is decided in dogmatics."[39]

Again, Barth denies that by dogmatics he means simply the work of professorial dogmaticians; rather, he means the "working out of this central question concerning the content of Church proclamation, in so far as the subject of this labour is the whole Church without excepting even a single one of its members." The academic form of dogmatics is merely its most obvious feature. All teachers must first be listeners, and listeners may well be teachers.[40] The two sides must cohere in the unity of the body of Christ. The congregation that is merely passive in relation to the exegesis of Scripture is already in secret rebellion.[41]

Behind Barth's prose lies a clear warning against the dangers of a permanent hierarchy or an elite corps of theologians and a strong encouragement of a sense of equality in the "brotherly [sic] christocracy."[42] The realization of such an understanding of order implies, of course, the participation of the whole church in Christian education. To this extent, Barth is less tolerant than was Schleiermacher of the natural distinction between leaders in the church and the mass of the people—reflecting, no doubt, the higher general standards of education in the twentieth century. But even Barth acknowledges the fact that there will be "stronger and weaker, older and younger, higher and lower brothers [sic]," the former possessing what he terms an "actual and not an institutional authority."[43]

Barth's marked reluctance to relate order in the community to any known sociological model ("understanding itself in terms of the world's misunderstanding")[44] has serious consequences for the realism of his prescriptions. Even if it is granted that the community's self-understanding is to take precedence over established models of organization, at the very least such models could assist the community in escaping from self-deception in the assessment of its fulfillment of its goals. In this connection one has every reason to reflect on the example of leadership in the church set by Barth himself in his theological activity. The fact that it was both intended and spoken of as service cannot disguise its accessibility only to an elite, and the maintenance of such an elite in the church has a decisive impact on its distribution of power. Despite the fact that Barth's theology is presented by him as a *consilium* and not as a law, the "Barthian movement" showed clearly what would happen in a church where pastors were taught by a coherent and determined elite and where the major content of the church's worship was in the control of the pastor.[45] There is no exercise of power that may not be legitimated as service. But those who intend that power should not fall into the hands of an elite need the assistance of sociological realism in the penetration of its disguises.

If we ask why it should be that Schleiermacher's position should strike us as more persuasive, indeed more open, than Barth's in this matter, this has in all probability to do with the fact that Schleiermacher regards the assistance of propositions borrowed from nontheological disciplines as clarifying rather than threatening the structure that is inevitably imposed upon the dogmatic material. Barth, in so many words, acknowledges this to be the case in criticizing Schleiermacher's willingness to understand church proclamation in connection with different types of human speech and in relation to the historical being of human persons.[46] The issue of the power of the theologian is something of a test case, and Barth's rigorous holding-apart of the immanent creaturely power and the transcendently free divine power of God is indicative of his sense of the dangers of their being intermingled or confused.[47] By contrast, Schleiermacher's preparatory work enables the fact to be openly recognized that in the history of the church these powers *are* frequently confused.

Allowing, therefore, for the imperative governing Barth's passion for the freedom of the Word of God, one may well want to insist that Schleiermacher's method opens the church to a critique that is essential to the performance of its mission. The contemporary definition of the essence of Christianity would have to take seriously the modern equivalents of Schleiermacher's oddly named preparatory disciplines, ethics and the philosophy of religion. By ethics, I believe we should understand something analogous to the contemporary disciplines of psychology and sociology. There is no doubt of the impact that psychological theories have had upon Western consciousness. The only question is whether contemporary persons realize how pervasive their influence is in modern culture. There is no way the contemporary understanding of religion can escape from a searching psychological critique of its concepts of sin and guilt, of sexual stereotyping, and of dependency. It is ironic that Schleiermacher's own extensive deployment of the concept of absolute dependence should itself be the object of psychological suspicion, as Barth's response to Freud in the *Römerbrief* already indicated.

Sociology, likewise, has contributed, not least in the form of classic Marxism, to the requirements of a modern prolegomenon to Christianity. To understand what a church is, which is Schleiermacher's aim in the introduction, entails taking account of the nature and function of ideology. Again, Barth's perceptive self-distancing from the Christianity of Nazi Germany indicates his own response to what is required of the practice of a hermeneutics of suspicion, little theoretical justification though he gives it.

Finally, the philosophy of religion entails, in Schleiermacher's scheme of things, a taxonomy of religions, which figures among the earliest attempts at a study of comparative religion. Here we have a difficulty because of the contemporary divorce between the disciplines of social anthropology, on the one hand, and philosophy of religion, on the other. Nor is Barth's practice in respect of either in any way encouraging. But if I may cite a single example, how can what is signified in Christianity by either gift or sacrifice be understood without an extensive exposure to the demands of contemporary anthropology? At the very least, one must suppose that a theologian who neglects social anthropology may be likely to miss either the distinctiveness or the universality of what Christian doctrine has to say about the structure of the divine-human relationship. But Schleiermacher's intention for what he termed the philosophy of religion was precisely the location of the *differentia* of Christianity, a distinctiveness that would be advanced and confirmed by the match between inquiries external and internal to Christianity.

CONCLUSION

My suggestion, therefore, is that we misread Schleiermacher and Barth if we suppose that their practice is as different as their theories would lead one to expect. I do not deny the differences, largely the result of sharply divergent contexts and needs. But I see between them a community of practice deriving ultimately from their common perception of the indeterminate future of Christianity. What Christianity will become for the men and women of the future is not decided. Nor will it have a future unless, with Schleiermacher, one is open to the contemporary secular disciplines by which its nature and history are exposed to the public gaze, and with Barth, one is open to the Word at whose gracious invitation it has been brought into existence.

NOTES

1. In English the last major study was W. A. Brown's *The Essence of Christianity: A Study in the History of Definition* (New York: Charles Scribner's Sons, 1904). The title is more than a little misleading, since the work is concerned less with specific instances of definition than with the nineteenth-century history of Protestant theology as a whole.

2. *Die Religion in Geschichte und Gegenwart*, vol. 1 (Tübingen, 1975), 1721–29.

3. R. Schäfer, "Welchem Sinn hat es, nach einem Wesen des Christentums zu suchen," *Zeitschrift für Theologie und Kirche* 55 (1968):329–47.

4. H. Wagenhammer, *Das Wesen des Christentums* (Mainz, 1974), 256.

5. Stephen Sykes, *The Identity of Christianity: Theologians and the Essence of Christianity from Schleiermacher to Barth* (Philadelphia: Fortress Press; London: SPCK, 1964).

6. R. Morgan and M. Pye, eds. *Ernst Troeltsch: Writings on Theology and Religion* (London, 1977), 145. This is a translation of the revised 1913 version of the original article, but the passage quoted is unaltered.

7. R. Schäfer, "Wesen des Christentum," in *Historisches Wörterbuch der Philosophie*, vol. 1, ed. J. Ritter (1971), 1015.

8. E.g., M. Schmaus, *Vom Wesen des Christentums* (1947), 16; R. Guardini, *Das Wesen des Christentum*, 3d ed. (1949); and K. Adam, *The Spirit of Catholicism* (London, 1934).

9. K. Rahner, "Christianity, Essence of," in *Sacramentum Mundi*, ed. K. Rahner, vol. 1 (New York: Herder & Herder, 1968), 299–311; see esp. 301.

10. Sykes, *Identity*, chaps. 1–3. What follows is a brief summary of the themes of those three chaps.

11. What I wrote about conflict in the primitive church has now been reinforced by Elisabeth Schüssler Fiorenza's fascinating study of dispute about

the role of women, *In Memory of Her: A Feminist Theological Reconstruction of Christian Origins* (New York: Crossroad, 1984). Her view of how women, despite having early occupied positions of leadership, were eventually excluded from the hierarchy and increasingly marginalized strongly confirms my argument that the development of theology as a solution to conflict inevitably entails the exercise of power.

12. F. D. E. Schleiermacher, *On Religion: Speeches to Its Cultured Despisers,* trans. John Oman (New York: Harper & Bros., 1958), 241, 242, 246, 249.

13. Ibid., 248. The 1st ed. had used the words "participated in the fundamental intuition of Christ" (*Reden über die Religion,* ed. G. C. B. Pünjer [Braunschweig, 1879], 285).

14. Schleiermacher, *On Religion,* 242.

15. F. D. E. Schleiermacher, *Brief Outline on the Study of Theology,* trans. T. N. Tice (Richmond: John Knox Press, 1966), §§54–62.

16. Ibid., §32.

17. F. D. E. Schleiermacher, *The Christian Faith,* trans. H. R. Macintosh and J. S. Stewart (Edinburgh: T. & T. Clark 1928), §§21–22.

18. S. W. Sykes, "Theological Study: The Nineteenth Century and After," in *The Philosophical Frontiers of Christian Theology: Essays Presented to D. M. MacKinnon,* ed. B. Hebblethwaite and S. Sutherland (Cambridge, 1982), 95–118.

19. Schleiermacher, *The Christian Faith,* 85.

20. Karl Barth, *Church Dogmatics* 1/2:862.

21. Ibid., 862.

22. Ibid., 864

23. Ibid., 865.

24. Ibid., 860.

25. Ibid., 867.

26. Ibid., 859.

27. Barth derives this phrase from Erik Wolf's "Zur Rechtsgestalt der Kirche," in *Bekennende Kirche: Martin Niemöller zum 60. Geburtstag* (Munich, 1952), 261; cited in Barth's *Church Dogmatics* 4/2:680.

28. Barth, *Church Dogmatics* 1/2:866.

29. Ibid., 868.

30. Ibid., 850.

31. Ibid., 864.

32. Karl Barth, *Anselm: Fides Quaerens Intellectum,* trans. I. Robertson (London, 1960), 41. In P. J. Rosato's *The Spirit as Lord: The Pneumatology of Karl Barth* (Edinburgh, 1981), an account is given of the pneumatology of the Anselm book, culminating in the statement that "in Anselm's work Barth unearths a pneumatic understanding of theological method as well as of faith itself" (p. 41). This seems a little too strongly put.

33. Karl Barth, *The Theology of Schleiermacher: Lectures at Gottingen, Winter Semester of 1923/24,* ed. Dietrich Ritschl, trans. Geoffrey W. Bromiley (Grand Rapids: Wm. B. Eerdmans, 1982), 278.

34. Schleiermacher, *Brief Outline*, §§3, 267.

35. Edward Farley, *Theologia: The Fragmentation and Unity of Theological Education* (Philadelphia: Fortress Press, 1983), chap. 4, pp. 73–98.

36. Schleiermacher, *Brief Outline*, §§236, 307.

37. Friedrich Schleiermacher, *Sämmtliche Werke*, vol. 3/1 (Berlin, 1846), 586.

38. Schleiermacher, *Brief Outline*, §259.

39. Barth, *Church Dogmatics* 1/2: 766–67.

40. Ibid., 798.

41. Ibid., 715.

42. Cf. ibid. 4/2:708.

43. Ibid.

44. Ibid., 687.

45. S. W. Sykes, *Karl Barth: Studies of His Theological Method* (New York and London: Oxford Univ. Press, 1979), 51ff. A comparison is drawn there with the impact of theology in a church with a more formal liturgical tradition.

46. Barth, *Church Dogmatics* 1/2:799.

47. See further Sykes, *Identity*, 206–7.

On Speaking of God—
the Divisive Issue for
Schleiermacher and Barth:
A Response to Frei and Sykes

6

RONALD F. THIEMANN

I could not help wondering, as I read the irenic prose of the two important contributions by Hans Frei and Stephen Sykes, what Karl Barth himself might have thought of these essays. One can almost envision a wry smile coming to his face as he read these discussions about essence definition, correlation, and philosophical foundations, and his asking at the end, "But gentlemen, what does all this have to do with God?" Or to use his own words from an essay of 1922, "We ought to speak of God. We are human, however, and so cannot speak of God. We ought therefore to recognize both our obligation and our inability and by that very recognition give God the glory. This is our perplexity. The rest of our task fades into insignificance by comparison."[1] Precisely because Barth thought that Friedrich Schleiermacher gives us so little help on that issue, he accused him in the same essay, in words both arrogant and uncharitable, of attempting to speak of God "simply by speaking of man in a loud voice."[2]

Barth, of course, mellowed with age, and toward the end of his life, in the "Concluding Unscientific Postscript on Schleiermacher,"[3] he wrote a remarkably sympathetic account, inviting just the kind of inquiry in which we find ourselves engaged in the essays in this volume—that is, seeking some rapprochement between himself and the one he rightly called the father of modern Protestant theology. Yet despite the remarkably irenic conclusion of that essay, in which he himself seeks some common ground with Schleiermacher and even expresses the hope that his own harsh criticisms might be mistaken, his final judgment differs only a little from the blunt assessment he made some forty-five years earlier. For in the 1968 essay, he writes,

> The common denominator under which I see [Schleiermacher] as well as his followers ... is the consciously and consistently executed anthropological starting-point which is evident as the focus of their thought and utterances. ... Until better instructed, I can see no way from Schleiermacher, or from his contemporary epigones, to the chroniclers, prophets, and wise ones of Israel, to those who narrate the story of the life, death, and resurrection of Jesus Christ. ... For the present I can see nothing here but a choice. And for me there can be no question as to how that choice is to be made.[4]

The twentieth-century epigones of Barth and Schleiermacher have agreed that their theological forebears have forged mutually exclusive options. Theologians who would follow in their train must choose, so the common wisdom goes, between anthropocentrism and theocentrism, between philosophical theology and biblical theology, between foundational and dogmatic theology. Frei and Sykes, however, have posed in these essays sharp challenges to the tradition of interpretation that relies upon such unimaginative dichotomous categories. Both essayists dispute the common view that Schleiermacher is engaged in phenomenological analysis in which philosophy serves as the indispensable foundation for theology.[5] Rather, Schleiermacher, quite like Barth, is engaged in a process of *Ortsbestimmung*, that is, "locating the language of evangelical piety on the language map."[6] That effort, says Frei, involves for Schleiermacher a "direct correlation" between theology as "positive Christian skill and *wissenschaftliche* understanding." But that correlation does not involve a "formal transcendental scheme under which the two can be unified," nor does it require a "philosophically founded technical phenomenology." In the opening paragraphs of *The Christian Faith*, Schleiermacher is engaged in a "simple psychological deliberation" or "a little introspection." Consequently, Schleiermacher, like Barth, retains the distinctive and irreducible character of Christian language even as he seeks to correlate that language with general philosophical and cultural principles.

Barth, on the other hand, emerges from these pages not nearly as averse to philosophical reflection as the common wisdom would suppose. Philosophy for Barth is not excluded from theology—indeed, it cannot be—but it is firmly subordinated to the rules of Christian self-description. Thus Barth is far more eclectic than Schleiermacher in his use of philosophy as a tool for theological clarification. But both theologians grant primacy to the distinctive language of the Christian faith.

Frei and Sykes are further agreed that Schleiermacher's theology, including his attempt at "essence definition," is thoroughly practical in orientation. On this point both essayists disagree with the position set forth by Edward Farley in his *Theologia*.[7] Farley argues that Schleiermacher asserts both a "teleological" and a "material" unity for theology. Insofar as theology is the vehicle for professional preparation for ministry, it is unified by the "clerical praxis external to the university and the faculty of theology."[8] Theology, like medicine and law, is a *positive* science. But despite its practical orientation, theology remains a *science* and so moves beyond its teleological rationale to seek the "distinctive essence of Christianity," that is, the "reality and truth of this particular historical form."[9] In seeking the essence of Christianity, Schleiermacher relates Christianity to a "fundamental ontological structure and requirement of the human being" through a "correlation between the determinate redemption of Christianity and the general structures and needs of the human being as such."[10] This philosophical investigation is not guided by theology's practical function but is a true *wissenschaftliche* activity.

The disagreement between Frei and Sykes, on the one hand, and Farley, on the other, turns on the interpretation of the role Schleiermacher assigns to "philosophical theology" in the theological task. Philosophical theology is the discipline through which the "self-identical essence of piety" is identified. The discipline is required, Schleiermacher argues, because the "diverse expressions of piety," that is, the first-order utterances of Scripture, worship, teaching, proclamation, and prayer, are themselves disordered and unreliable. In specifying the essence of piety in terms of the "consciousness of being absolutely dependent," Schleiermacher designates a universal human feeling as the foundational experience of all religious piety. Because that experience is one of feeling or immediate self-consciousness, it is precognitive, present to but always beyond knowledge and action. The validity of the claim that human beings are "in relation to God" depends therefore on a self-authenticating claim to immediate self-consciousness through which one feels absolutely dependent upon "the Whence of our receptive and active existence."

The important issue here is not whether philosophical theology entails a full-scale phenomenological analysis or simply "a little introspection." The key issue concerns, rather, the rationale and function of philosophical theology. Philosophical theology is required, Schleiermacher argues, because the first-order utterances of faith, including those of Scripture, are hopelessly confused and disordered. Philosophical theology provides the coherence that those primary utterances lack. On this point the converging Barth and Schleiermacher appear to part company. Although Barth never suggests that theology simply repristinates or repeats the first-order language of faith, he strongly asserts that the primary Christian language, and particularly the language of Scripture, possesses an inner coherence that the theologian must identify and restate. Theology discovers and clarifies the coherence of first-order discourse; it does not create or provide that coherence. A fortiori, theology does not provide that coherence by discovering the essence of Christianity in a self-authenticating feeling of absolute dependence. The grounding of Christian talk of God in human interiority cannot yield access to the God whose identity is depicted by the "chroniclers, prophets, and wise ones of Israel [and] those who narrate the story of the life, death, and resurrection of Jesus Christ."

The central difference in Barth's and Schleiermacher's conception of the relation of philosophy to theology lies in the function each assigns to the philosophical endeavor. For Schleiermacher, philosophy is inherently epistemological and foundational. An epistemological inquiry is one that seeks to justify beliefs by attention to the origin, sources, or causes of our knowledge. Schleiermacher's philosophical theology must be epistemological because the religious self-consciousness is immediate and precognitive. Consequently, the religious self-consciousness eludes *description*. Though absolute dependence can be experienced or felt, it cannot be fully or directly described. That is why we must engage in "a little introspection," because only through introspection can we become conscious "that the whole of our spontaneous activity *comes from a source outside us.*" Schleiermacher's quest for the source of our spontaneous activity marks his inquiry as epistemological. Further, his appeal to immediacy, to a noninferential form of experience, as the *mode* of self-consciousness marks his epistemological inquiry as *foundational*—by which I mean an understanding of rational justification as a form of causal explanation.[11] In foundational epistemologies a belief is justified not by the reasons we give in support of the belief but by the fact that we have been caused to believe it. According to Schleiermacher's account we assert God's reality as Whence of our existence because we are compelled upon introspection so to assert it. Thus it appears that Schleiermacher's correlation is both epistemological and foundational—not in the sense that an autonomous philosophical inquiry establishes the prior philosophical foundation for theology but that the conceptuality of a foundational epistemology is imported into the theological task itself.

My identification of Schleiermacher's correlation as epistemological and foundational should not be taken as an invitation to engage in a new round of theological name-calling. The issue is clearly not what we call the correlation but the implications of that correlation for the central question of the theology: the question of God's reality. My argument supports Farley's contention that there is in Schleiermacher's thought a second rationale for theology, logically distinct from the practical or clerical justification. Insofar as Schleiermacher sought to grant *wissenschaftliche* status to theology, he granted an independent, epistemological, and foundational function to philosophical theology that Barth was unwilling to grant. Because Barth believed the first-order language of the Christian tradition to be roughly coherent, he was unwilling to grant to philosophy or theology the explanatory role Schleiermacher assigned to philosophical theology. The issue between Barth and Schleiermacher, and their contemporary epigones, is the issue of whether the truth about God is to be found in the first-order language of the faith, particularly in the biblical narratives that identify God, or in a theological reconstruction that provides a coherence and explanatory power the texts do not and cannot possess. On this issue, Barth and Schleiermacher appear to remain unreconciled.

In his concluding comments, Hans Frei identifies the limiting dangers that theologians must avoid if they hope to be faithful to the theological convictions Barth and Schleiermacher share. Whatever differences remain between these two fathers in the faith, it has become clear that we can no longer speak simply of a choice between these two powerful theological traditions. The essays in this volume offer the first stage in what must become an ongoing conversation among theologians of divergent perspectives. If that conversation becomes a genuine dialogue that looks not only to the past but toward new opportunities for theological construction, then a true convergence might emerge not between these two theological masters but within the company of their followers. But such a convergence is conceivable only if we contemporary epigones seek to become what Schleiermacher and Barth have always been, true teachers of the church and thereby of the culture.

NOTES

1. Karl Barth, "The Word of God and the Task of Ministry," *The Word of God*

and the Word of Man, trans. Douglas Horton (Boston and Chicago: Pilgrim Press, 1928), 186.

2. Ibid., 196.

3. Karl Barth, *The Theology of Schleiermacher: Lectures at Göttingen, Winter Semester of 1923/24,* ed. Dietrich Ritschl, trans. Geoffrey W. Bromiley (Grand Rapids: Wm. B. Eerdmans, 1982), 261–79.

4. Ibid., 271–72.

5. The most thoroughgoing contemporary interpretation of Schleiermacher as phenomenologist is Robert Williams's *Schleiermacher the Theologian* (Philadelphia: Fortress Press, 1978). In my own work on Schleiermacher, I have stressed the importance of his philosophical analysis for providing a necessary and universal basis for theology. See Ronald F. Thiemann, "Piety, Narrative, and Christian Identity," *Word and World* 3/2 (Spring 1983): 148–59; and idem, *Revelation and Theology: The Gospel as Narrated Promise* (Notre Dame, Ind.: Univ. of Notre Dame Press, 1984), 24–31.

6. Brian A. Gerrish, *Tradition and the Modern World* (Chicago: Univ. of Chicago Press, 1977), 38.

7. Edward Farley, *Theologia: The Fragmentation and Unity of Theological Education* (Philadelphia: Fortress Press, 1983).

8. Ibid., 84.

9. Ibid., 93.

10. Ibid.

11. For a fuller account of the problems inherent in the confusion of rational justification with casual explanation, see Thiemann, *Revelation and Theology,* 43–46.

7

ROBERT F. STREETMAN

Friedrich Schleiermacher is recognized by friend and foe alike as a dialogue partner par excellence. We have also seen that Karl Barth relished the opportunity for dialogue with him, which was to take place "in heaven," during which time he and Schleiermacher could engage in a "very serious" exchange of theological views, without forgetting to laugh at themselves. Barth's desire is undoubtedly surprising to some of his conservative followers, to whom association with the likes of Schleiermacher is synonymous with exposure to the plague.

Nevertheless, in that classic meeting, which presumably began in December 1968 shortly after Barth's demise, there surely must have been laughter in abundance, and it is likely to recur from time to time during their frequent exchanges. On such occasions, after the merriment subsides, the discussion must surely assume the character of a vigorous theological debate. One can almost hear Schleiermacher saying, "Well, young Karl, you and those other young theological Turks have had quite a field day at my expense. Since all of you came after my time by several decades, you were able to criticize my system without any possibility of a reply from me, yet I have a goodly number of questions concerning the criticisms you have made of me. So hold on to your hat!"

That Schleiermacher's response should be made in the form of questions rather than a more conventional defense of his position will not be surprising to readers of his two "open letters" to his friend Gottfried Christian Lücke. They were written in 1829, after Schleiermacher had received considerable criticism for the first edition of his *The Christian*

Faith (1821–22) and two years before the appearance of the greatly revised second edition. In the first open letter, he discusses his view of his relation to critics of his work: "In general, I acknowledge opponents only in matters of intention and deeds. The thinker has only co-workers, the author has only readers, and I know of no other relations between them." Now, since he has no "intention of founding a sect or school," he sees no valid reason why "opponents" should rise up against him. When a critical reader writes a review of Schleiermacher's work, then the author-critic "relationship is reversed"—*if*, that is, Schleiermacher should choose to read this review. Yet the critic of his work

> does not have a greater right than any other author to demand that I read his work. And if I become his reader, I do not owe him anything but to make the best possible use of his book. Of some sort of obligation to reply to objections and to become a writer again for the sake of those readers who have written, I know nothing at all.[1]

Instead of acting as a defender of his position against Barth's criticisms, Schleiermacher prefers to be the reader, or critic, of Barth's reading of him, and thus he would become a questioner of Barth's reading of *The Christian Faith*. In other words, his basic question to Barth would be, "Dear Karl, are you certain that you have 'made the best possible use' of my magnum opus?" It is clear, then, that Schleiermacher would share Barth's desire for dialogue and would claim the right to initiate this exchange with questions arising from his reading of Barth's criticisms.

Indeed, Schleiermacher relished dialogue to such a degree that he could scarcely be expected to pass up an opportunity to *question* a natural dialogue partner. And what partner would be more "natural" than Barth, who was the formative theological catalyst for our century that Schleiermacher was for the last one? Since the issues that may be debated between these epigones are myriad, which ones should command our attention in this essay? Probably the most striking point of opposition is to be seen in their doctrines of the Trinity. If we place these views alongside each other, we discover that Schleiermacher was widely held to be an antitrinitarian (or at best, only a very half-hearted trinitarian), who deigned to broach the subject only in the conclusion of *The Christian Faith*, as a pedagogical summary of the Christian doctrine of God. By contrast, we then see that Barth was perceived to be *the* trinitarian theologian of our age, who understood the Trinity to be the beginning, yea, the be-all and the end-all, of Christian theological reflection rather than a pedagogical ploy. In this essay, I shall attempt to play the role of a medium whereby Schleiermacher may have his first opportunity to pose some questions for Barth concerning that theologian's criticisms of his doctrine of the Trinity (or the alleged lack thereof).

This essay rests upon a much more detailed study,[2] in which I have argued that the previous interpretations of Schleiermacher that have minimized his trinitarian views have been principally misunderstandings of what he attempted to do. On the contrary, I have argued (*a*) that he was a serious, if critical, trinitarian; (*b*) that his reinterpretation of Sabellius's view of the Trinity was essentially correct (and was largely accepted by Schleiermacher's major critics); (*c*) that critics have erred in restricting their investigations to his explicit discussion of the Trinity in the conclusion of *The Christian Faith*, instead of reading and evaluating it within its larger setting in his theological method and in his treatment of the divine attributes, as well as in the light of the essay on Sabellius; and (*d*) that he still has a catalytic role to play in contemporary trinitarian discussion. Thus, in *The Christian Faith*, he was attempting *not* to denigrate this doctrine but to achieve three objectives: (1) to lay hold of an essential core of underlying truth concerning the Christian doctrine of redemption and to liberate it from the anchorage of "orthodox" trinitarian theology in speculative philosophy (§170); (2) to undercut classical problems such as the eternalizing of personal distinctions and the preferential treatment of the Father (§171); and (3) to show that the Trinity qua doctrine as yet remains unfinished, since, as he believes, Protestants have not yet made their distinctive contribution nor has there ever been a complete return to the origins of the situation that evoked the doctrine (§172).

BARTH'S CRITICISMS OF
SCHLEIERMACHER'S TRINITARIANISM

In Barth's estimation, Schleiermacher erred in reversing the Reformers' order of the correlation of Word and faith by proceeding from a starting point of human initiative. The Reformers, as Barth reads them, correlated the divine and the human, because the correlation is based, "created and sustained," entirely in and by "the Word of God." Conversely, he regards Schleiermacher's correlation as a tour de force of human initiative.[3] The problem for Barth, then, is that Schleiermacher has *reversed* the original terms of the correlation, giving primacy to human spirit over the divine Word. By virtue of this reversal, Barth believes, the primary "centre" of the Reformers (the divine Logos) is transposed into a "subsidiary centre" to the "theology of awareness," which now assumes primacy. Even so, Barth holds that a "pure theology of the Holy Spirit," grounded in the divine initiative from the first to the last, might have been a viable approach. For him, the question is

> whether [Schleiermacher] will be in a position, in trinitarian terms, to recognize and ensure as much validity for the divinity of the *Logos*, which forms for him this second centre, as for the divinity of the Holy Spirit, which is his actual centre or rather is apparently meant by what he presents as his actual centre.[4]

Barth holds that anything short of a full affirmation of the divinity of the Holy Spirit could only undercut Schleiermacher's intentions— however commendable they may be in themselves. The result would leave the divine factors in the correlation vulnerable to the subjective oscillations of the Christian self-consciousness between the poles of sin and grace. In this case, the Christology would admit of only a "quantitative superiority, dignity and significance of Christ as opposed to our own Christianity." And presumably, the Holy Spirit would turn out to be little more than the principle of esprit de corps of the Christian community. The verdict of Barth, therefore, on the completed system, is that "the Word is not so assured here in its independence in respect to faith as should be the case if this theology of faith were a true theology of the Holy Spirit."[5]

The root of the difficulty, for Barth, lies in the desire of Schleiermacher "in all circumstances to be a modern man as well as a Christian theologian." Barth holds, however, that the apologetic and cultural interests of modernity conspired to keep the theology of faith in the center—to the detriment of the substance and objectivity of the Christian revelation. What he is saying, then, in so many words, is that Schleiermacher's theological method—theology as *Glaubenslehre*—does not permit the integrity of revelation to shine through.

A second area of criticism has to do with a question Barth feels obliged to ask of all formulators of Christian systems of dogmatics. If it may be assumed that the espousal of some kind of a doctrine of the Trinity is central to Christian dogmatics, then Barth's question may be posed as, What is the *formal location* of the doctrine of the Trinity in the system, and what is the *material effect* of this placement on the system as a whole?

Barth thus infers from the location of the Trinity at the end of *The Christian Faith* that, for Schleiermacher (as for P. Marheinecke and A. Schweizer as well), "no constitutive meaning attaches to it, so that here, too, the fact is more important than the purpose and manner in which it is used."[6] Notice, however, that Barth is not at all disturbed that Schleiermacher treats the doctrine of the Trinity as a special case outside the spectrum of associated doctrines, because the former's own location of it as the very starting point of the system gives it a special status. For Barth, the problem is that placement at the conclusion seems to undercut any significant material effect that the doctrine of the Trinity might have on the previous doctrines in the body of the system.

The opposition of methods is, indeed, fundamental. Schleiermacher's method requires him to locate the Trinity at the conclusion of the system, whereas for Barth, by contrast, theological method dictates that the Trinity *begin* the system, for reasons that we are about to see.[7] In a *Leitsatz*, Barth writes,

> God's Word is God Himself in his revelation. For God reveals Himself as the Lord and that according to Scripture signifies for the concept of revelation that God Himself in unimpaired unity yet also in unimpaired difference is Revealer, Revelation, and Revealedness.[8]

As Barth sees it, the doctrine of the Trinity must begin the system, because the Trinity is "God Himself in his revelation." The church is the fellowship of those who have been claimed, remolded, and reconciled by that revelation. The theological task of the church, then, is to analyze and to proclaim the same in its witness to the Word.

The proclamation of the church is answerable to the Scriptures, and thus there can be no appeal to any external or hermeneutical canons, since the underlying concept of revelation—which is, for Barth, the sole warrant of scriptural authority—is to be found only in the Scriptures. This scriptural revelation therefore claims uniqueness, so that dogmatics cannot set for itself any problems that do not spring from the scriptural account of that revelation. Revelation, then, is to be considered only "from the side of its subject, God"[9] And once it is so considered, Barth holds, we do have God in His triniform revelation as Revealer, Revelation, Revealedness. The remaining propositions of dogmatics are then to be derived systematically, but not necessarily by strict logical deduction,[10] from this foundation. The "root of the doctrine of the Trinity," for Barth, is the biblical statement "God reveals Himself as the Lord." Thus the actual doctrine of the Trinity is a "work of the Church," or in other words, the "analysis" the church makes of the revelation that it has received, as witnessed to in the Scriptures.[11]

Since, as we have just seen, Barth holds that theology must take its methodological point of departure "from the side of its subject, God," the free and gratuitous self-unveiling of that divine subject must be the starting point of his dogmatic system. Thus, the Trinity is the *foundation* of dogmatics. And Barth believes that this foundation upholds the rest of the system at every point. Any attempt, therefore, to explain away a direct, formal opposition in the placement of the doctrine of the Trinity between him and Schleiermacher is doomed to failure. Much remains to be said, yet what is said must be limited to those areas of Barth's trinitarianism that elucidate his evaluation of Schleiermacher's position on the Trinity. And here a distinction must be made between criticisms by implication and explicit critical evaluations of Barth concerning Schleiermacher's trinitarianism.

Because Barth never subjected Schleiermacher's trinitarianism to a full-scale systematic evaluation, some of the points in Schleiermacher's reformulation of Sabellianism would be subject to criticism only by implication. If Schleiermacher attempted to advance trinitarian thinking from the perspective of a revised interpretation of Sabellius's doctrine of the Trinity, Barth by contrast emerges as a champion of Athanasian interests (without, however, claiming such a title). In the light of this basic contrast, certain emphases of Schleiermacher's program are implicitly criticized by Barth's affirmations. Indeed, so obvious is the opposition that these implicit points can merely be mentioned in passing.

In the first place, it is not clear to Barth, as his earlier criticisms imply, that Schleiermacher is firm enough in asserting the full divinity of the Holy Spirit. It seems to Barth that the divine side of the correlation is systematically undercut by the human side. Conversely, he wishes to let the divine side be the point of departure from first to last. Second, there are problems arising out of the phenomenal and developmental nature of the *prosopa* of Sabellianism. Here, specifically, Barth opposes Schleiermacher's denial of the preexistence of the *prosopa* as well as his repudiation of the ability to draw distinctions within the godhead. Conversely, Barth wishes to affirm a full-blown doctrine of eternal distinctions anchored within an immanent Trinity.[12] Also, as we shall see, Barth suspects that the phenomenal character of the *prosopa* may be a denial of the reality of revelation.

One of Barth's more explicit criticisms is that the modalistic scheme —which proceeds from the (commendable) intention of safeguarding the unity of God—undermines the reality of revelation:

> And when, finally, the modalistic Monarchians, . . . a Sabellius in particular, a Priscillian—in whose footsteps Schleiermacher and his school have walked in modern times—asserted equality in essence of the Trinitarian "persons," but only as phenomenal forms under which God's real essence was concealed as something different and higher—it must still be asked whether revelation can be believed in, with the thought in the background that in it we have to do not with God as He is, but only with God as He appears to us.[13]

In context, Barth presents the Sabellian tradition as arising for the purposes of protecting the unity of God against subordinationist attempts in the Christology of Origen and adoptionist tendencies in Paul of Samosata. Thus, modalism saw its role as protecting the unity of God through the positing of the *monas* hidden behind the *trias* of the *prosopa*, all of whom share equally in the *monas* as their essence.

It is noteworthy that Barth accepts Schleiermacher's most basic point in the reconstruction of Sabellius—a point that also proved to be acceptable to the majority of Schleiermacher's critics, as I have argued elsewhere[14]—as probably representing the thought of Sabellius. That central point is that Sabellius conceived the *monas* to be the godhead, which he then distinguished from God the Father, whom he conceived to be one of the three *prosopa* and therefore of no greater, nor of any lesser, dignity than the other two *prosopa*, by virtue of their common relationship to the godhead.

But beyond this initial point, the agreement does not go. The very idea that there might be a *monas* hidden beyond the *trias* raises real problems for Barth. The basic difficulty would be that the believability of the revelation through the *trias*, whom Barth describes as "only phenomenal forms under which God's real single essence was concealed as something different and higher," is now called into question. He maintains that such an approach—through the *prosopa*, which are the three revealed modes of the *monas*—"means that God in His revelation is not properly God."[15] Whatever the *monas* may be then, it is, in Barth's reading, different enough from the *prosopa* to undermine the integrity of revelation.

A second explicit criticism concerns Barth's assessment of the implications of Schleiermacher's modalism on the doctrine of the "inconceivable element in revelation as such." To Barth, the inconceivable element is the appearance of the Son of God as the Reconciler in the face of "our enmity towards God."[16] There is for him no logical necessity that the God who sees his good creation turned into our sinful world should send his Son to reconcile that world unto himself. It is one thing to love one's creation in its freshness and goodness; it is quite another thing to love so much one's creation now gone wrong that one would give oneself, or one's Son, to restore it. For Barth, the distinction in the "mode of existence" of the Father from that of the Son is seen precisely in these two acts of creation and reconciliation.

Because he believes this distinction to be grounded solely in the "inconceivable" mystery of the divine love and grace, Barth looks askance at any approach that would rationalize trinitarian distinctions. In such a case, he charges, the different modes of existence follow one upon another by virtue of a logical necessity. Such he takes to be the case with Schleiermacher:

> In this way [of alleged rationalization of a mystery] Schleiermacher regarded sin quantitatively as a mere deficiency, and consequently reconciliation (redemption) as the crowning of creation, and again, consistently, he viewed the Trinity modalistically, that is, regarded the difference of the three modes of existence as one that was abrogated in the profundities of God.[17]

In the quotation, Barth sees two rationalizations. First, there is the quantitative opposition of sin and grace, with the Reconciler being separated from the reconciled by virtue of the perfect degree of his sinless God-consciousness. Second, Barth depicts the three modes as following one another of logical necessity—not as miracles that defy theological justification.

The substance of Barth's reactions to Schleiermacher's trinitarianism, therefore, may be summarized as follows. In the first place, Barth has charged that Schleiermacher overbalanced the divine and human correlation to the detriment of the divine factor. Thus, the integrity of the divinity of each of the *prosopa* would be in question (as in the first implicit criticism above). In the second place, Barth charges, as we have noted, that the formal location of the Trinity at the end of *The Christian Faith* undercuts any significant material effect of this doctrine on the body of the system. Among the implicit criticisms of Barth, we have noted his misgivings concerning (*a*) Schleiermacher's ability to do justice to the full divinity of the Holy Spirit; (*b*) the denial of the preexistence of the *prosopa;* and *(c)* the phenomenal character of the *prosopa*. Explicitly, Barth criticized Schleiermacher for rationalizing the "inconceivable element in revelation as such," by subjecting it to a *logically* triniform modalism, and he explained that he read the phenomenal character of the *prosopa* as signifying a denial of the reality of the revelation of God (if God, in fact, is a higher, hidden *monas*). We must now examine these criticisms.

SCHLEIERMACHER'S QUESTIONS CONCERNING BARTH'S CRITICISMS

Schleiermacher's first major question to Barth is, Do you fully comprehend the concept of the center?

It is Barth who brought the concept of the center into the forefront of discussion, yet his interpretation of that concept has drawn fire from critics. His belief is that for Schleiermacher the ultimate aim of religious affirmation is the surmounting of all pairs of *relative* antitheses. Barth's charge, then, is that "the good of salvation is to be sought not in a *relation* between God and man but in their *undifferentiatedness*."[18] The center functions as the ground, beyond the antitheses, of this "undifferentiatedness."

This understanding of the function of the center, "as signifying peaceful indifferentiation" has been called into question by Gerhard Spiegler. According to Spiegler, the difficulty is found in "Barth's conviction that the very notion of relative difference must be rejected." Consequently, Barth could entertain only two possible courses of interpretation—"in terms of either identity or difference."[19] Since Barth cannot really regard the second option as a possible interpretation of Schleiermacher's position—because, as Spiegler argues, Barth reads the "relativization of difference" as implying the erasure of the "absolute difference between God and man"—Barth's only recourse is to construe Schleiermacher's system in terms of a subtle philosophy of identity. Yet this line of interpretation leads Barth into some areas of at least apparent contradiction. For example, after placing great emphasis on the principle of "religion in life," Barth does not make it clear enough to Spiegler how he can place so much emphasis on the "notion of life" in Schleiermacher and then "claim that for Schleiermacher the truth lies only in the 'middle' or in the 'point of no distinction.'" In Spiegler's words,

> It certainly would be difficult to assume that Schleiermacher's "higher realism," which breaks through in the notion of life and ends in his

insistence on the reality of individuality, stands in no meaningful relationship to what Barth calls his formal and material philosophical-theological principle, the "principle of the centre."[20]

Because of Barth's reading of Schleiermacher as a subtle philosopher of identity, Spiegler argues, Barth must understand Schleiermacher to be advocating "the *deus in nos*." This supposition leads Barth to the reading of a radical internalization of the concept of *Gefühl*, so that "feeling" becomes an all-inclusive category and God is, as Barth claims, "shut up" in feeling. Consequently, the God-concept "cannot signify anything else but the expression of feeling concerning itself, the most immediate self-reflection."[21] When this understanding is applied to dogmatics, the result is theology as *Glaubenslehre*, as the reflection of faith in upon itself, and not an interpretive recital of divine revelation, as Barth would wish.

Spiegler, who has championed the concept of "relative difference," holds that Schleiermacher and Barth both err in applying the concept of "absolute difference" in their distinctive ways to the relation of God and man. It is not within the limits of this study to consider the details of Spiegler's study of the attempt of Schleiermacher to affirm an "eternal covenant" between faith and culture, but the question of the relation of God to man requires further examination. On the way to this theology of culture, the thesis of Spiegler is that Schleiermacher's thought rests on an unsteady foundation. The problem does not occur, however,

> because he worked with the principle of relativity, but because he failed to apply that principle also to his doctrine of God. Schleiermacher, by exempting God as the Absolute from relativity altogether, is forced to make God a *totaliter aliter*. Thereby he makes possible the interpretation of his theology—which depends on the relationship between God and the world—as an anthropology.[22]

As I follow the dispute of Spiegler with Barth's interpretation of Schleiermacher and then consider Spiegler's own criticism of Schleiermacher, I find myself drawn toward a dialectical conclusion. That is to say, I agree basically with Spiegler's criticism of Barth's interpretation of the center, yet I disagree with Spiegler's own interpretation of what Schleiermacher is affirming in his doctrine of God. As I see it, the antipodes of "identity" and "difference" do not exhaust the range of possibilities. Nor has either critic given sufficient attention to the invaluable essay on Sabellius, with its crucial implications for the doctrine of the Trinity.

To ignore the essay on Sabellius is to underestimate, or even perhaps to miss entirely, the distinction between the hidden God (the *monas*, or godhead) and the *trias* of *prosopa*, revealed in the Christian *oikonomia* of redemption. As we have seen, Barth criticizes a modalistic scheme of this sort as a phenomenalism in which there is no valid revelation of the hidden *monas*. In his criticism of Schleiermacher's Christology, Barth is concerned that there was only a quantitative difference between the Redeemer, who realizes perfect God-consciousness at all times, and believers, whose God-consciousness constantly fluctuates between the antitheses of sin and grace. This is a point at which Spiegler's charge that Barth suffers in his interpretation from his failure to recognize the validity of the "notion of relative difference" seems very much in order. Or, it might be suggested, when one reaches a quantitative contrast of the proportions mentioned above, it becomes difficult to avoid the conclusion that such a contrast also becomes a difference in kind. But perhaps a significant relative difference is a better description. For in the absence of such a concept—amid Barth's awareness of Schleiermacher's emphasis on the transcendence of God—Barth finds the weight of theology falling on the human side of the correlation of Word and faith. This may, in fact, be an oversimplification on his part based on the assumption that the relativization of antitheses cancels out any meaning these polarities might otherwise have.

I maintain that—by virtue of the evident failure of Barth to delve more deeply into Schleiermacher's doctrine of God as the *monas* revealed as the *trias* for the sake of finite humanity—he fails to do justice to the terms of Schleiermacher's theological dialectic of the divine causality. Specifically, he seems to have failed to acknowledge the grounding of the finite side of Christology within the infinite divine causality. Schleiermacher distinguishes two aspects within a single causality. One aspect is the eternal side, or the eternal decree itself, as unconditioned by time and space, and the other is historical effectuation by virtue of the gracious divine accommodation to a humanity bound to experience reality through spatiotemporal categories revealed in the fullness of time through the agency of the *trias*. Schleiermacher's concept of the organic wholeness of doctrine both sustains and elaborates the above view of the divine causality.[23]

In the light of these two affirmations, what I am arguing is that Barth seems to lose sight of—or at least to take insufficient cognizance of—this divine initiative as grounding but also working consistently within finite human history until, in the fullness of time, the Redeemer is born as a human person in whom there is a "veritable existence of God." The divine initiative has been at work, I have argued,[24] from creation onward and is now continuing its operation in preservation, in redemption, and in sanctification. Not to emphasize this side of the dialectic is to undercut the working of the divine activity *within* the finite human order—and thus to convey the (mistaken) impression of a merely humanistic, anthropological theology.

Consideration of a related issue will advance the argument and lead directly into the heart of the assessment of Barth's criticisms of the trinitarian aspects of Schleiermacher's thought. The second question of Schleiermacher to Barth, then, is, Does your charge of "phenomenalism" really stand up to a closer reading of my doctrine of the Trinity? In other words, the question is whether the *monas* can be related to the *trias* in such a way that both poles of the trinitarian relationship can be acknowledged as *God*, thereby undercutting Barth's charge of phenomenalism. For Barth, the difficulty is that the *trias*— insofar as the *prosopa* composing it should be understood as the modes of the manifestation of a godhead more transcendent than they—ought not to be called "real" revelation. We have seen that in Barth's view what is revealed in such a modalistic *trias*, however impressive it may appear to be, is not worthy to be called God. Is it possible, however, to discover a way of affirming Schleiermacher's view of the reality of the revelation of the *monas* in and through the *trias*?

DIPOLARITY AS SCHLEIERMACHER'S "NAME" FOR GOD

I have already shown that in Schleiermacher's view (on the basis of the influence of Sabellius), the *trias* is "God revealed" by virtue of the eternal divine causality accommodating itself in time as the triniform *oikonomia* of redemption. Something more can now be said from the standpoint of a concept of deity which is called variously surrelativism, panentheism, or dipolar theism. Whatever the term, it serves as an alternative to the supposed dilemma of identity and difference described above, because it embraces both factors and holds them in creative tension.

At the outset, it must be emphasized that, in his day, Schleiermacher had only the most limited access to fully developed expressions of this position. Nevertheless, the proponents of this position in our own day find their roots not only in Plato—whose works Schleiermacher translated—but also in Schelling, a contemporary of Schleiermacher who shared some of the common philosophical influence of Romanticism while differing on other matters. Moreover, it must be noted that an approach similar to the one I am about to develop has already been examined and found wanting by Richard R. Niebuhr, in an extremely illuminating essay.[25] I accept his presentation of certain points both of similarity and of difference between Schleiermacher and dipolar theism in our day, yet I carry the data to a conclusion different from Niebuhr's.

On the side of similarity, Niebuhr discerns "one formula" that is applicable to the developed positions of Charles Hartshorne and Schleiermacher. Therefore,

> God is not all but all that exists is in God and is intelligible only within the arena of the divine action. Moreover, both Schleiermacher and Hartshorne differ from Spinoza in a common way. The world is the instrument of God's intention. The Self-Surpassing Surpasser takes up each finite occasion and bends it to purposes transcending the present worldly state of affairs. Similarly, *The Christian Faith* places the order of finite being in the domain of the divine good pleasure. The dynamic, teleological idea of God informs both views.[26]

There is a remarkable similarity between the two positions.

Nevertheless, Niebuhr concludes that dipolarity cannot be an adequate "name" for Schleiermacher's doctrine of God. He sees "overwhelming differences" between the positions of Hartshorne and Schleiermacher, "the chief being the opposition in the values that Hartshorne and Schleiermacher place on the possibility of God."[27] Other points of distinction are the "difference between Hartshorne's theomorphism and Schleiermacher's agnosticism" and Hartshorne's agreement with Barth "that the word 'person' receives its meaning from the divine nature and that man is personal only in a derived, secondary, analogous fashion." Elsewhere I have shown Schleiermacher's abhorrence of the application of anthropomorphic categories to God and his view that applications of the term "person" and "nature" to Christology (and of the former term to the *prosopa* of the Trinity) are fraught with difficulties.[28] "Where Hartshorne is speculative," Niebuhr concludes, "Schleiermacher is empirical and parsimonious."[29] Though I find no reason to question any of the similarities *or* differences cited by Niebuhr, I do have strong doubts about the legitimacy of his conclusion that the differences between Schleiermacher and Hartshorne are "overwhelming" enough to rule out any possibility of identifying Schleiermacher as a dipolar theologian. Even if Hartshorne's position should be acknowledged as *the* normative expression of this approach—a concession Hartshorne himself might well regard as prejudicial to his claim for the long historical rootage of his argument[30]—I do not see the logical force for denying that positions of such striking similarity, which have preceded the putatively normative expression of this approach by more than a century and which also vary in some important respects from this norm, could merit membership in a common school. Surely we must allow for significant deviations from the norm—without just reading a dissenter out of the party. Thus, I cannot see the logical justification for Niebuhr's denial that Schleiermacher is a dipolar theist merely because some aspects of his position conflict sharply with Hartshorne's later position. And I am not alone, as the words of Claude Welch indicate: "If a single term were to be used to denote Schleiermacher's idea of the relation of God and the world, the most useful would doubtless be 'panentheist.'"[31]

Hartshorne believes that Otto Pfleiderer (1839–1908) "was perhaps the first [among German theologians] to adopt the surrelativist position." The former's judgment of Schleiermacher is limited to a parenthetical remark: "Schleiermacher had indeed turned decisively away from classical theism toward pantheism, but he failed to safeguard the full reality of the Many, as free and temporal, within the One."[32] In Hartshorne's terms, this means that Schleiermacher allegedly failed to give adequate expression to *temporality*, the ground of the reality of the Many, in polar correlation with *eternity*, which is the ground of the reality of the One.[33] Thus, Schleiermacher appears to Hartshorne to be a pantheist. Although this charge is certainly not a new one, Niebuhr's essay argues—and it seems to me conclusively—against such an interpretation.[34] But what concerns me more is the omission by Hartshorne of any consideration of the role of the single divine causality that, as I have so often stated, is expressed dialectically, by virtue of its *eternal* and *temporal* poles.[35] This is an expression of the same polarity that is central to Hartshorne's position, yet he gives no evidence of being aware of this crucial aspect of Schleiermacher's doctrine of God.

On the basis of the foregoing discussion, I conclude that Niebuhr, Barth, and Hartshorne have all failed to trace Schleiermacher's doctrine of God back to its dipolar rootage in the theology of Sabellius (although Barth does reveal some acquaintance with modalistic elements in this doctrine). When we combine the similarities to dipolarity that Niebuhr cited above with Schleiermacher's espousal of dipolar deity (the *monas* revealed as the *trias*) and then interpret this dipolarity by means of the divine attributes and the careful qualifications undergirding the *single* divine causality in its two tensional aspects (eternal and temporal), the result is Schleiermacher's sophisticated, dipolar view of God. And it is this dipolarity that makes God both the hidden *monas* and the revealed *trias*. By virtue of Schleiermacher's affirmation of the dipolar reality of God, then, it seems that Barth is incorrect in charging that the *prosopa* of the *trias* do not bring authentic revelation. Schleiermacher's reply would then be that they yield as much revelation—and that only by virtue of gracious divine accommodation—as the finite human spirit is capable of receiving.[36]

OVERCOMING OPAQUE SYMBOLIZATION

In order to express the concept of God that is seen in Schleiermacher's dipolar position, I must appropriate a term coined by Paul Tillich—"the God above God." As Tillich has argued concerning his own use of the term, this is the God who is often *obscured* by the opaqueness of the symbols used to reveal God. In Tillich's view, the very concreteness of the symbols of ultimate concern tempts the adherents of a particular path of faith "to elevate its symbols to absolute validity."[37] When thus absolutized the symbols become opaque and vulnerable to the possibility of idolatrous worship. Thus, in Christianity, "the symbol of the cross stands against the self-elevation of a concrete religion to ultimacy, including Christianity."[38] It is on the cross that Jesus as the Christ triumphs. For, notwithstanding his undeserved suffering, he overcomes the final temptation to become an opaque symbol. Instead, he is transparent to his own divine Ground; he points through and beyond himself to the God who transcends *all* concrete symbolization.

Schleiermacher's concept of the *monas* is an anticipation of the concept of "the God above God." A concept from the history of religions will help us to find our way, by means of Joseph Campbell's description of a rite of passage:

> Among the Keraki of New Guinea bull-roarers play a prominent role in the ceremonies of initiation. The boys are made to sit with their eyes covered by older men and then the bull-roarers begin to sound. The boys think they are hearing the voice of the presiding crocodile-deity of the ritual; the sound comes nearer, as though the monster were approaching to swallow them, and when it is directly over their heads, the old men's hands are removed and the boys see the bull-roarers. Thus they become aware of the sound that throughout their childhood had been thought to be the voice of a living monster.[39]

Although the details of this account are not analogous to the views of

Tillich and Schleiermacher on the subject of transcendental theism, Campbell's underlying principle of the "biological function of myth" is in some respects helpful. Essentially, he regards myth as a kind of second (cultural) womb, within which persons live until they reach the time of delivery to full spiritual maturity. When that point is reached, myth can be acknowledged by each neophyte as myth, as in the above account.

For our purposes, it is important to note that, in Campbell's view, the major Western religions have tended to absolutize their myths—thus keeping their adherents confined to the psychobiological womb for their entire lives—whereas other religions (especially the Oriental ones) have built demythologization into their initiation for adulthood. The truly mature religious spirit, therefore, is symbolized by Campbell's concept of the wild gander who flies higher than the gods so as to catch a glimpse of the God above God.[40]

Without actually using the term, Schleiermacher's God above God is the God encountered through the action of the four fundamental attributes (omnipotence, eternity, omnipresence, and omniscience). God can be called the "God above God," because God can only be for the believer who looks through the lens of the *trias*. For they are gracious redemptive *prosopa*, who as transparent lenses mediate and manifest the nature of this godhead *as efficacious, loving intention*. For Schleiermacher, the statement "God is love" is the nearest thing to a description of the divine essence. And since God is also wisdom, this love is also efficacious.[41] Creation (and preservation), redemption, and sanctification are the three paramount expressions of this efficacious loving intention of the God who can be real only when believers cease focusing on the surface of the triniform symbols and look *through* them toward the *monas*.

Against Barth's charge that such a concept of a *monas* undermines the integrity of revelation in the *prosopa*, Schleiermacher is able to make a twofold reply. First, on the basis of his dipolar, triniform theology, he can say, as we have noted, that the *trias* yields the only authentic revelation of the *monas*, and further, that this Trinity of *prosopa* yields as much revelation as the finite human spirit can absorb. The second possible reply is that Barth's focus on the persons of the Trinity (even after taking due note of criticisms of the concept of person)[42] runs the risk of absolutizing the concrete symbols (in the senses of Tillich and Campbell). To the extent that he focuses exclusively *on* the symbols and does not look *through* and *beyond* them (since presumably for Barth there can be no God above them), it might be charged of Barth that there is a risk here of *idolatry* (Tillich). Or in Campbell's terms, Barth runs the risk of forcing believers to dwell within the womb of myth throughout their lives—never aspiring to transcend the concrete symbolic expression of Christianity. Tillich's interpretation of Christ as the fully and selflessly transparent symbol would function as a corrective to such vulnerability (especially the persistent charge against Barth of Christomonism). The love of Christ then becomes the transparent lens through which we see the efficacious, loving intention of God (the *monas*) as realized for us in the cross.

In sum, I have argued against Barth's charge of phenomenalism in the following ways. First, I have maintained that—the denials of Niebuhr and Hartshorne notwithstanding—the "name" of God that best describes the dialectical doctrine of the Trinity and the operation of the divine causality is "dipolarity." Moreover, dipolarity takes the discussion of the center beyond the debate of Spiegler and Barth concerning the alternatives of identity and difference. Since dipolarity correlates these antipodes, Schleiermacher's position is not comprehended by either of the prior interpretations. Thus, by virtue of Morris Cohen's "principle of polarity," absoluteness (the *monas* pole) and relativity (the *trias* pole) can no longer be regarded as antipodes that are mutually exclusive in all respects. Second, I have argued that dipolarity undercuts the charge of phenomenalism by affirming that the *trias* is the *divine* polar correlate of the *monas,* or as Schleiermacher terms it, the *trias* is "God revealed" by way of divine accommodation. The *trias* manifests symbolically the *monas* (the godhead, as in Tillich's "God above God") as efficacious, loving intention. Third, I have emphasized the necessity of overcoming the opaqueness of revelatory symbols lest the believers, in focusing their devotion on the symbols themselves, turn them into idols and thereby miss the fullness of revelation.

Another question that Schleiermacher would wish to ask of Barth would be, Do you seriously believe that your charge that I have rationalized the "inconceivable element" will hold up?

We have seen that Barth charged Schleiermacher with the rationalization of the mystery of the "inconceivable" manifestation of the divine love and grace. It seemed to him that Schleiermacher's three *prosopa* must follow one another by logical necessity. Moreover, he charged that the mystery was rationalized because of Schleiermacher's emphasis upon the quantitative opposition of sin and grace, as between the Redeemer and the redeemed.

As to the first charge, Schleiermacher asserted that the only reason for speaking of the *prosopa* as being three in number was not the sacredness of the number three—which number most theologians before and after him have sought to anchor in the godhead on the basis of a doctrine of eternal and immanent distinctions—nor even the force of rational deduction. The only basis of the number three was the three manifestations of the divine *oikonomia* in creation (and preservation), redemption, and sanctification. It was nothing more nor less than the movement of the *oikonomia* itself that demanded at each of these moments that there be an authentic and full manifestation of divinity.[43] The mystery of why there should be an *oikonomia* could be approached only by delving into the deeper mystery of the divine love as the *prosopa* reveal it. But for Schleiermacher, there could be no rational explanation as to *why* the *monas* (the hidden godhead) is love. On this aspect of the charge, therefore, there seems to be very little difference in Barth and Schleiermacher.

It might be said that for Schleiermacher *every* action of the divine causality is an inconceivable expression of the divine love. That is expressed in these early words, so often criticized:

> Miracle is simply the religious name for event. Every event, even the most natural and usual, becomes a miracle, as soon as the religious view of it can be the dominant. To me all is miracle. In your sense the inexplicable and strange alone is miracle, in mine it is no miracle. The more religious you are, the more miracle would you see everywhere. All disputing about single events, as to whether or not they are to be called miraculous, gives me a painful impression of the poverty and wretchedness of the religious sense of the combatants.[44]

The standard reply to these words would probably be that if everything is miraculous, then nothing is really miraculous. To this charge, Schleiermacher would perhaps be content to reiterate the above words—to the effect that one who can discern the inconceivable miracle of the divine love only in one of the "mighty acts of God" has spiritual myopia. Conversely, in the light of Schleiermacher's dialectical understanding of miracle, what is really inconceivable to him is that the world should have been created at all, and since it has been created, the truly religious person discerns the loving hand of God at work even in the most seemingly ordinary events such as the rising of the sun and the falling of the rain on the just and the unjust.[45]

As for the second charge—concerning the quantitative opposition of sin and grace—there are two things to say. First, we have already noted that Barth interprets Schleiermacher's treatment of the Redeemer in a nondialectical fashion. In other words, he does not seem to pay due attention to the undergirding of the entire process—the creation, development, and bringing to completion (in the advent of the Redeemer)—of the human race by the activity of the divine causality. Schleiermacher wished to affirm this divine undergirding of the human race at every transitional point in its development. The Redeemer is both suprarational *and* natural, but not either to an absolute degree (in the sense that being the one would exclude being the other). Barth seems to overlook this theme of the divine undergirding of human nature. Therefore, the impression is given that Schleiermacher develops a mainly humanistic (low) Christology growing out of a kind of deistic initiation of the human process, with the deity thereafter remaining apart from it, or at least in a subservient position.[46] It should be clear that virtually the entire understanding of the divine activity in this study would refute that point of view.

There is a second thing to say in answer to the charge of a merely quantitative opposition of sin and grace which reinforces my previous argument. The difficulty is that I may gain reinforcement at the cost of bringing to light an equally disturbing problem for many interpreters of Schleiermacher. Although Barth sees the accent falling on the human side of the correlation of divinity and humanity in the Redeemer, some other critics have raised questions that imply that they see an imbalance on the *opposite* side. For example, some critics regard Schleiermacher as an overprotective parent in his treatment of the Redeemer.[47] What they are concerned about is seen particularly in his apparent fear of admitting even the *possibility* of sinning on the part of the Redeemer, and only the most limited possibility of his being tempted. Sin or serious temptation would cause a fluctuation in his otherwise constant God-consciousness.

For reasons that I have detailed elsewhere, I find myself in agreement with those critics who see the problem of emphasis falling on the *divine* instead of the human side (as Barth would have it).[48] At the same time, it should be clear that this conclusion of mine stands in agreement with the emphasis upon the divine undergirding that has been stressed throughout this essay. This overprotection is an unfortunate overemphasis. Yet the self-manifestation of the *trias* is still the only basis that Schleiermacher accepts for threeness. Thus he would reject any suggestion of undermining the mystery of the inconceivable manifestation of the divine love and grace. The issue between him and Barth is as to the location of the point wherein the element of divine inconceivability shows itself. Schleiermacher sees it *everywhere,* from creation, throughout nature and history; Barth sees it only in the mighty acts of God that tend to fall, *senkrecht von Oben,* into history at specific points.[49]

The final question of Schleiermacher to Barth is, Dear Karl, have you correctly assessed the effect of my placement of the Trinity on the system?

We have seen that Barth criticized Schleiermacher for placing the doctrine of the Trinity at the conclusion of the system and that, partially by way of compensation, he placed his own doctrine of the Trinity at the beginning. Barth's assumption is that the formal placement of this doctrine determines for the most part its material effect within that system. And as we saw, Barth inferred from Schleiermacher's placement of the doctrine that "no constitutive meaning attaches to it."[50] Now we must come to terms with this judgment.

Confronted with this criticism concerning placement, Schleiermacher would surely have attempted to turn the cutting edge back upon Barth. He would surely have agreed with Barth that a mere threefold division of a dogmatic system (as in Marheinecke and Schweizer) is not sufficient to yield an operative doctrine of the Trinity. But after noting Barth's location of the Trinity as the prolegomenon to the system, he would have dogged Barth's every step throughout the *Church Dogmatics* so as to ascertain whether this doctrine actually permeated the system. Unless he could be convinced that it did, location at the beginning would be no better than location at the end. He would remind Barth at the outset that Barth himself had stressed the organic wholeness of the system of doctrine for Schleiermacher. He would undoubtedly wish to capitalize on Barth's view that the concept of the center consistently pervades the system, as an example of Barth's understanding of the organic wholeness of Schleiermacher's thought.

Yet Schleiermacher's main appeal would be to organic wholeness in other respects. It was obvious to him, as a believer in the organic wholeness of doctrine, that authentic doctrines must permeate systems. As he emphasized, the treatment of the doctrine of God under a single heading within a system gave it an inescapably abstract character and obscured its relation to the other parts of the system (§§31.2, 50.4). Thus, the formal placement of the doctrine at the conclusion of *The Christian Faith* was deliberate, for the purpose of making explicit the unifying connection of the divine causality of the *monas* with the three *prosopa* which has been functioning implicitly throughout the body of

The Christian Faith. Therefore, Schleiermacher would have felt no obligation to favor the doctrine of the Trinity with placement at the conclusion if it had held *no* discernible organic connection with the rest of the system. Had he felt obliged to maintain a rudimentary doctrine of the Trinity merely for traditional reasons, he would have followed his established procedure for the treatment of certain of the divine attributes that he did not consider essential to his system (as, e.g., in §56). In other words, he would have restricted discussion of the Trinity to a modest postscript to the final divine attribute discussed (§168, on the divine wisdom).[51] On the contrary, he acted systematically in response to his earlier statement that only *The Christian Faith* in its entirety would be sufficient to describe his doctrine of God,[52] by making the explicit doctrine of the Trinity in the conclusion serve as the "composite" doctrine or *meta*doctrine that caught up *all* the divine attributes and forged them into an organically whole system. By this means, he gave unified expression to the operation of the divine causality in the *monas*, which is revealed by virtue of dipolarity, in and through the *trias*.

By way of contrast to the point of view of Barth (and of Welch), I have argued in chapters 2 and 4 of "Schleiermacher's Doctrine of the Trinity" for the implicitly trinitarian character of *The Christian Faith*. The movement of thought in chapter 2 stressed that the derived attributes were expressions of the divine causality through the agency of the *trias* (and the fundamental attributes by the *monas*). The entire argument was undergirded by a detailed discussion of Schleiermacher's dialectical understanding of the divine causality which, although unconditioned in itself, graciously accommodates itself to the exigencies of human need in nature and history. Chapter 4 argued for the organic wholeness of trinitarian doctrine in Schleiermacher's understanding by showing the centrality of the relation of the causality of the religious self-consciousness and by illustrating its origin and growth more specifically in the case of the sinlessness of the Redeemer.[53] In both cases, the concept of a "vital human receptivity" to the influence of the divine causality was seen to be a crucial ingredient in human nature, from its creation through its subsequent development to its completion and perfection in and through the Redeemer, and in the susceptibility of this receptive human nature to the influence of the Holy Spirit as the Common Spirit of the redeemed community and the basis for the propagation of the new Christian God-consciousness.

By virtue of the foregoing arguments, as well as in the light of the essay on Sabellius with its *monas/trias* polarity and its trinitarian analogies, in light of the presentation of the Christian *oikonomia* of redemption, and in light of Schleiermacher's view of the organic wholeness of doctrine, I must conclude that the doctrine of the Trinity is functioning—albeit in implicit form—*throughout The Christian Faith.*

NOTES

1. F. D. E. Schleiermacher, *On the Glaubenslehre: Two Letters to Dr. Lücke,* ed. James A. Massey, trans. James Duke and Francis S. Fiorenza (Chico, Calif.: Scholars Press, 1981), 34.

2. Robert F. Streetman, "Friedrich Schleiermacher's Doctrine of the Trinity and Its Significance for Theology Today" (Ph.D. diss., Drew Univ., 1975).

3. Ibid., 364–67.

4. Karl Barth, "Schleiermacher," in *Protestant Thought: From Rousseau to Ritschl,* trans. Brian Cozens, rev. H. H. Hartwell et al. (New York: Harper & Bros., 1959), 341.

5. Ibid., 352.

6. Karl Barth, *Church Dogmatics* 1/1:348.

7. Our focus must be on the relation of his theology to Schleiermacher's.

8. Barth, *Church Dogmatics* 1/1:339 (§8, "God in His Revelation").

9. Ibid.

10. In an analogy by Robert Osborn, Barth does not deduce a second doctrine from a prior one as though moving outward from the center of a wheel (Christology) to point *a* (e.g., election) on the surface and then by deduction to point *b* (e.g., universal salvation). After establishing point *a,* he returns to the center for a new reading.

11. Barth, *Church Dogmatics* 1/1:353–54.

12. Ibid., 401ff.

13. Ibid., 405.

14. Streetman, "Schleiermacher's Doctrine of the Trinity," chap. 5.

15. Barth, *Church Dogmatics* 1/1:405.

16. Ibid., 469.

17. Ibid., 469–70.

18. Karl Barth, "Schleiermacher," in *Theology and Church: Shorter Writings, 1920–1928,* trans. Louise Pettibone Smith (London: SCM Press, 1962), 173.

19. Gerhard Spiegler, *The Eternal Covenant: Schleiermacher's Experiment in Cultural Theology* (New York: Harper & Row, 1967), 26.

20. Ibid.

21. Barth, *From Rousseau to Ritschl,* 348.

22. Spiegler, *Eternal Covenant,* 29.

23. Streetman, "Schleiermacher's Doctrine of the Trinity," 206–17.

24. Ibid., 431–32 n. 136.

25. Richard R. Niebuhr, "Schleiermacher and the Names of God: A Consid-

eration of Schleiermacher in Relation to Our Theisms," in *Schleiermacher as Contemporary*, ed. Robert W. Funk (New York: Herder & Herder, 1970), 176–215.

26. Ibid., 203.

27. Ibid.

28. Streetman, "Schleiermacher's Doctrine of the Trinity," 197–98.

29. Niebuhr, "Schleiermacher and the Names," 204.

30. In *Philosophers Speak of God*, Charles Hartshorne and William L. Reese, eds. (Chicago: Univ. of Chicago Press, 1953), 29–57, Hartshorne makes the attempt to anchor this view in the thought of Ikhnaton, Lao-tse, Plato, the Hindu scriptures, and the Judeo-Christian Scriptures.

31. Claude Welch, *Protestant Thought in the Nineteenth Century*, vol. 1 (New Haven: Yale Univ. Press, 1970), 81 n. 40. For a similar judgment, see Robert R. Williams, *Schleiermacher the Theologian: The Construction of the Doctrine of God* (Philadelphia: Fortress Press, 1978), 62–71, 170.

32. *Philosophers Speak*, ed. Hartshorne and Reese, 269.

33. Hartshorne's formula is, "God as Eternal-Temporal Consciousness, Knowing and Including the World in His own Actuality (but not in His Essence)" (ibid., 16–17). The principle of polarity of Morris R. Cohen (to whom Hartshorne is indebted) supports the dipolar position of Schleiermacher: "The law of contradiction does not bar the presence of contrary determinations in the same entity, but only requires . . . a distinction of aspects . . . in which the contraries hold" (Morris R. Cohen, *A Preface to Logic* [New York: Henry Holt & Co., 1944], 74–75). As presented in this essay, Schleiermacher's eternal/temporal Trinity should satisfy both Hartshorne and Cohen.

34. As reasons Niebuhr cites Schleiermacher's "respect for appearances, for the phenomenal world," his "belief in the reality of human freedom," and "Schleiermacher's conviction that the idea of God and the idea of the world are ideas that function in thinking in two different ways" ("Schleiermacher and the Names," 200–201).

35. See also Streetman, "Schleiermacher's Doctrine of the Trinity," 434 n. 151.

36. Cf. the biblical accounts, such as of Moses and the sheltering rock (Exod. 33:13–23).

37. Paul Tillich, *Dynamics of Faith* (New York: Harper & Bros., 1958), 97.

38. Ibid., 122–23.

39. Joseph Campbell, *The Flight of the Wild Gander: Explorations in the Mythological Dimension* (Chicago: Henry Regnery Co., 1969), 57.

40. In the Kena Upanishad, the gods send such a free spirit up above where they themselves are able to go, in order to *discover* the nature of the supreme reality *(Brahman)* and report back to them. Schleiermacher's *trias* is gracious *revelation* rather than the result of human discovery.

41. See Streetman, "Schleiermacher's Doctrine of the Trinity," 74–77; cf. Niebuhr's "Schleiermacher and the Names," 95, which emphasizes the polarity in Schleiermacher's view of God as love.

42. Streetman, "Schleiermacher's Doctrine of the Trinity," 435 n. 160.

43. Ibid., 190–91, 193.

44. F. D. E. Schleiermacher, *On Religion: Speeches to Its Cultured Despisers,* trans. John Oman (New York: Harper & Bros., 1958), 88–89.

45. Streetman, "Schleiermacher's Doctrine of the Trinity," 85–86 n. 22.

46. Ibid., 391–92.

47. Albert Schweitzer, *The Quest of the Historical Jesus: A Critical Study of Its Progress from Reimarus to Wrede,* trans. W. Montgomery (New York: Macmillan Co., 1968), 62: "The uniqueness of His self-consciousness is not to be tampered with."

48. Streetman, "Schleiermacher's Doctrine of the Trinity," 407–10.

49. Karl Barth, *Epistle to the Romans,* trans. Edwyn C. Hoskyns, 6th ed. (London: Oxford Univ. Press, 1957), Rom. 1:23, p. 50; cf. Streetman, "Schleiermacher's Doctrine of the Trinity," 435–36 n. 175.

50. See above, n. 6.

51. Streetman, "Schleiermacher's Doctrine of the Trinity," 436 n. 178.

52. Ibid., 57–58.

53. Ibid., 206–17.

The English Tradition of Interpretation and the Reception of Schleiermacher and Barth in England

8

DANIEL W. HARDY

In discussions about two theologians so much aware of the importance of interpretation as Friedrich Schleiermacher and Karl Barth were, it should not be necessary to indicate that as we receive them, they themselves are interpreted by others. From the beginning, they were received by others who viewed them from independent vantage points; certainly they are so now, even by those who most want to do them justice. Barth's attempts to understand Schleiermacher were only prominent instances of such interpretive reception. Likewise, any reception of the two participates in a history of interpretations. Barth's successive attempts to understand Schleiermacher showed that there is even within one theologian a history of the interpretation of his predecessors. It should not, therefore, be forgotten that present-day attempts to understand Schleiermacher and Barth in their interrelation are interpretations and participate in—and are influenced by—the history of such interpretations. There is no such thing as a "clean" or "new" interpretation; it is always, at least to some extent, affected by its own vantage point and the history of interpretations within which it stands.

Though there is undoubtedly much cross-trafficking between the places and people who carry on this interpretive history, in the end the interpretations—and the interpretive histories—are deeply particularized and affected by the milieus within which they occur. This is true not simply in the geographical sense but also in a more fundamental sense. The geographical proximity of interpreters to one another tends to bring particular "styles" to interpretation and to interpretation history. One can, for example, identify an American style and tradition of

Schleiermacher interpretation. But perhaps more important is that each milieu in which interpretation goes on is affected by what is considered possible there. It was such a sense of what was considered possible in a particular place, for the cultured despisers of religion in Germany, that led Schleiermacher to his particular reinterpretation of Christian faith. Likewise, the sense of what is possible in the milieu of the interpreter affects present interpretations of Schleiermacher and Barth separately and in their interrelation.

So it seems that every attempt to understand the relation between Barth and Schleiermacher is itself an interpretation (of each and both together) participating in a history of such interpretations and "local" in its style and in what is considered possible. For this reason, it is important in considering Schleiermacher and Barth in their interrelation to readjust one's sights and look at the interpretation to which they are subjected. By looking at a particular tradition of interpretation, we may find the effects for the study of Schleiermacher and Barth of a particular tradition of their reception. Perhaps this may have several additional benefits: it may serve to relocate a potentially scholasticizing debate—about the "correct" interpretation of Schleiermacher and Barth and their interrelation—more firmly as one manifesting varieties of historical interpretation; it may reveal areas where "accepted" interpretations of the two theologians are at variance with the originals; and it may show analogies to this tradition of interpretation that operate elsewhere, in America or Europe, for example, and similarly affect the reception of Schleiermacher and Barth.

We shall focus on England, identifying features of current theological work there, finding their roots in a longstanding tradition of interpretation there, and then finding the effects of this tradition for the reception and interpretation of Schleiermacher and Barth in England today. But it may be best first to consider how a tradition of interpretation might operate.

THE OPERATION OF TRADITION

I do not suggest that a tradition, as in English theology, is easy to get at. Its position is somewhat akin to the "fiduciary framework" that Michael Polanyi discusses, one operating as an unarticulated position underlying all our knowing and doing.[1] It is the bearer of central concerns and as such is often difficult to identify and appreciate. It seems to operate as the reference point around which important issues rotate, or (to change the metaphor) the *cantus firmus* of the music which is made, itself not fully exposed while being used as the medium through which relationships with the world are made and as the standard that judgments must meet. How this framework, with its concerns, is appropriated, perpetuated, and used is a fascinating matter: if one "has" it, one does not fully "know" it or how it originated even if one uses it constantly. It and its accompanying concerns must emerge for one over the period of one's use of it, partly from oneself and partly from training, and do so slowly and perhaps never fully. It and its concerns are also the slowest to change.

Such a framework and concerns come into operation, of course, in the work of any theologian and also in the interpretation of the theologian made by another. They are the stuff of which theological—indeed any rational—work is made, whether the direct work of a theologian or that of an interpreter, and they lie at the heart of what is done. One might see Schleiermacher's piety and Barth's ontology as examples of such frameworks or concerns. Each is central to the theologian's position and interpretation and is rendered consistent and elucidated by him only with difficulty, over a period of time and perhaps never fully satisfactorily. This is not to suggest that they are simply "personal," "human," "culturally conditioned," or whatever: that would prejudge the issue of what in fact the framework and these concerns *are,* and in individual cases they may actually be "located" very differently. In a broader sense, one can call these frameworks or concerns the bearers of traditions in which people participate, as Schleiermacher's and Barth's (despite their differences) were bearers of a Calvinist tradition. Here again, this is not to say that they were merely culture bearers.

Two other things need to be said in this very basic indication of the operation of traditions. One is that the framework and concerns that a theologian employs are a product partly of the sources to which the theologian feels responsible and partly of what is considered possible in the particular milieu in which the theologian works. Schleiermacher and Barth considered themselves responsible to the tradition of Reformed Christian theology but also responded to what was "possible" in their time and place. The other thing that needs to be said is that the theologian is heir to and figures in an ongoing dynamic, an interaction with others of the time, and times before, who accept the same responsibilities to tradition and their own time and place. The way in which this dynamic actually goes on is crucially important for theological work. It is quite possible, for example, for a theologian to be so laden with the tradition in an earlier form as to lose a sense of responsibility to his or her time and place; conversely, the theologian can be so much preoccupied with what is possible in his or her place as to lose a sense of responsibility for the tradition to which the theologian belongs. In other words, the issue of "modernity" is a crucial one for the operation of traditions.

IS THERE AN ENGLISH TRADITION OF INTERPRETATION?

Having recognized how a tradition of interpretation might operate, can we say that there is a particularly English tradition of interpretation? If there were to be such a thing, it would need to appear in theology in England today (or in that of previous periods) and be traceable to a heritage from the past. There is assuredly a fair amount of chaos in recent English theology, but we can find a number of characteristics that may indicate a common way of going about things. Of course, the appearance of these characteristics might be accidental; they might not of themselves indicate a common tradition. We shall therefore need to determine whether they have a common source. The brief compass of this discussion will limit us: where we should provide a much more thoroughgoing analysis of current work, we will have to content ourselves with some brief indications of common characteristics, and where we should engage in a more detailed history of English thought, we will have to limit ourselves to a panoramic view of history. Within these limitations, let us first identify some of the characteristics common to current English theology and then attempt to find their source.

One of the most striking features of modern English theology is the strong attention given to *norms*. Those who are active in English theology today have strongly developed views about what may and may not be said, though without much awareness of the distinctiveness—historical or cultural or religious—of those views. Likewise, English theologians today identify certain ways of doing things, whether in thought or practice, as "natural" to human understanding and behavior as such, as if things could not be otherwise, without realizing that these ways may be not so much natural and universal as the products of a particular history that continues with its own dynamic to shape present convictions and practices.

Closely allied with this is a concern for the importance of *rhetoric*. What can be said, it is supposed, can be said clearly, in a fashion that renders it nearly picturable. And there is a particular premium placed on lucid presentation and expression. Anything else that may arise from the attempt to present what is beyond easy expression had best be passed over in silence as unspeakable. This leads one to suppose that Wittgenstein's famous dictum "What we cannot speak about we must pass over in silence"[2] has particular importance (and perhaps a special meaning) for the English, lending authority to the supposition that obscure matters should not be spoken about directly without first being reduced into "clear" language, for example, language that can be taken to refer to observable events.

There is a question of *self-awareness* implicit in the attention to norms and rhetoric. English theologians live and work in a unified English culture that has its own largely hidden standards of value, such as its particular norms and rhetoric. They are largely unaware that these are peculiar to England even where they apply them, testing and interpreting others by the standard of their convergence with a unified English culture. There is no overt exclusion of others simply because they are not English, and there is no overt barrier that prevents the importation of foreign thought. But the application of norms and standards of rhetoric as if they were natural and universal—in other words, without self-awareness that they are particular to the English—serves as an effective covert barrier. Quite apart from the acceptability of particular positions that may be presented, there appear to be barriers preventing them from being fully accepted in England. For example, one must ask why it is that Schleiermacher and Barth, who have had a determining influence on theology in so many places, have really had very little effect on English theology. It seems to be because they do not accord with the norms or rhetorical standards of the English, and because these are naively—that is, without self-awareness—accepted by the English as natural and universal.

There is also the question of *individuality*, the individuality of the English as persons and in their institutions. English thought and practice are peculiarly individual, based in the positions adopted by individuals, whose right to take their positions must not be challenged except where it conflicts with the rights of others. Likewise, English society and institutions are largely the products of cooperating individuals. Those who enjoy privilege are those with the freedom and power to exercise their individual choice in cooperation with others, and they have these because of the position they have been accorded by others who have chosen them. (For English thought and practice to be individual in this way is not, however, to be confused with being "personal.") It is because of this that recent English theology gives such importance to individual *decision* and loyalty: the essential characteristic of faith is seen as activity exercised through choice in belief and interpretation. Furthermore, this individuality allows each religious person to stand over the tradition to which he or she is heir and to reshape it as seems best or to accept or reject influences from the past. It may also allow a theologian, under the disguise of historical scholarship, to reshape the history of theology according to his or her own view and to persuade others to share the same view. Because of this, even the English tradition of interpretation is subject to drastic reshaping at every point in the modern scene.

There is also the issue of theological *integrity*. The identity and continuity of Christianity in England is also frequently seen in individualist terms: Christianity comprises those who have chosen it and is continued through the cooperation of those faithful. Except in the rather few places where those who identify themselves as Christians proceed to give a systematic or historical account of their faith in academic terms, this view of Christianity gives it a rather peculiar place in academic circles. Since Christianity is the beliefs and behavior of individuals, it is taken that it cannot be directly studied. Instead, it is properly approached through the disciplines best qualified to deal with the products of the activity of cooperating individuals: historical criticism of texts, church history, philosophy of religion, or (less frequently) history of religions, each of these conducted as a descriptive or critical inquiry. In many English universities, therefore, these disciplines take the place of, and are confused in the public mind with, the direct and self-coherent statement of faith. And the effect of this is to place the responsibility for the "theological" elucidation of Christian faith in the hands of those whose main concern is with history, philosophy, and the like, and not with Christian faith itself. Broadly speaking, since these deal with "appearances" of Christianity in the products of individuals, they give English "theology" the character of phenomenology. And because the criteria of selection are those of the broader disciplines of history, philosophy, and so forth, it is no accident that primary attention is given to figures who are considered, in this broad sense, historically or philosophically important rather than those who are important within Christian faith. Where the choice is from those in the Christian tradition, furthermore, the selection will be made from "classical" figures, chiefly biblical and patristic, because the English—still under the influence of the habits of the ancient universities—have not yet admitted the importance of modern theology. Hence, one is much more likely to find Augustine or Hume or Kant given attention than Schleiermacher or Barth, who will be treated as oddities to be considered in special connections if at all.

Finally, there is the question of the *durability* of accomplishments. In England, singular figures from the past do not—as persons—normally have a "lasting" influence on their successors, in the sense that they can be considered to have an importance beyond their time. Important figures in nineteenth- or early twentieth-century English theology, for example, do not appear to have "lasted" in mid- and late twentieth-century British theology; nor do Schleiermacher and Barth. This is not to say that they are not the subject of substantial and expert study by a few specialists. But such attention is confined to those few places with a commitment to the history of modern theology or to the international conversation in modern systematic theology, and where there are scholars to perpetuate that study. This means in practice that attention is given them only in universities, and only in the handful of universities with these commitments. Elsewhere, the more common attitude is neatly summarized, Who do these dead men think they are?[3]

This is rather peculiar in view of what we found earlier about the importance accorded to individuals in English theology, for is it not individuals who should continue to be studied? But there is a sense in which the English concern is always with events and issues as more really the stuff of truth than can be the views of individual human beings. Any accomplishment by an individual, therefore, is through the contribution of the individual's action (as an event) or the individual's ideas (to an issue). Once a contribution has been made, it is dissociated from its author, becoming an occurrence or a position that should be considered in its own right insofar as it is taken as important by history, philosophy, and the like.

But this list of the features of modern English theology does not in itself justify the conclusion that there is a common English tradition of interpretation unless the features can be shown to be traceable to a common heritage. To this task we must now turn.

THE MODERN TRADITION OF
ENGLISH THEOLOGY

It can be claimed that English thought, if not also English society as a whole, took on its modern form in the post-Reformation period, primarily during the seventeenth and eighteenth centuries. Its main features might be considered three:

At least from the time of Francis Bacon, but loosely following Calvin, *human knowledge* was placed at the intersection of the influences of nature and revelation, of the "waters flowing from below and above"; chief attention was to be given to the development of this human knowledge as the organ of the two. In this, primacy was given to humility, weighting the "wings" of knowledge to prevent it from soaring and thereby depriving the "book of nature" and the "book of the Word" of their determinative importance. But very early and increasingly the emphasis changed: the analysis of human knowledge and its machinery became important in its own right, and the results became determinative for the content of legitimate piety. In this way the implicit tendencies of British practice coincided well with Kant's strategy for knowledge though not with his transcendental derivation of the possibility of knowledge. The strategy, like his, was to put piety "in its place." The effect of this combination was to place human standards of knowability in a determinative position.

Closely allied with this was the *question of morality*. When Calvinism arrived in England, it was spread in a scholasticized form in which the will of God for man—the decrees of election—was treated as a foundational principle from which human life and virtues, or their converse, were to be deduced as a logical system. That had the effect of logicizing the action of God in creation and salvation, and encouraging Christians to check their salvific status "against the chart." One's relative position as more or less moral became important in its own right, and the longstanding tradition of moralism in British religion began. This was further enhanced by the "Anglican" attempt to use religion as an instrument of national unity: proper morality was as important for civil reasons as for religious. Unlike American moralism, however, this did not give rise to a work ethic (and still does not!); it was associated with a hierarchical class system, morality being measured by moral codes proper to classes, not by a single chart of salvation. In a sense, this also prepared the English for Kant's strategy of morals, which made the necessity of moral behavior (the moral imperative) important in its own right and allowed for the use of particular moral symbols as possible extras. The English agreed with the moralistic tendency inherent in this view while associating with it code systems as operative symbols particular to each class. Only later, with the Industrial Revolution, did achievement become important, and even then the social differentiations to which achievement gave rise were codified in a manner that adapted the older hierarchical class system. Nowhere else could one find a gulf between artisans and managers which so paralleled that between the old classes.

A third element in British understanding that is as important as the views of knowledge and morality is the *aesthetic*. The ancient ideal of a pure interaction with God, a beatific vision whereby God in his glory is found to be near—present for—one who is pure in heart, and through being near perfectly actualizing human being by the light of the Spirit, underwent a complete transformation in eighteenth-century England. It was now associated with the sensuous vastness of Newton's cosmology, the infinite and eternal of extended space and time. This spatiotemporal vastness, taken up in the romantic idea of the sublime, was to be participated in through an expansive sensuous imagination. But this imagination was also seen to have its own dynamic and to serve as an "interior vastness." Both object and means of participation were thereby changed from those of the supernatural beatific vision to those of natural sensuous imagination. As a result, there arose a confusion between God's transcendence and natural vastness, and ontological differentiation in this transcendent vastness such as had occurred in the doctrine of the Trinity became unintelligible. There also opened up an interior vastness that could not readily be thought. These vastnesses could not be appreciated properly through scientific thought: the only appropriate expressions were artistic or literary.

Our purpose has been to look at a particular tradition of interpretation in order to find the effects for the study of Schleiermacher and Barth of a particular tradition of their reception. We have now looked at some of the characteristics of modern English theology which may show the presence of such a tradition of interpretation, on the one hand, and the main features of seventeenth- and eighteenth-century English thought, on the other hand. We have still to find continuities between these two, the recent and the earlier. We are now in a position to do this and at the same time to show the effects of the tradition of interpretation for the interpretation of Schleiermacher and Barth.

THE PRESENCE OF THE ENGLISH TRADITION
IN RECENT INTERPRETATION

Most of the characteristics of present-day English theology which we have found seem to be traceable not so much to single aspects of the heritage of the seventeenth and eighteenth centuries as to combinations of them that have developed over the years.

Norms

For example, the recurrent English concern with *norms* appears to be the outgrowth of all three of the elements of the modern tradition of English thought. Following the practice from the seventeenth century onward of giving central place to *human knowledge* in its theoretical and practical forms, human knowledge is used as determinative of what may be believed, but the standard used within this knowability is that of naturalistic aestheticism; this is applied as an inflexible rule and thereby becomes what could be called a cognitive moralism. But, again following the tendency in the earlier moralism (i.e., to check one's own salvific status), this is more individualized in recent times. The "but that I cannot believe" attitude widely found in English theology today places individual or social consensus about what is possible in the position of a criterion. This "moralism of naturalistic knowledge" is, of course, closely linked to the specifically modern problematic of most theology.

It also seems to be responsible for the usual English interpretation of Schleiermacher and Barth. It is interesting to see how this is so. The English norms involve the use of naturalistic human knowledge as determinative of what can be believed. Employing these norms in interpreting Schleiermacher and Barth, however, makes them—and indeed most important theology—seem always to some extent either to conflict with or to stretch the bounds of what is considered possible. So far as Schleiermacher and Barth themselves are concerned, that is no accident. They intended to unsettle the comparable norms operative in their times and places. Operating within one set of norms, Schleiermacher intended to extend the sensitivities of the "cultured despisers" of religion to show them that their view, if properly understood, implied Christian faith. Operating within another set of norms (partly derived from Schleiermacher), Barth intended to displace the prevailing habit of basing Christian faith in the extension of human capacities, to show that it could only be based in God's speaking of himself to human beings. The norms within which the two operated were thus somewhat different. But in any case, they also treated the norms very differently, the one extending them, the other reconstituting them. Therein lies the great difference between them and also the great difficulty Barth had in arriving at a view of Schleiermacher.

But English theology employs such different norms, and applies them so moralistically, that neither stretching nor reconstitution is permitted. The problem is not just that the English norms are different—which goes without saying—but that they are differently applied. And the combination of different norms and different applications disallows the fundamental strategies that Schleiermacher and Barth employed.

Self-Awareness

What of the lack of *self-awareness* which we found to be characteristic of recent English theology in its supposition that its own norms are natural and universal? The distant ancestry of this view is twofold: in the seventeenth-century English supposition that the Reformation would be completed (and the millennium come) in England, and in the successes of the empire in world exploration and in scientific and technological advance. These generated a strong sense of the identity and destiny of the English. But the original religious basis for this sense of identity and destiny conflicted with the existing social structure of the nation, organized under monarch and bishops. "Being favored" was therefore not only a matter of God's election, it was also a matter of one's position in the structure of society or church. Either election or position should be capable of being checked by reference to an obvious order. The eventual result of this state of affairs was that a morality that seemed to be religious yet allowed positions for leaders in state and church became the instrument of national unity. But in the process, attention was shifted from its basis in God's election to "obvious orders" that made one's status clear. In other words, clear moral and social codes became the basis for national unity, and obedience to the moral codes (moralism) became the basis for membership in church and state. Of course, this constituted the English way of life and in time came to be so much identified with life itself that for the nation as a whole no other right way of life could exist. Hence there could be no self-awareness that this way of life was a particular one generated by a particular history.

One other thing must be noticed. From the start the unified morality coexisted with a diversified social structure. So English society was unified by its morality as one nation under law, but within the one nation—both in state and in church—there were "obvious orders" by which people were positioned in strata, each class of people distinguished from the others and also unified by its own code of belief and behavior, and as time went on, by its own history. So within the one English way of life there were various ways, each the "natural way," the only conceivable right way, for that stratum. There was no self-consciousness about this.

This natural, unselfconscious national morality, with its associated stratifications, remains a dominant feature of English life. But it has suffered two major shocks at least. One was the arrival of another standard by which to position people, that of achievement and its correlative, measurable success. That had two sides, the spiritual one found in the various kinds of religious revival and "enthusiasm," and the industrial one found in those responsible for scientific and technological advance. Both gave a large place to willing, choice, and perseverance. The effect of positioning people by their achievement was not to disrupt the moral basis for national identity but to provide alternative means of religious and social stratification that were largely at odds with the traditional ones. Even now, after two hundred years or so, these are held alongside the traditional ones and remain alternatives. But they have produced a measure of self-consciousness in those who live by the traditional ones. The other shock has been the arrival of substantial numbers of people of different racial and religious origins. On the whole, they have been debarred by both existing forms of stratification, the traditional and the achievement-based, from the existing strata. But their presence, with distinctive forms of morality and religion, raises self-awareness (if not outright self-protection) among the traditional and achievement-based strata that theirs are particular moralities generated by particular histories. Ironically, the new arrivals often refuse the habitual moralism of the English, insisting that religion not be subsumed within a national morality. Religious faith, they say, is the basis for moral life; for national morality to subsume religion within moralism short-circuits the development of a more fundamental understanding of religion and of morality. But even without such explicit challenges to English ways, their very presence provides a massive shock to the national moral code and its associated stratifications, provoking an unprecedented and unwelcome self-awareness.

Of these two shocks to the traditional basis for national identity and diversity, neither could be said to have made significant inroads in changing it. But the achievement-based one has become strong enough to coexist with the traditional one, and on occasion to collide with it, while the new arrivals seem to have no position at all. In fact, they hardly constitute a shock; they are simply a presence, as voiceless as were the achievers of the early industrial era who left "civilization" in the South of England for places in the Midlands and North where they could make positions for themselves.

What is significant about all of this for our purposes is its formative effect on the English tradition of interpretation. The reception and understanding of views seem to be conditioned by considerations drawn from the bases of English national identity and diversity, whether traditional or achievement-based. For example, the work of important modern theologians contains a challenge to the basis of English society in a self-sufficient morality (moralism) that constituted the grounds for membership in the society as a whole and for membership in the strata of society. Equally they challenge the stratification of society by achievement and its rewards. Major thinkers such as Schleiermacher and Barth, or indeed others such as Hegel, Kierkegaard, and Bonhoeffer, have all been concerned with finding the proper basis for a nation's identity and internal diversity. But, on the one hand, none would allow that this basis could be an independent national morality (no matter how "good" it was), particularly one formulated as codes (a unified one for the nation, associated with those proper to social strata) to be obeyed by citizens according to their place. Rather they sought to establish the suprascientific, supramoral position of Christian faith which served to displace human sciences and moralities from dictating "orders" of creation and society. And, on the other hand, none would allow that society should be stratified by achievement. For the human will and its freedom, as well as the circumstances within which it could flourish, were not self-grounded: they were granted and reformed by the activity of God. Therefore, they maintained, the only appropriate identity and diversity for each nation and stratum were constituted by response to God in lived faith within the different spheres of life ("mandates" was Bonhoeffer's word) in the world.

Such views, however, cannot be received or understood within a society whose identity and structure are constituted by a morality and moral codes whose religious basis has been lost or whose structure is provided by achievements. The very tradition of moralistic national life found in England has, in other words, proved a barrier to the reception of one of the most significant contributions of modern theology, rendering it as voiceless and positionless as are the new arrivals in England who wish also to challenge the loss of a truly religiously based morality.

It is not only the importance of religious faith that is not understood.

The tradition of moralistic national life can produce a blindness to religion per se. For at least some people in England the shock of the arrival of new people of different religious and racial origins has produced acute self-awareness. But, peculiarly enough, the self-awareness is only about religion, not about the particularity of the bases of English society and of the history that generated them. Hence the moral identity of the nation remains untouched, while there arises a strong awareness of the historical conditioning of religious views. The English morality that has traditionally held religion captive to its own purposes, keeping it as a marginal backing for the accepted morality, remains unquestioned, with no awareness of its own particular history. At the same time, evidence is found for further marginalizing religion: it is found that religion has regularly been captivated by the influences of different eras—by the philosophical influences of the early era of Christianity, or by the ideals of the Victorian era, or even by the claims of Christian tradition to exclusive truth, for example.

It seems therefore that those who have always marginalized religion can understand it in no other way. Ironically, they go on to promote and defend adapted forms of Christian faith that are primarily moral in character, whether moral in the sense of providing a justification for a particular kind of living or moral in the sense of providing a justification for a particular interpretation of living. They therefore show every indication of remaining in thrall to the English tradition of interpretation, based as it is on the captivation of religion within the moral basis of English society. But their adaptations are primarily individualist and so do not provide a means of reconciling the diversities found in England today: they do not provide a religious basis for a supracultural national identity for England.

This too constitutes an interpretive barrier to the possibilities offered by major modern theologians such as Schleiermacher and Barth who have attempted to unite diverse traditions within a single religious one. Indeed, they have attempted to do so in two ways, by according a suprareligious placement to God and by giving an account of the history of religions that unites them within the higher position that is to be given to Christian faith. But by employing the religion blindness of the English tradition, these attempts are blocked, for they are thought to produce forms of culture-bound ideology:

> Now in Barth's theology it seems that theological statements do not have to be proved by philosophical argument, or historical research, or empirical evidence. Theology is church ideology, purporting to be divinely

revealed. Barth's own vast picaresque theological romance is a strange construction: its intellectual status is very uncertain, to say the least, but it rather resembles ideology. And there are considerable doubts about just how it is to be applied to the problems of late industrial society.[4]

Individuality

Can *individuality* be part of a longstanding tradition also? In the form of Calvinism, which was implanted in England in the sixteenth century, much importance was accorded to the task of testing one's own salvific status by reference to a schematized system of salvation. This made the individual pivotal, and it was accompanied by a thinly disguised view of faith as an act of the individual will. According to that view, nation and church were considered to be the "company of the predestinate," together by virtue of election rather than by natural or human bonds between its members.[5] Among those not so much attracted by the predestinarian view, nation and church were, severally and together, unified by their common morality, which took the form of codes that had to be obeyed. But when the reference to the foreordaining purpose of God was removed by the application of the norms of human knowledge (see above) and the religious foundation of unity between people in the nation was subsumed within moral codes demanding obedience, what resulted? One could "know about" other people or "get along" with them by together following the established codes of behavior. But neither of these courses involved bonds of recognition and concern or any relationships of mutual responsibility beyond those required by obedience to codes of behavior. Even now, English society is conceived in this fashion, as essentially made up of individuals knowing about one another more than knowing one another, and getting along by mutual recognition of common standards of behavior more than recognizing one another.

This view is reflected in the peculiar concentration on individuality and pluriformity in believing and behavior which is so characteristic of recent English theology. This is not simply a renewal of the emphasis on individual commitment and responsibility within corporate Christianity. Now it seems to be presumed that such unity as may have characterized Christian belief and behavior has largely disappeared, leaving each issue a matter for individuals to resolve through private struggle:

> To speak of the Bible as the "Word of God", or the "Word of God in the words of men", is just as much a judgement of faith as to speak of some

historical event as an "act of God". It is not a proposition that can be proved. There are many Christians who wish to keep this language when talking of the Bible; there are others to whom it does not come easily. But no one who seriously intends to be a Christian can avoid wrestling with the Bible as part of that tradition with which, if he would follow Jesus at all, he must come to terms. And when he does so, then, whatever his presuppositions, he finds there "words of eternal life".[6]

There is a corresponding timidity about ecclesiology and associated issues such as ministry and sacraments to be found in the churches. All these, the manifestations of corporateness from God, are passed over in silence or with protestations about the importance of individual growth. The same phenomenon is indicated by the universal absence of ecclesiology from academic theology as that is found in universities.

It is also significant, for our purpose of understanding the actual use of the English tradition of interpretation, that it results in a subtle reinterpretation of the ecclesial basis of most modern theology, or a preference for the individualist emphasis of modern existentialism. So far as Schleiermacher and Barth are concerned, the English reception of them construes them as based in individual religious experience and faith, respectively. While both conceive their primary focus of attention as the church's faith, the English understand this as *individual* faith found in members of the church.

What is thus lost through the emphasis on the individual is not infrequently compensated for through an expansion of the importance of a sound or deepening meaning system for the individual. It is at this point that the dynamic of personal imagination or moral responsibility, that "interior vastness" mentioned earlier as an aspect of the transformation of aesthetic understanding in English thought, becomes important. When the individual is freed of the constraints that arise from responsibility to a wider historical community, the way is opened for the individual to explore faith in terms of the "interior vastness" of a human life, with faith seen as comprising a meaning system with which the individual may confront the world. This kind of "aesthetic" path is far from the realistic tendencies found in Schleiermacher, despite his generally idealistic position, and Barth.

Durability

Despite the importance given to individuals, we saw before that present-day English thought does not seem to allow *durability* to the accomplishments of individuals as such; instead their accomplishments are seen as contributions to events and issues, and their influence diffused into the discussion of such events and issues by historians (or historians of thought) and philosophers. Is this also part of the tradition of English thought?

It seems to be the indirect product of a number of characteristics deeply embedded in the modern English tradition. We have already seen the importance of the translation of Calvin's piety, the heartfelt relationship of faith in God, into a logical system of what had been done by God and its evidences in human life against which the believer could check his salvation. In the process of this translation, a personal relationship was transformed into a factual one, and evidences within the person that might guarantee that the relationship was indeed one with God were transformed into logical checks the believer could carry out in order to check whether in fact he or she was saved. This is a striking change that depersonalizes salvation and changes Christianity into the process of checking one finished product against another—God's deeds and human deeds.

It is well also to remember that the whole development of modern understanding in England took place in close association with the development of science as the most appropriate means of finding out what is the case, and there too the personal gave way to the logical. English science moved from the dynamic relationship to the world advocated by Bacon to the nearly mechanical one advocated by John Locke. There was a significant difference: the one was concerned with guiding the process by which knowledge was formed, the other with analyzing and judging finished products by whether they had been formed according to the mechanical pattern of perception and thought. The one was improving upon the achievements of great figures from the past, the other was much more skeptical about their achievements—indeed about whether the past was accessible in any reliable way at all. So at least from the time of Locke a particular way of considering the achievements of the past became characteristic of English discussions: the past was "finished products," which were to be judged as rational (or not) by their conformity to established rules of a mechanical kind. If these finished products measured up to the standards of rationality, they were durable.

The same procedures were employed in all spheres. But it is significant that persons and the personal dimension, including their lives, their language, their imagination, and even their knowledge or belief, were not susceptible to these procedures until they were depersonalized by transforming them into finished products. Before they could be treated by this rational method, they had first to be replaced by an analytical counterpart. In Locke's account of Jesus, for example, the person is replaced by ideas such as "that he fulfills prophecy," which can then be tested.

There is one further consequence of these procedures that needs to be noticed. In the context of these procedures, anything that has not yet been translated into a finished product that can be subjected to mechanical rationality is seen as metaphysical, in that it is beyond treatment by the only acceptable rational method. It must therefore be translated out of the metaphysical sphere. That includes not only persons and personal capacities and statements about God and the physical world but also statements about historical continuities. So not only must the achievements of persons be translated into the finished products of ideas in order for them to be rational, so too must cosmology, theology, and historical continuities. Interestingly, that produces a situation where personal achievements disappear and where the dynamics of historical tradition do also! It is not surprising that there is no awareness of the existence of a dynamic English tradition.

For a faith with its roots in historical events that are understood in personal, cosmological, and theological terms, all of which are subject to the dynamics of history, the consequences of such views as these are severe. On the one hand, the connection of historical events to divine purpose in creation, providence, incarnation, and eschatology (all of which are metaphysical within the context of the views we have been discussing) become obscurities that are the products of previous understandings laden with myth or ancient philosophy:

> Others might praise the marvels of Barth and Brunner, Moltmann and Pannenberg, Küng and Schillebeeckx; to me they were repetitious, and often idle rhetoric.[7]

On the other hand, there comes the imperative to use the rational method dictated by a tradition that does not recognize itself as a tradition. This requires the translation of the "data" of theology into "finished products" analytical in form and testable by the mechanical method. For example, one must translate claims about the action of God in the world into "clear" differences made in a situation by the action of God and then test these against observations.

If such theologians as Schleiermacher and Barth are viewed from within the tradition as we have now seen it, their position will be seen quite differently from how they intend it; an interpretive barrier or filter will operate. Their approaches, and indeed those employed by nearly all modern Continental thought, are quite different. For a start, they refuse to require the translation of data into "finished products," recognizing not only that the achievements of previous ages must be allowed to be themselves (implicit in Barth's recognition of Scripture as a "new world") but also that they cannot simply be translated into the kind of data capable of being assimilated by an alien rationality. Nor can the rationality that is used for them be a static, quasi-mechanical one; it must be dynamic and historical, though it is not the less disciplined for that:

> The understanding of history is an uninterrupted conversation between the wisdom of yesterday and the wisdom of tomorrow. And it is always conducted honestly and with discernment.[8]

The major division between Schleiermacher and Barth is not on this score at all but on whether theology is to be a function of anthropology (i.e., anthropology with a transcendent reference) or whether anthropology, and indeed everything else, is to be understood from its reference to God and God's purposes.

Hence their common approach is to concentrate on the proper way of understanding the formation of "facts" and their meanings, rather than supposing that one has from the past those finished products that English thought likes to consider facts. Likewise, their understanding of cosmology and theology cannot be subdivided into analytical units; one cannot find differences between this unit and that, which might be traced to the causation of an axiomatized God. Instead, their understanding of cosmology and anthropology, whether in general or in reference to a particular situation, is to frame them within their reference to the divine purpose.

There is an interesting question of *rhetoric* associated with this. As we saw earlier, the English tradition and its norms require clarity of statement. We may now see that this emphasis is based on the supposition that language should function as *communication* of facts or analytical units, and should be measured, as language, by its suitability for this task. But this is a rather restricted notion. Language and its function might equally well be considered as providing "actuality" or what could be called a "key to the world." This would be akin to the much more fundamental notion of word as "bringing to be." And with such a notion of language, the task of understanding would be more that of recovering the possibility afforded by language for the achievement of "actuality." There is little doubt that this is the notion of language used by Schleiermacher and Barth and that the notion of rhetoric implicit in the English tradition conflicts sharply with it.

Not all notions of language in the English tradition are so restricted. In some quarters, for example, more attention is given to discursive presentation (narrative, e.g.) that follows the sequence of historical occurrences without reducing them to analytical units. And another use of language has developed to meet the needs of expressing the "interior vastness" we discussed earlier. These two uses may unite in the presentation of "worlds of meaning" that are related to "reality" only very loosely if at all. They prove attractive to those whose tradition of language reaches elsewhere (e.g., farther back) than to the analytic notion, and there are many English theologians whose thinking is more rooted in classical study or literature than in the more exact world of modern science—whose "aesthetic" is of the one kind rather than the other.

Interestingly, they will have their own ways of understanding Schleiermacher and Barth. If they are attracted to Schleiermacher at all, it will be to the Schleiermacher of the speeches *On Religion* and not the Schleiermacher who systematizes religious piety in *The Christian Faith*. If they are interested in Barth at all, they will be interested in his presentation of the story of God with man, though as a meaning world whose connection with "reality" is uncertain. But whichever view is taken, there is no attention given to Schleiermacher and Barth in their more "scientific" aspect, the one using highly exact language in the service of phenomenology, the other doing the same as ontologist. This contrasts sharply with the treatment they are accorded in Europe. But it is as much a reflection of the preference for a different notion and use of language, and there is no mistaking the sharp cleavage from the more "analytical" view of language which it represents.

Consequence for Ethics

It is interesting to notice one other effect of the rhetorical cleavage for ethics. For those whose thought and language are those of the "analytical" aspect of the English tradition, ethics has become the study of theories—Kantian, utilitarian, for example—and of their application to situations. As a rule, this understanding of ethics finds a place only in English university philosophy. For those whose thought and language are discursive or literary, ethics is more a matter of the presentation of the character of persons alone or in relationships. And since English life itself can be seen in this way, as the presentation of people, there need be no study of ethics; there need only be *presentation* of people in history and literature from which their character can be found. In fact, such presentations constitute the most widely read (and seen) study in England; there is little importance given to any more formal study of ethics by the public.

Likewise, the central question of ethics, responsible freedom, is differently handled. For the "analytical" study, responsible freedom consists of finished states that provide the conditions for living such freedom, very much as the analytical approach analyzed "finished products" for consideration by mechanical procedures of rationality. To be sure, there is widespread opposition nowadays to the suggestion that such finished states can provide freedom, responsible or otherwise. From no matter what source they might come, they are in principle incapable of yielding freedom. For the discursive and literary approach, however, responsible freedom is more practical: it consists of the behavior of people within whatever moral code has been provided, whether historical or literary. But in this case, the behavior presented comes from "elsewhere," whether history or literature, and cannot therefore provide responsible freedom for anyone beyond the realm being presented—that is, for someone "now" and in the "real world." Perhaps more important, in neither case is there the necessity or the possibility of more radical emancipation, except perhaps from one who *frees himself or herself* by criticism of those substitutes for responsible freedom which are provided by the two approaches and *grounds freedom* in a "higher morality" or meaning system that he or she finds.

It is interesting to reflect on Schleiermacher and Barth in this light. For were they not presenting finished states from Christian history, whether the historical foundation of Christian piety (Schleiermacher) or the fixed facts of God's self-revelation (Barth), from which ethics is derivable by deductive rationality? That is, of course, the way in which they are conventionally seen in England, a way that seems exactly to follow the demands of the English analytical tradition as it bears on ethics. And this interpretation draws heavy criticism upon them for their offensiveness to human freedom. But neither one finds the basis for ethics in such finished states or uses such a deductive method; the basis for ethics is in a living relationship to God that finds itself through recognizing God's past and continuing history with human beings.

An alternative sometimes suggested is that Schleiermacher and Barth have constructed a "special history" as the basis for ethics which is so unlike "normal history" that it amounts to a special story or meaning system that embraces just human beings who use it to interpret their freedom and give it direction. This way of understanding the two theologians seems to derive from the other aspect of the English tradition that gives importance to discursive or literary presentation. But neither theologian is concerned to provide such a history or story unless it is directly related to the history of the world and human beings and is more real than this "reality." That "history" is seen by them as the motive force for true emancipation, the emancipation that is otherwise missing from ethics. It is also seen by them as the proper guide by which one may criticize false substitutes, whether those provided by "finished states" or those provided by "telling history" or building "meaning worlds." Their purpose in finding the true history of God with man is in fact to provide a more profound basis for ethics and responsible freedom than is available through the channels of the English tradition. But the barriers of that tradition prevent this from being heard.

The Dispersion of Theology

Associated with this, there is the question of *theological integrity*, the dispersion of the subject matter of theology as a discipline in its own right among other disciplines presumed capable of selecting from and of treating this subject matter. Is this too the product of the English tradition that we have found operative in the other areas we have discussed?

Now that we have seen the sources and effects of the various aspects of the English tradition, the transference of theology into other hands— or into other disciplines operated by "theologians"—is not surprising. For it has repeatedly been subjected to naturalistic cognitive and aesthetic norms applied with little awareness of their particularity to the English tradition of interpretation. It has repeatedly been submerged within the moral identity of the nation and its associated groupings, thereby losing its identity—for the public and for itself—by being marginalized. As we have seen, there have been movements that have challenged the moral identity of English life and its displacement of religion. These have been based on spiritual and material achievement or have arisen from the presence of new arrivals whose identities and religious life do not fit the moral identity of the English nation. But no fundamental readjustment has occurred either in the moral identity of

DANIEL W. HARDY

English life or in the displacement of religion as its basis. The consequence of this is that religion has been seen as the product of individuality and the province of special interests, whether those of individuals or groups.

And when religion is put in this position, it can be pursued by those
who are "interested" and may produce its own statements about history, cosmology, and theology. Those who are interested have every
right, it is said, to produce their own discursive meaning worlds but not
to suppose that their meaning worlds have any intrinsic connection to
history, science, and philosophy as such, which must continue to be
studied with a rigor learned through "neutral" history, science, and
philosophy (and latterly, social science). Neither should it be supposed
by the interested people responsible that their convictions or meaning
worlds have any natural bearing on the moral identity of the English
people.

Since the origin and status of such meaning worlds is so much at
variance with the techniques proper to the "neutral" disciplines, they
can only be treated indirectly, as artifacts subject to these disciplines
with their methods and principles of selection. If they are discursively
presented, this makes them amenable to treatment by techniques appropriate to history or literature; if they are analytically presented, this
makes them subject to treatment by historians, scientists, or philosophers. But altogether, "academic" study requires that "special interest"
be set aside.

Not only does this treatment reconstitute the study of theology,
diffusing its concerns into the hands of those whose discipline is learned
elsewhere, it also establishes a gulf between places where theology is
studied in this fashion and places where the "special interest" and its
accompanying meaning worlds are maintained. The two "sides," academic study and special interest, may in fact meet in the lives of those
who engage in both, and this is well enough accepted in English
practice. But significantly enough, a uniting of the two sides can be
achieved only by these people as individuals. If they require a rationale
for what they do, they must find it elsewhere than in the English
tradition.

Seen against the background of the dispersion of theology required
by the English tradition, the work of Schleiermacher and Barth can
only appear as the pseudoacademic products of special interests. The
foundations they provide for their views in the universal religious
intuition of human beings (Schleiermacher) or in the fact that all

creation and history stand under the Word of God (Barth) are unavailable. For this reason the coherence of their systems is radically suspect, whether as providing truth or as constituting a theological encyclopedia, except as ideology. It is obvious what must be done with them: let the different "neutral" disciplines consider them if they consider them worth the effort.

In this respect also, the practice of theology deriving from the English tradition of interpretation disallows the challenges that Schleiermacher and Barth offer. Meanwhile, theology is carried on by experts whose norms are drawn from elsewhere. The "science" of theology is shared out among historians, linguists, textualists, philosophers, historians of religion, and phenomenologists. Although these may give a place to the study of Schleiermacher and Barth, the study will in effect "bracket" their most important feature, the exploration of the determinative presence of God for human beings under the particularity of the Christian mode of that presence.

If the connections we have found between the characteristic features of modern English theology and the main tendencies of earlier English thought and life are legitimate, it appears that there is a case for the existence of an English tradition of interpretation. Becoming aware of such a tradition, derived ultimately from the three features found in British understanding and life from the seventeenth and eighteenth centuries—knowability as a determinant, moralism through moral codes, and naturalistic aesthetics—enables us to appreciate concerns that underlie and inform British theology and that form its views on most subjects as well as its interpretations of most theological work. The tradition is found in different mixtures in the work of different theologians, not necessarily very clearly but functioning in an important way to form their views.

Most theologians prominent in England today work within this English tradition without being aware of its full implications. Among them, one might mention Don Cupitt, John Hick, and Maurice Wiles. As a result, they can be seen to present and defend Christian faith in a form adapted to the difficulties they have found, making themselves impervious to attack so far as possible. Their presentations are largely personal and individual and consist of meaning systems or coherent revisions of cognition, history, or doctrine which can be used to identify them as religious, whether through their cognitive interest or as the basis of moral behavior. But as such they are adaptations to the English tradition that we have reviewed and do not substantially challenge it.

From within this stance, they look unkindly at Schleiermacher and Barth, perhaps because from within the English tradition they cannot understand them, perhaps because the tradition they embrace forces upon Schleiermacher and Barth naturalistic and moralistic norms foreign to them, perhaps because they cannot countenance the challenges those two offer to the practices established within the English tradition.

The question remains whether a better challenge can be offered to the English tradition than is provided by the theologians just mentioned. One way to begin this project will be to become more aware of the features of the English tradition that we have tried to trace. Then we may face this tradition with a clarity that will enable us to criticize it from the basis offered by Christian faith, not necessarily following the examples provided by Schleiermacher and Barth but at least learning from their effort to do something similar.

NOTES

1. Michael Polanyi, *Personal Knowledge: Towards a Post-critical Philosophy* (Chicago: Univ. of Chicago Press, 1958), chaps. 8 and 9.

2. Ludwig Wittgenstein, *Tractatus Logico-philosophicus* (London: Routledge & Kegan Paul, 1961), 151.

3. Ninian Smart, oral comment.

4. Don Cupitt, review of *The Future of Creation*, by Jürgen Moltmann, *Theology* 83 (1980): 215.

5. R. T. Kendall, *Calvin and English Calvinism to 1649* (New York and London: Oxford Univ. Press, 1981), 59.

6. *Christian Believing—the Nature of the Christian Faith and Its Expression in Holy Scripture and Creeds: A Report of the Doctrine Commission of the Church of England* (London: SPCK, 1976), 31.

7. Michael Goulder, in *Why Believe in God?* ed. Michael Goulder and John Hick (London: SCM Press, 1983), 27.

8. Karl Barth, *The Epistle to the Romans*, trans. E. C. Hoskyns (New York and London: Oxford Univ. Press, 1933), 1.

THE PROSPECTS
FOR FURTHER DIALOGUE:
ASSESSMENTS

Part

3

A Historical Demurral

9

RICHARD CROUTER

It is disquieting to see how frequently the discussion of Karl Barth and Friedrich Schleiermacher is dominated by sets of theological concerns that are legitimate but that minimize the historical-contextual side of each figure's work. It is especially appropriate for historians of Christianity to recognize and give weight to the fact that both Schleiermacher and Barth belong to historical theology. The sooner we recognize this, the better our chances will be of getting clear on what the debate between them is all about. The point is that, strictly speaking, neither thinker belongs to contemporary systematic theology. Without wishing to deny the constructive implications of such comparisons, I think the task of comparing the two figures must use the perspectives and tools of historical theological work in order to be persuasive. One should frankly recognize that both of them belong to historical theology, accept Barth's "Postscript" of 1968 with this in mind, and then go to work. In other words, I would argue that one ought to try to contextualize not just one figure but both of them rather more than is usually done.

It seems to me that Hans Frei, for example, is arguing for a (hypothetical) convergence in the thought of both figures, which arises from their orientations to the historical (and unresolved) problem of how best to relate *Wissenschaft* and theological truth. I would argue for an even wider sort of convergence that calls for greater attention to historical setting and context. Although I agree with Daniel Hardy, particularly in what he has to say about historical theology, I would want to carry it further. He says that historical theology has the task of assessing whether, for instance, Barth's criticisms are correct. It seems to me that this is not all historical theology ought to be about; in addition to determining the "correctness" of Barth's critique, we need to ask, assuming for the moment that Barth does go astray in his view of Schleiermacher, why this is the case. What are those problems and horizons of thought in Barth's world that lead him to his view of Schleiermacher? How do those factors—social, political, intellectual— relate to similar factors operating in the climate of theological work of Schleiermacher's own time and place? The task of comparison needs to be contextualized at both ends of the spectrum. I am not sure we really get to the bottom of these issues by a judgment merely that Barth may be wrong in the case of Schleiermacher. (I think, incidentally, there is some weighting of the present panel toward endorsing the latter thought.) But if that is the case, just where does Barth go wrong? How do these two thinkers in fact differ? It seems to me that, were there time to do so, a contextualizing of the outstanding systematic problems of interpreting the Barth-Schleiermacher relationship would need to consider three perspectives on the problem:

1. The first point is that both Schleiermacher and Barth were deeply involved in two quite different but equally momentous cultural crises of Europe, the one brought on by the French Revolution, Napoleon, and the fate of Prussia, the other brought on by the breakdown of nine-teenth-century European society with the First World War and its aftermath. The Germany of Schleiermacher wears Prussian colors and is a victim of aggression, whereas the Germany of Barth's day is aggressor. The overall direction of each writer's work is not unrelated to their radically different cultural settings, which provide a means of gaining some outside leverage on the two projects that might shed light on at least some of the difficulties in comparing them.

2. Aside from the fact that both Schleiermacher and Barth were deeply involved in cultural crises, each figure was a polemicist in his own right. Schleiermacher, however, was a relatively quiet polemicist. That is why his critical talk about culture has sometimes been confused with silence. But anybody who knows anything about Schleiermacher and reads him in context knows how deeply he is involved in the sharpest sort of criticism of his predecessors and of his rivals and contemporaries—Hegel and the Idealist philosophers, Friedrich Schlegel and the Romantics, as well as the numerous Pietists and biblical literalists of his day. Barth, on the other hand, is a noisy polemicist of an outspoken sort. I think we ought not to mistake that

they have this polemical ingredient very much in common. Schleiermacher and Barth have in common the fact that, like so many magisterial minds, they have a fundamental set of commitments that they adopt early on and continue to develop over an entire career. This large span of thought also argues for the task of historical theology in sorting out what the contours and evolution are of each thinker's thought over time.

3. One could add to this list of historical commonalities and parallels the suggestion (noted most significantly in recent work of Brian Gerrish) that each thinker stands in the historic Calvinist tradition. That vantage point on their contributions to Christian teaching needs considerably more work and development.

Thus far I have expressed some thoughts on the overall task of comparing Schleiermacher and Barth. A few remarks on specific aspects of the preceding presentations are in order.

I will not try to respond in detail to the papers, although I note that Daniel Hardy's paper may make the case that at least on the British scene, Schleiermacher and Barth are more apt to be seen as points of departure for contemporary theology than as direct, contemporary options for today. I do not have comments on the trinitarian discussion set forth by Robert Streetman, partly because it seems to me that the point is well taken. In a certain sense the critique that Streetman makes has much merit. Schleiermacher's whole system is implicitly trinitarian; it strikes me that within the scheme of Christian theology there has always been a place for expressing difference in the matter of trinitarian thought. Consequently, this angle of vision does not give us a firm, and thus independent, point of comparison for the projects of Barth and Schleiermacher.

I would, however, make a few remarks about John Thiel's account of Barth's early Schleiermacher criticism. I would pick a quarrel with Thiel on the notion that prior to 1947, Barth was engaged in a monologue. Such a judgment strikes me as lacking objectivity on several grounds. First, nobody who polemizes is really engaged in a monologue. Persons who polemize have a significant other as their focus even if this other consists mainly of arguments within themselves. Thus to call Barth's utterances a monologue strikes me as overstating the matter even though it may be an arresting way to point out the apparent one-sidedness of Barth's critique. What I am saying here is in line with what I said earlier about wanting to contextualize Barth and the work of historical theology, not just to identify *where* Barth goes wrong but also to ask *how and why* he goes wrong. Otherwise we must restrict ourselves to Barth's own accounts and intentions, a restriction that to my mind is entirely too limiting.

With regard to the notion of peace, there is a certain surprising ambiguity in Barth's attitude toward Schleiermacher that is expressed in the Göttingen lectures, an ambiguity that continues throughout Barth's many utterances on Schleiermacher. Sometimes there is no ambiguity at all, as in the resounding disclaimers and denunciations of the *Römerbrief* that Thiel cites, which are outbursts of one-sided criticism. But the odd thing is that in introducing his analysis of the household sermons, Barth, somewhat reluctantly I gather, acknowledges that Schleiermacher—and this is characteristic of Barth; one can see him scratching his head before those students at Göttingen—Barth acknowledges that Schleiermacher, even though his presupposition is totally wrong and we all are supposed to know that, is aware of what he calls the "social question." In his household sermons, Schleiermacher is aware that the blight of society, the hostile jealousy among the social classes in Prussia, is something that demands attention of the preacher. Schleiermacher himself is deeply concerned with the material causes of social unrest. I must say that I was quite surprised to see this side of Barth when I first read these lectures. I started wondering whether part of the animus, and the thing that starts Barth's early critique of Schleiermacher, which is then carried through over the years, is really rooted in the question of the social responsibility of a constructive theology. At the end of his paper, Thiel notes that in 1968 Barth begins by asking whether Schleiermacher would have been a signatory to the petitions on behalf of the Kaiser in the First World War. This sort of issue was also on Barth's mind when he started out. Faced with quite a different German social-political agenda, Schleiermacher's line in the perennial quest for social justice was as directly related to his situation as Barth's resounding *Nein* was related to the collapse of European culture as he knew it. Each was a theologian in the midst of cultural turmoil and carried the anguish of his age into the heart of his theological work. Each thinker responded as a theologian of his own time and place. So I think we would be better off to recognize more fully the historical dimension of both thinkers' work.

Barth on Schleiermacher, Yesterday and Today

10

DANIEL B. CLENDENIN

In all of our reflections on Karl Barth's interpretation of Friedrich Schleiermacher, we would be negligent if we did not attempt to synthesize our results so that they affect our own theologizing today. We find ourselves obliged to draw out some issues of their own dialogue which impress themselves upon us and demand further research and reflection. How is it, to use Barth's own words, that through studying these two church fathers we can "win for theology a little more honor"?[1] As he writes in another place, good theology today depends upon our ability to respect, sustain, and incorporate our ties to the past.[2] Accordingly, and after the fashion of Schleiermacher, let me propose three areas from the Barth-Schleiermacher debate that remain relevant for the theological task today, one each from the areas of philosophical, historical, and practical theology.

According to Schleiermacher, "Everyone's philosophical theology essentially includes within it the principles of his whole theological way of thinking."[3] The task of philosophical theology, in its twofold form of apologetics and polemics, is to articulate the distinct nature or peculiar essence of Christianity. The discipline reminds us that theology can proffer either a "pure expression" or a "deviation" or "diseased condition" of the Christian message.[4] With this in mind, philosophical theology must give ongoing attention to two matters.

First, to what extent does the essence-definition paradigm provide a fruitful way to read Barth's critique?[5] If it does represent a productive matrix, we must go on to inquire whether Barth and Schleiermacher represent two mutually exclusive ways of viewing Christianity,[6] and if so, whether either theologian makes a convincing "power claim," to use Stephen Sykes's nomenclature. On the other hand, we might read the two theologians as offering viewpoints that deserve to exist in a productive, more fruitful tension. As Sykes has shown, the former alternative seems doomed to fail for many reasons (he notes three in particular). It is unrealistic, inconceivable, and even undesirable to expect any final agreement on defining the "true" essence of Christianity.[7] This first path open to us, of making an either-or choice on the two thinkers, has been tried and found wanting. I shall discuss the second option of coexistence and convergence below.

The second question that philosophical theology must continue to address and that the Barth-Schleiermacher dialogue highlights is the function and adequacy of language in theologizing, a point on which both Daniel Hardy[8] and Robert Streetman[9] touch in their essays. Above all things, theologians are "vendors of words,"[10] and we must continue today to analyze their role. As Wolfhart Pannenberg wrote recently, "There is no doubt that theologians must engage in theoretical reflection on language, because, as Gerhard Ebeling has aptly said, 'that which the gospel contains cannot come to us except in the form of a linguistic communication.'"[11]

Barth's entire critique illustrates this issue with graphic clarity. He bristled at the role that he perceived Schleiermacher had assigned to human language (in contrast to music, especially). "We come directly to a most important characteristic of Schleiermacher's theology, if we select, from the plenitude of questions which have been raised, those which bear on the general relation between the factor finally presented as 'speech' and the reality . . ."[12] According to Barth, Schleiermacher distrusted words and their ability to communicate reliable knowledge about the divine. As a result, he felt, dogmatic statements become only derivative and take a back seat to the more original, inner feeling.

Barth directs our attention to *The Christian Faith* and *Christmas Eve* to substantiate his charge. In the former work, of course, Schleiermacher distinguishes the three types of speech (poetic, rhetorical, and didactic) and contends that the poetic form is most appropriate to religious expression while the didactic, although necessary, is least appropriate. Furthermore, of the three types of dogmatic propositions (descriptions of human states, conceptions of divine attributes, and utterances about the world's constitution), it is well known that Schleiermacher would have preferred to omit the last two altogether.[13]

Thus, words are at best only shadows of our inner religious experience. Even the best use of language requires a *kenosis*, even a distortion of the inner reality.[14] Sykes, who has something like this in mind in a chapter of his book on the "tradition of inwardness," writes, "No matter how precise theological formulations may strive to be, or indeed actually are, they are never immune from the charge that they have failed to capture the ultimately mysterious meaning and truth of the heart."[15] Thus, philosophical theology must continue to explore the adequacy and role of human language. Whereas Schleiermacher tends to emphasize the inherent limitations of words,[16] Barth stresses God's overcoming of these limitations.

BARTH'S DISTORTION OF SCHLEIERMACHER

We now turn to our second question, which falls to historical theology and which likewise demands further research: Did Barth interpret Schleiermacher correctly or even fairly? Is Barth correct, to recall an incident full of symbolism for him, that Schleiermacher watered down the rich wine of the gospel to the point that it was no longer even wine?[17] The present studies have resulted in two tendencies.

On the one hand, there seems to be some agreement that Barth distorted Schleiermacher's work and resorted to emotional rhetoric that shed much heat and little light. Terrence Tice concluded from his dissertation research, for example, that Barth's critique was "seriously mistaken at every juncture,"[18] a verdict he reaffirms in his current essay. Likewise, Richard Niebuhr chides Barth for seeking a theology of revelation in Schleiermacher's *Christmas Eve*, and he rejects Barth's criticisms as "impossible to take seriously."[19]

Evidence for this distortion abounds. One could cite Barth's preplanned attitude in his Göttingen lectures of 1923–24, which constituted his "open assault" on Schleiermacher and by which he declared war.[20] Boasting that "the muzzle of my gun is trained on him,"[21] Barth freely confessed this biased predisposition before he ever began the semester: "I have no reason to conceal the fact that I view with mistrust both Schleiermacher and all that Protestant theology essentially became under his influence."[22] It is no wonder, then, that when he had completed the semester he concluded that he had been prepared for something bad and had, to his amazement, found something far worse—a gross, deep, and horrendous distortion of Protestant theology by Schleiermacher.[23] Thus, it does seem true that Barth stubbornly imposed his own agenda on Schleiermacher.

Let me add a further reason for Barth's distortion of Schleiermacher, that of his entire methodological assumption that Schleiermacher's preeminent mode of theologizing was preaching—"not the professor's platform, nor the writing desk, but the pulpit."[24] Streetman addresses this briefly in his essay.[25] Barth recognized that his approach to Schleiermacher was original,[26] but I wonder if he realized it was a potentially strategic mistake. My questions revolve around Schleiermacher's views on language, in which he delineated three types of speech communication: the poetic, the rhetorical, and the didactic. In his second letter to Lücke, Schleiermacher warned that "the language of dogmatic theology is not designed to be carried over into such popular forms of communication as the sermon or catechism; in fact, it would be unwise to make this transition too easy."[27] In *The Christian Faith*, he warned that dogmatics moves about in a "special realm of language" that is peculiar to it (the didactic); it is a "terminology which is as sedulously avoided in the homiletical and poetical communication of religious consciousness as it is eagerly sought after in the dogmatic."[28] Hence, for Schleiermacher, sermonic and dogmatic language were two very different things and only the latter was sufficient to accomplish the tasks of scientific theology. Is Barth justified, then, in using the sermons as his main source of interpretation?

Even if we admit the validity of this sermonic interpretation, the method has created large gaps in Barth's treatment of Schleiermacher's corpus. He spends over half the semester lecturing on the sermons, while his lectures on *The Christian Faith* are truncated. Except for a twenty-page survey, Barth does not even consider the content of *The Christian Faith*. In fact, he only discusses Schleiermacher's introduction, and even then only the first fourteen subsections (through the propositions borrowed from apologetics). In short, Barth addresses only the first seventy-five pages of Schleiermacher's 750-page magnum opus, and that despite Schleiermacher's insistence that the introduction was only a "preliminary orientation" and not the "main subject and core of the book."[29] Further, Barth never got to his planned discussion of Schleiermacher the scholar or philosopher; one searches in vain for any interaction with Schleiermacher's *Christliche Sitte*, the *Ethik*, or the *Soliloquies*.[30]

Despite this widespread agreement concerning Barth's distortion of Schleiermacher, the renewed analysis of their dialogue has also resulted in another, slightly different interpretive tendency that should remain the focus of further investigation. This "revisionist" reading of the two takes a more positive approach, which discovers points of similarity or convergence between Barth and Schleiermacher. Here we note the clear stages in Barth's five treatments of Schleiermacher, stages that become progressively more irenic. Thiel, for example, characterizes Barth's first three encounters as polemical monologues, whereas the last two attempts (the article in *Protestant Theology* and his "Postscript") take on the character of honest dialogue.[31]

Barth says as much himself in the "Postscript," where instead of declaring all-out war he offers to Schleiermacher a "song of praise."[32] He tells us now that he remains in "conscious perplexity"[33] about his interpretation of Schleiermacher, that his disagreements are only until he is better instructed.[34] In spite of all his vituperative criticisms, Barth can write, "I never think of him without feeling what Doctor Bartolo so well articulated in *The Marriage of Figaro*: 'an inner voice always spoke to his advantage.' "[35]

It is not without reason, then, that Hans Frei explores not only hypothetical but real lines of convergence, that Sykes highlights similarities and agreements,[36] and that Tice points to possible continuities. The key here rests in distinguishing between Barth's *attitude* regarding Schleiermacher (which clearly became more conciliatory) and the substance of his disagreement (which might remain but is now open to correction). Tice's interviews bear out Barth's softening, less polemical attitude and his desire to dispel the popular conception of an adversarial relationship with Schleiermacher.[37] Indeed, Barth can tell Tice that Schleiermacher is his "finest comrade"[38] and that while their points of agreement are more formal than material, there is still a type of "togetherness" in their christocentric methods.[39] Tice thus suggests that despite the "fundamental differences not only in temperament but also in both method and doctrine between Barth and Schleiermacher, many of the widely accepted, positive contributions of Barth actually constitute a revival of the genuine Schleiermacher."[40]

RECIPROCAL DYNAMICS IN
PRACTICAL THEOLOGY

Further interpretations of Barth on Schleiermacher must recognize, therefore, in addition to Barth's material differences and even distortions, a softened tone, a change in attitude, and even potential lines of convergence. We now turn from historical theology to practical theology, that science which Schleiermacher described in the first edition of the *Brief Outline* as the "crown of theological study."[41]

Both Barth and Schleiermacher serve as examples for us today in their demand that theology serve the church and in their demonstration of that truth in their personal lives. Frei rightly notes throughout his essay how both men placed a high premium on practical theology.[42] The question that practical theology must continue to ponder is that of the reciprocal dynamic between religious experience and scientific doctrine. Sykes formulates this in terms of the relationship between the *lex orandi* and the *lex credendi,* especially in terms of the question of their "normative relations."[43] This question surfaces several times in different ways throughout Barth's critique of Schleiermacher.

On the one hand, he cannot praise Schleiermacher highly enough as a genuinely Christian man: "For all my serious objections that I have against his theology, I regard Schleiermacher not just as an outstandingly clever person but also as a sincerely devout Christian."[44] Elsewhere: "He had a personal relationship to Jesus which might well be characterized as love."[45] Barth sings his "song of praise" to Schleiermacher and rejoices in his "eschatological peace" and long-awaited "reunion" with him in heaven.[46]

On the other hand, one is tempted to ask how all this can be. It sounds too good to be true, for to the very end Barth insisted that, although he was open to correction, he still agreed with Schleiermacher "in *no* fundamental sense whatsoever."[47] While at Göttingen he had branded Schleiermacher's Christology a "heresy of gigantic proportions."[48]

The upshot of this whole question for practical theology to consider rests in an ironic twist. Given the dichotomized judgment of Barth, that Schleiermacher's doctrine could not have been worse while his piety could not have been better, one is left wondering if there is any relationship at all between scientific doctrine and religious experience. In fact, does not Barth implicitly affirm Schleiermacher's definition of true religion as inward feeling when he praises him as a Christian and damns him as a theologian? Further, if Barth is correct, this whole third question for practical theology might turn out to be of no significance whatsoever. Why waste time in doctrinal dispute if, as Barth suggests, he and Schleiermacher will discuss these weighty matters in heaven amid hearty laughter?[49] Why not laugh at ourselves this side of heaven? If Streetman is correct, though—and I think he is—vigorous theological debate will follow the laughter, for the substance of their exchange is of importance.[50] Sykes also suggests some constructive guidelines for deciphering the reciprocal dynamic of the normative relationship between doctrine and experience. While we should never expect or even desire total doctrinal agreement about the essence of Christianity, "too much is at stake for mere toleration."[51] With no intention of detracting from the significance of doctrine, Sykes proposes that the community at worship provides the right context for a balance between dissent and unity.[52] Like philosophical and historical theology, the practical theologian has his or her work cut out, for the matters at hand have a vital bearing on theology's service to the church.

NOTES

1. Karl Barth, *Protestant Theology in the Nineteenth Century* (Valley Forge, Pa.: Judson Press, 1976), 427. See Richard R. Niebuhr's similar comment in his essay in this vol., "Christ, Nature, and Consciousness," 23.

2. Karl Barth, *The Humanity of God* (Richmond: John Knox Press, 1960), 12. See also idem, *Protestant Theology*, 12: "We need openness towards the interest in particular figures with their individual characteristics, an understanding of the circumstances in which they worked, much patience and also much humour in the face of their obvious limitations and weaknesses, a little grace in expressing even the most profound criticism and finally, even in the worst cases, a certain tranquil delight that they were as they were."

3. Friedrich Schleiermacher, *Brief Outline on the Study of Theology*, trans. Terrence Tice (Atlanta: John Knox Press, 1977), 39.

4. Ibid., 30.

5. See Stephen Sykes, *The Identity of Christianity: Theologians and the Essence of Christianity from Schleiermacher to Barth* (Philadelphia: Fortress Press, 1984), esp. chaps. 4 and 8, which focus on the contribution of Schleiermacher and Barth to the whole question of essence definition.

6. See ibid., 149, where, e.g., Sykes shows how "in Troeltsch and Barth we encounter . . . rival epistemological strategies, whose implications allow no place to the other's position."

7. Ibid., 11–34.

8. Daniel W. Hardy, "The English Tradition of Interpretation and the Reception of Schleiermacher and Barth in England," 141–42, 156–57 above.

9. Robert F. Streetman, "Some Questions Schleiermacher Might Ask about Barth's Trinitarian Criticisms," 117–18 above.

10. Malcolm Muggeridge, *Chronicles of Wasted Time, Chronicle I: The Green Stick* (New York: William Morrow & Co., 1973), 11. Muggeridge is referring to a statement by Saint Augustine.

11. Wolfhart Pannenberg, *Anthropology in Theological Perspective*, trans. Matthew J. O'Connell (Philadelphia: Westminster Press, 1985), 389–90. See his entire section on this matter, "Theology and the Religious Implications of Language," 384–96.

12. Karl Barth, *Theology and Church: Shorter Writings, 1920–1928*, trans. Louise Pettibone Smith (London: SCM Press, 1962), 161. Barth continues in

this passage, suggesting that Schleiermacher "is convinced, as few men have been, of the inexpressibility of the divine."

13. Schleiermacher did not omit the last two types of propositions, because such a dogmatics would have isolated itself. It would not have had the desired and necessary historical continuity with previous theologies, and as a result, would have been of little practical use. For Schleiermacher's explanation of this matter, see his *The Christian Faith*, trans. H. R. Mackintosh and J. S. Stewart (Philadelphia: Fortress Press, 1976), 126; and his *On the Glaubenslehre: Two Letters to Dr. Lücke*, ed. James A. Massey, trans. James Duke and Francis S. Fiorenza (Chico, Calif.: Scholars Press, 1981), 70ff. Schleiermacher did, however, envision a day when theology could and would follow the preferred method.

14. Barth, *Theology and Church*, 161.

15. Sykes, *Identity*, 46.

16. See Schleiermacher, *On Religion: Speeches to Its Cultured Despisers*, trans. John Oman (New York: Harper & Bros., 1958), 51, 59, 119; see esp. 121, 152, where Schleiermacher praises the virtues of music in light of the built-in inadequacies of language.

17. Barth, *Theology and Church*, 191–92. Barth refers to Schleiermacher's deathbed celebration of the Eucharist in which, because of the doctor's orders, he replaced the wine with water. Cf. idem, *Protestant Theology*, 432.

18. Terrence Tice, "Schleiermacher's Theological Method" (Th.D. diss., Princeton Theol. Sem., 1961), 17; cf. idem, "Interviews with Karl Barth and Reflections on His Interpretations of Schleiermacher," 55 above.

19. Richard R. Niebuhr, *Schleiermacher on Christ and Religion: A New Introduction* (New York: Charles Scribner's Sons, 1964), 43 n.54; see also 52 n.65, 55 n.72.

20. Karl Barth, *The Theology of Schleiermacher: Lectures at Göttingen, Winter Semester of 1923/24*, ed. Dietrich Ritschl, trans. Geoffrey W. Bromiley (Grand Rapids: Wm. B. Eerdmans, 1982), vii.

21. Ibid.

22. Ibid., xv–xvi.

23. Ibid., 259.

24. Barth, *Theology and Church*, 156.

25. Streetman, "Some Questions," 118 above.

26. Karl Barth, "Concluding Unscientific Postscript on Schleiermacher," *Studies in Religion* 7 (1978): 122.

27. Schleiermacher, *On the Glaubenslehre*, 80.

28. Schleiermacher, *The Christian Faith*, 118.

29. Schleiermacher, *On the Glaubenslehre*, 56. Without even having lectured on the content of *The Christian Faith*, Barth consoles his students, "And might it not be that we can find consolation for being forced to stop here [due to time constraints] in the confidence that in these twelve sections we have perhaps in some sense come to know the whole of this version of the Christian faith?" See Barth, *Theology of Schleiermacher*, 243.

30. In his "Concluding Unscientific Postscript," 122, Barth says that he did cover the *Soliloquies* in his Göttingen lectures, but I do not see that he did, at least not in any formal way.

31. John Thiel, "Barth's Early Interpretation of Schleiermacher," 11 above.

32. Barth, "Concluding Unscientific Postscript," 128.

33. Ibid., 135.

34. Ibid., 131.

35. Ibid., 123.

36. See Stephen W. Sykes, "Schleiermacher and Barth on the Essence of Christianity," 88–89, 92–98, 98ff., 100ff. above.

37. Tice, "Interviews," 49–50 above.

38. Ibid., 50.

39. Ibid., 50.

40. Ibid., 55. Cf. p. 57, where Tice envisions a "profound agreement" between Barth and Schleiermacher.

41. Schleiermacher, *Brief Outline*, 125.

42. Hans Frei, "Barth and Schleiermacher: Divergence and Convergence," esp. 67, 71, 73 above.

43. Sykes, *Identity*, 275.

44. Barth, *Theology of Schleiermacher*, 106.

45. Barth, "Concluding Unscientific Postscript," 130.

46. Ibid., 134.

47. Ibid., 130; emphasis in original.

48. Barth, *Theology of Schleiermacher*, 104.

49. Barth, "Concluding Unscientific Postscript," 133. Despite all this praise, Schleiermacher will have to wait his turn, and that for a long time, as Barth's letter of March 16, 1968, to Karl Rahner reveals: "To spend a few *hundred* years in eternity with . . . Schleiermacher . . . would please me very much should I myself get to heaven—so long as I could have a few *thousand* years with Mozart first" (emphases added). See *Karl Barth, Letters, 1961–1968*, trans. Geoffrey W. Bromiley (Grand Rapids: Wm. B. Eerdmans, 1981), 288.

50. Streetman, "Some Questions," 114 above.

51. Sykes, *Identity*, 262.

52. Ibid., 265, 295.

Barth, Schleiermacher, and Theological Decisions

11

JAMES J. BUCKLEY

The Barth-Schleiermacher conversation is much more than a debate and dialogue between two theologians. It is a conversation that stands surety for the two major theological alternatives available on issues of Christian life, God, and theological method.

The crucial importance of the dialogue and debate between Friedrich Schleiermacher and Karl Barth can be read off what David Kelsey calls the "array of decisions" theologians currently make in the course of doing theology.[1] On this view, we can roughly distinguish "orthodox," "liberal," and "narrative" theologies. Orthodox theologians' "proximate" *subject matter*, says Kelsey, is the church's doctrine; the contemporary *cultural context* is as a whole incompatible with these Christian doctrines as a whole. Such orthodox theologians address the *audience* of the community of faith in such doctrines from a *vantage point* within this community. They *aim* to construct a conceptual scheme that proves the intelligibility and perhaps the truth of such doctrines *by means of* showing that these doctrines have their foundation in objective reality. *God,* the "ultimate" subject matter of theology, is the being who has given us these doctrines as the means to think theologically. Some forms of Eastern Orthodoxy, pre–Vatican II Roman Catholic theology, and confessional Lutheran and Calvinist theologies represent such "orthodox theologies." Like these orthodox theologians, Schleiermacher and Barth were concerned with issues of doctrine, the former locating doctrine as one form of didactic speech and the latter locating doctrine as one form of the Word of God.[2] But despite their different ways of locating doctrine, Schleiermacher and Barth stood opposed to "orthodox" theologies thus described. All the authors in this collection rightly presume this common ground. The issues orthodox theologies would surely raise for Schleiermacher and Barth depend on their recognizing the differences between the two—as follows.

"Liberal" theologians, says Kelsey, decide that their subject matter is not the doctrines but the biblical and traditional symbols of Christian faith; modernity is the inescapable context, requiring this theology to reinterpret its symbols or to use them to challenge this culture. Liberal theologians address the Christian community of the faith which occasions and evokes biblical and traditional symbols from the vantage point of this community of pious faith, a shared modern consciousness, or some oppressed group within and outside this community (e.g., the poor, blacks, women). They aim to construct a conceptual scheme that proves the intelligibility and perhaps truth of Christian symbols or to display the structures of consciousness all people share by showing that these symbols express this universally shared experience or refer to objective reality. Their God, then, is the one who has given us these symbols as the public expression of God's presence to each individual's personal, social, or historical life. Schleiermacher is often hailed as the father of theological liberalism; his contemporary heirs include Rudolf Bultmann and Paul Tillich, Edward Farley and Gordon Kaufman, John Macquarrie and Schubert Ogden, David Tracy and Karl Rahner.

Narrative theologians decide that their subject matter is the biblical narratives; they handle the cultural context in ad hoc rather than systematically exclusive or inclusive ways. They address all humanity "from the perspective of those who acknowledge that they are at once within the circle of faith and somehow outside it," some focusing on all humanity and others on oppressed groups among us. They aim to offer self-description of the Christian community (in the manner of some cultural anthropologists) by exhibiting the rules that govern Christian discourse and offering reasons for believing that their theological proposals are true. God, then, is the One who acts in particular histories (e.g., in the Bible, in contemporary acts of liberating the oppressed, or in Jesus Christ). Barth is sometimes hailed as the father of one kind of narrative theology; his contemporary heirs include the likes of Hans Urs von Balthasar, Gustavo Gutiérrez, and Jürgen Moltmann.

No good theologian would claim that her or his theology solves all its own internal problems, much less the difficulties presented by the existence of competing theologies. To study such theologians is to map the set of interconnected decisions made in a way that does justice to the unfinished character of that theology. But Barth and Schleiermacher are rare precisely in the way they confidently build the unfinished character of their thinking into their theologies. When Barth, after asking some probing questions of Schleiermacher, finally asks whether his questions for Schleiermacher "provide a basis for a meaningful and relevant discussion about the way he worked out the details of his position," he shows the unfinished character of his critique of Schleiermacher, and therefore of his own theology.[3] One can hardly imagine a living Schleiermacher treating Barth any differently; indeed, one can very well imagine Schleiermacher putting Barth's final question first. Schleiermacher is not a "liberal" theologian if this suggests that the category of symbol is tyrannical and the cultural context determines Christian faith. Instead, Schleiermacher's theology deals, as Barth notes, with two foci of an ellipse—Christ and us—irenically balanced.[4] Schleiermacher, we might say, is a quintessential mediating theologian precisely because he offers no methodological way of stating the mediating enterprise (say, a "method of correlation") prior to the exercise of the mediating task. Barth, for his part, is not a narrative theologian if this means that the particular scriptural narrative rules out "secular parables of the kingdom" in our world at large[5]—or that the general category of narrative provides the key to unlock all theological doors. Instead, Barth's theology is focused on offering volume after volume of descriptions of the storied Christ interacting with friends and enemies, strangers and God, and offering these thick descriptions in ways that maximize the "self-attestation" of Jesus Christ. Once given these descriptions, all else is ad hoc (i.e., honed to particular purposes).[6]

In sum, if asked to categorize Schleiermacher and Barth as "orthodox" or "liberal" or "narrative," we ought certainly to put Schleiermacher in the second and Barth in the third category. But neither fits neatly into either group. This, I think, is the main accomplishment of this collection of essays: Barth and Schleiermacher are read as paradigms for those interested in constructive conversation between these two groups. The Barth-Schleiermacher conversation is much more than a debate and dialogue between two theologians among many; it is a conversation that stands surety for the two major alternatives to the "orthodox" theology described by Kelsey.

Beyond this, however, there is little consensus among the authors in this collection on how the dialogue ought to proceed. All would probably agree that we need to continue studying Barth's early (John E. Thiel) and later (Terrence N. Tice) readings of Schleiermacher—but I find no consensus on whether Barth was wholly or partly right or wrong in his diagnosis and prescription. All would probably agree that we need continued study of the relation of Barth and Schleiermacher to the theological culture of non-European nations (Daniel W. Hardy) and important theological issues that seem initially alien to the internal workings of their theologies (Stephen W. Sykes)—but I find no consensus on how far Schleiermacher and Barth can move or be moved from their historical contexts (Richard Crouter) without distorting the internal shape of their theologies. All would probably agree that the issues of God (Robert F. Streetman) and human being (Richard R. Niebuhr) are central—perhaps the most central—issues of the debate, but there is no consensus on which of these crucial theological and anthropological issues provides best access to the other. All would probably agree that we need the construction of more hypothetical dialogues between Barth and Schleiermacher that seek less for ways to repeat the dialogue than to recast it in terms that remain internal to Barth and Schleiermacher (Hans W. Frei). But it is difficult to do this (Ronald F. Thiemann) without returning to the central theological issues Barth himself posed.

In these circumstances, any proposed agenda can only seem arbitrary. But proposals must be made, if only to assure that the accomplishments of this volume are further pursued. I will comment on three of the issues Kelsey raises: the debate between Barth and Schleiermacher on the "proximate subject matter of theology" (i.e., symbol or narrative), the "ultimate subject matter of theology" (i.e., God), and what Kelsey calls "undoubtedly the most important debate about method in Christian theology" (i.e., foundationalist and nonfoundationalist theological methods).

THEOLOGY'S PROXIMATE SUBJECT MATTERS

Barth's attention to Schleiermacher's sermons—as well as the attention by almost all the above authors to "preaching," "rhetoric," and "first-order" Christian discourse—are instances of the centrality of theological decisions about the "proximate subject matter" of theology. For both Schleiermacher and Barth, theology is a "practical" enterprise, and we engage theologians as we listen to their ordinary, common-sensical, and idiomatic uses of language as the background for their discussions of more technical theological issues. What, we need to ask ourselves and others, are the "paradigmatic ideals" of Christian "praxis"? Who are the "competent speakers" of Christian idiom?[7]

"Symbol" and "narrative" condense two quite different ways of construing this idiom. They refer not primarily to single things or events but to a posture toward first-order Christian discourse—the one suggesting that this idiom is very different from the theological idiom, the other that this idiom provides the indispensable context within which theological wisdom functions. The contrast emerges clearly in two of the respondents: Daniel B. Clendenin claiming that Barth's focus on Schleiermacher's preaching is a prime cause of Barth's "distorted" reading of Schleiermacher, and Thiemann contending that it is precisely the "hopelessly confused and disordered" character of Schleiermacher's theory (if not practice) of the Christian idiom that sets the world of *The Christian Faith* apart from that of *Church Dogmatics*.

Arguments over the Christian idiom are particularly difficult to adjudicate because they are debates over the context of dialogue and debate themselves. Even after (or precisely because of) this volume of essays, those of us persuaded by Barth's use of biblical narrative—especially his thick descriptions of Jesus Christ as an "agent in a narrative plot, in his particular narratable plot" (Frei)—await a thoroughgoing critique of their positions in Schleiermacher's own terms. In any case, the insistence throughout these essays on the "practical" character of theology in Barth and Schleiermacher challenges us all to pursue further the range of practices ruled in and out— from particular texts of Scripture and celebrations of the Lord's Supper to the Christian community's mission to the religious and nonreligious world—by Barth's and Schleiermacher's theologies. Only such a context can show us when we ought to debate and when to dialogue—as well as how to tell the difference between the two.

THEOLOGY'S ULTIMATE
SUBJECT MATTER

Barth's and Schleiermacher's opposition in unity on the doctrine of God is remarkable. For example, as Michael Root points out,[8] both theologians insist on the transcendent unity of God's creative and redemptive activity and a supralapsarian vision of Jesus Christ. This agreement is not captured in classifying them as liberal and narrative. And yet they have opposed notions of what it means to confess a triune God (Streetman) among human beings physically, socially, and historically circumstanced (Niebuhr). Accounting for this unity in opposition ought be a central feature of any future conversation.

If we explicate Barth's doctrine of God in the context of his *narrative* vision (Frei) and Schleiermacher's doctrine of God in the context of his system of cosmic *organism* (Niebuhr), the central issue is easily stated. For Schleiermacher, "to talk of God's *acts* (in the plural) is to relapse into anthropomorphism or, as we would say, mythology: it is to imagine God as one personal agent among others in space and time, making ad hoc decisions, doing this and doing that as the occasion demands. But Schleiermacher has no hesitation in speaking of the divine *activity,* or of the one divine act, provided it is not thought of as resembling the individual and temporal acts of human activity."[9] Barth would partly agree and partly disagree. Any apt description of God "is the description of an act of God [not, therefore, acts (in the plural)], or better, of God Himself in this act of his [not, therefore, divine activity in general]."[10] And there is "one divine act" that does not resemble our activity, because it is an eternal act of election—but more important, because this "electing God" is a central description of the Jesus Christ depicted in the Gospel narratives who is "God with us" and "we with God." The central issue generated by this unity in difference on the "ultimate subject matter" of theology is, How, if at all, shall we characterize divine and human agency?

The options here are various. Work seems to be headed in two different directions. On the one hand, Streetman's article suggests why some are interested in comparisons between Schleiermacher, Barth, and "panentheists." But dialogue here must surely await consensus on the sense in which Schleiermacher is (Streetman) and is not (Niebuhr, Brian Gerrish, and Root) a panentheist. On the other hand, those, including myself, persuaded that Schleiermacher's and Barth's common Reformed tradition outweighs whatever they might share with panentheism in the abstract might focus on Barth's and Schleiermacher's diverse and opposed views of the "paradox of double agency, divine and creaturely."[11] Exploration of this option is implicit in the essays by Frei and Thiemann above—and quite explicit in their other work.[12] It is undoubtedly only by moving in both these directions that we can move from debate to dialogue on the crucial issue of the ultimate subject matter of theology.

FOUNDATIONALISM AND NONFOUNDATIONALISM

On what Kelsey calls the "most important debate about method in Christian theology today," our essayists are divided among themselves into two groups. On the one side are those who take Barth and Schleiermacher as "foundationalists," who hold, roughly, that knowledge has some noninferential ground, source, or starting point. For Schleiermacher, on this view, the starting point of theology is the person of pious faith in Jesus as Redeemer or "persons in relation" (Niebuhr); for Barth, the starting point—or as Barth periodically says, the *Erkenntnisgrund*—is Jesus Christ. When Barth criticizes Schleiermacher for his "anthropological starting point" or Barth is criticized for "starting with revelation," the presumption is that both agree *that* there is a foundation of theology while disagreeing on *what* that foundation is. Niebuhr and Thiemann, for example, read Schleiermacher as a foundationalist; Streetman reads Barth's doctrine of the Trinity as a claim about the "*foundation* of dogmatics."

On the other side are those who imply that the choice between foundationalism and nonfoundationalism does not capture the movement of either theologian, though they do not deny that Schleiermacher and Barth have foundationalist moments. Frei and Sykes move in this direction; Thiemann reads Barth nonfoundationally and Schleiermacher foundationally. In Thiel we have hints of a nonfoundationalist reading of Barth and in Tice a nonfoundationalist reading of Schleiermacher. On the nonfoundationalist reading, the problem with Schleiermacher (from Barth's viewpoint) is not that he does or does not have a ground or starting point but that the storied Christ is swallowed up in the system of organic relations. The problem with Barth, on this second view, is not his christological foundation but the ad hoc way that theologians are called to think and behave in relation to the "secular parables" of our intellectual and political culture.

Thus, there is no consensus concerning either Schleiermacher or Barth on this issue, whether they are read with Schleiermacherian or Barthian eyes. My own sympathies are with the second, nonfoundationalist reading of both Schleiermacher and Barth. The issue, as Hans Frei suggests, is not whether theology ought to be "systematic" or ad hoc on these issues but whether we are about the task of "correlating" Christian and other epistemologies—or "subordinating" one to the other. But even those of us who agree with Frei's option for the latter might also agree that we need to pursue further the manifold patterns of relationships besides "correlation" and "subordination" between Christian and other ways of life and language, carefully distinguishing the manners in which such ways of living are resources for and rivals to the Christian God and the Christian life. This, it could turn out, is precisely what is involved in the work of the Holy Spirit, weaving all humanity into the *totus Christus* promised at the end of the Gospel narratives. But, whether we agree with this suggestion or not, it is fair to say that the dialogue between Barth and Schleiermacher can only proceed by continued focus on formal issues but also and primarily on the material issues of Christ, God, and humanity.

NOTES

1. See David Kelsey, "Method, Theological," in *The Westminster Dictionary of Christian Theology*, ed. Alan Richardson and John Bowden (Philadelphia: Westminster Press, 1983), 363–68. Kelsey isolates six such "decisions," listed in the following paragraphs. I have in the manner of Barth made our "decisions" about God a sui generis seventh decision.

2. Friedrich Schleiermacher, *The Christian Faith*, trans. H. R. Mackintosh and J. S. Stewart (Edinburgh, 1928; New York: Harper & Row, 1963), §15; and Karl Barth, *Church Dogmatics* 1/2, chap. 4.

3. Karl Barth, *The Theology of Schleiermacher: Lectures at Gottingen, Winter Semester of 1923/24*, ed. Dietrich Ritschl, trans. Geoffrey W. Bromiley (Grand Rapids: W. B. Eerdmans, 1982), 277. Note the similar strategy in the Barth-Bultmann correspondence as interpreted by Martin Rumscheidt in *Karl Barth in Re-View: Posthumous Works Reviewed and Assessed*, ed. H.-Martin Rumscheidt (Pittsburgh: Pickwick Press, 1981), 65–82.

4. Barth, *Theology of Schleiermacher*, 49.

5. Barth, *Church Dogmatics* 4/3: 110–35.

6. For this reading of Barth, see James J. Buckley and William McF. Wilson, "A Dialogue with Barth and Farrer on Theological Method," *Heythrop Journal* 26 (1985): 274–93.

7. On "competent speakers," see George A. Lindbeck, *The Nature of Doctrine: Religion and Theology in a Postliberal Age* (Philadelphia: Westminister Press, 1984), 79, 82, 99–100. On "paradigmatic ideals," see Francis S. Fiorenza, *Foundational Theology: Jesus and the Church* (New York: Crossroad, 1984), 304, 306.

8. Michael Root, "Creation and Redemption: A Study of Their Interrelation, with Special Reference to the Theology of Regin Prenter" (Ph. D. diss., Yale Univ., 1979), esp. chap. 3.

9. B. A. Gerrish, *A Prince of the Church: Schleiermacher and the Beginnings of Modern Theology* (Philadelphia: Fortress Press, 1984), 67. See also Gerrish's "Friedrich Schleiermacher," in *Nineteenth Century Religious Thought in the West*, vol. 1, ed. Ninian Smart et al. (Cambridge: Cambridge Univ. Press, 1985), 138.

10. Barth, *Church Dogmatics* 4/1: 6.

11. Austin Farrer, *Faith and Speculation: An Essay in Philosophical Theology* (New York: New York Univ. Press, 1967), v.

12. See Hans Frei, *The Identity of Jesus Christ: The Hermeneutical Bases of Dogmatic Theology* (Philadelphia: Fortress Press, 1975), and Ronald F.

Thiemann, *Revelation and Theology: The Gospel as Narrated Promise* (Notre Dame, Ind.: Univ. of Notre Dame Press, 1985), particularly Thiemann's use of Thomas Tracy's *God, Action, and Embodiment* (Grand Rapids: Wm. B. Eerdmans, 1984).